W9-BNU-656

Spindletop Boom Days

NUMBER NINE
Clayton Wheat Williams
Texas Life Series

Spindletop Boom Days

PAUL N. SPELLMAN

Texas A&M University Press : College Station

The paper used in this book meets the minimum requirements
of the American National Standard for Permanence
of Paper for Printed Library Materials, z39.48-1984.
Binding materials have been chosen for durability.

Library of Congress Cataloging-in-Publication Data

Spellman, Paul N.
    Spindletop boom days / Paul N. Spellman
        p.   cm.—(Clayton Wheat Williams Texas life series ; no. 9)
    Includes bibliographical references and index.
    ISBN 0-89096-946-9 (cloth)
        1. Petroleum industry and trade—Texas—Beaumont. 2. Gushers—
    Texas—Beaumont. 3. Beaumont (Tex.)—History. I. Title. II. Series.
    TN872.T4 S63   2001
    338.4'76223382'09764145—dc21   00-034398

*These stories are dedicated
to the memory of
W. A. "Al" Boatman, Jr.,
a storyteller in his own right,
an oil man, and a gentleman.*

Contents

Illustrations

Acknowledgments

The Center for American History at the University of Texas at Austin is the repository of the Pioneers of Oil Collection, whose oral history transcripts form the foundation of this manuscript. I am grateful to Ralph Elder and his colleagues John Wheat, Linda Peterson, and Janis Nelson for their patience and assistance over the course of one intensive summer's research and nearly two years of updating and long-distance communicating. The staff watching over the UT Archives and the library staff on the UT campus were very supportive of my endeavors.

In Beaumont I have been able to depend on D. Ryan Smith, executive director of the Texas Energy Museum, for his help throughout the process of photo collection and also for general research counsel on this subject; John Leggett assisted with the photo processing. Christy Marino, curator at the Gladys City/Boomtown Museum, was very helpful on several key projects for this book, and I appreciate the hard work of the staff at the Tyrrell Historical Library archives downtown. The library staff at Lamar University helped guide me to several significant theses and other manuscripts housed there.

In Liberty, Texas, the Sam Houston Regional Library proved a treasure trove of both newspaper articles and photo collections for Spindletop, and I am grateful to Robert Schaadt and his very helpful staff: Darlene Mott, Venus Booker, and Sandra Burrell. Jack Whitmeyer of Woodville was instrumental in getting a wonderful photo collection to the Sam Houston Center many years ago, and I appreciate his willingness to share with me the background on the materials there and at his home.

Janet Neugebauer worked through the Southwest Collection at Texas Tech University for me. Craig St. Clair helped me long distance at the Texaco Archives in White Plains, New York; so too the staff at the Ethyl Corporation archives in Richmond, Virginia; and Craig Orr did the same in the American Petroleum Institute Photo Collection now housed at the Smithsonian Institution's National Museum of American History in Washington, D.C. I always enjoy working with the staffs at the Texas

Room of the Houston Public Library and at the University of Houston M. D. Anderson Library.

I appreciate the technical assistance from Danny Goode at Wharton Junior College as I sent my work out on the Internet. I also thank the staff at Texas A&M University Press for their help putting the ideas and the manuscript together and then polishing it for me.

I received help and encouragement from two generations of the Texas petroleum community, including Michel T. Halbouty, Robert and Genevieve Behrman, Ralph and Charlie Cantrell, Jack and Mac Surko, Jim Funk, Charlie Read of the Hamill Foundation and Kay Hines, Dwight Smith in Oklahoma, the Houston Geological Society and Auxiliary, and my dear mother-in-law, Mrs. Al (Tuleta) Boatman, who knows the oil business oh so well and whose excitement for my work never wavers.

Nothing that I accomplish is possible without the remarkable, sustaining support of my family, from Corpus Christi to Austin to Denton. I am especially indebted to my wife, Tudy, for her unflagging love of who I am and what I do.

Spindletop Boom Days

Introduction

Pattillo Higgins stood at the edge of Big Hill, the familiar pungent odor of sour springs surrounding him. The sun had almost disappeared over the horizon, but it was far from the cool of the evening. The twenty-nine-year-old crooked his good right arm at the elbow, his hand clenched against his thigh. He stared across the slight rise as he had a thousand times before, but this time a frown creased his prematurely aging face. His pride and joy, the Gladys City Oil, Gas, and Manufacturing Company, was in desperate trouble. Again. The young driller Walter Sharp had had to quit at 418 feet, the oozing sands below the salt dome holding his pipe in a death grip. The money was almost gone, and so with it the last round of hope. Behind him, sleepy Beaumont cared not at all for his anguish or his bad fortune. Maybe it was time to return to the brick works. Give up on the crazy theory of limitless oil reservoirs beneath odd geological formations. Put the dream away for good. Or perhaps make one more try.

The Austrian captain opened the Washington, D.C. newspaper and casually read through the headlines of the day. In 1895 the news ranged from wars in central Europe to greedy sugar growers in Hawaii. President Grover Cleveland continued to deal with a range of domestic issues, and the gold standard controversy was building toward a confrontation between Western Populists and Eastern Republicans. As a mechanical and mining engineer by trade, Anthony Francis Lucas, his Americanized name for sixteen years now, looked through the ads and posted notices for potential business.

On this particular day a notice caught his eye that would soon change his life. The article had been released out of Houston, Texas, seeking consultation and financial sponsorship for a speculative drilling project. A Beaumont man, Pattillo Higgins, seemed to be courting expertise in both petroleum wells and geology. Interesting, Lucas thought to himself. The writer had included just a brief statement about salt dome formations, indicating the existence of one in southeast Texas. Lucas had studied geological formations at the Polytechnic Institute in Graz as part of his degree work, and since that time had continued to enjoy a curious fascination for the subject. Here was someone who seemed to have the same interest, and quite possibly an actual site where the salt dome theory could be put into practice. Although currently working on a project involving sulphur mining, Captain Lucas decided he would respond to the Higgins notice.

So what can a one-armed Sunday School teacher and an Austrian mining engineer contribute to our understanding of that "new" Texas frontier that was to be born in an eruption of crude oil on a cold winter morning? And what, if anything, can the Spindletop experience tell the modern twenty-first-century reader about the uniquely American frontier character that was reinvented in those early days of the twentieth?

CREATING THE SPINDLETOP
FRONTIER CHARACTER

The frontier was, and is today, and will continue to be borne out of the *character* of the women and men who participated at the edge of their respective socio-cultural world. Whoever takes a step, real or imagined, that no one else has yet taken, is contributing to the *dynamic* of the American frontier. Whoever dares to break a precedent, and in so doing breaks a new trail, leads others into a heretofore uninhabited wilderness. That wilderness can be measured by acre or by mathematical formula; it can be on dry land or on the high seas or in the infinite skies; it is a place where no one has ventured until that moment.

The character that came out of the Spindletop Era is not uniquely Texan or even American, but for our purposes it is certainly distinctive. And there are characteristics of this dynamic that help identify it for us.

Those who came to Spindletop were *self-confident* and *self-sufficient*. Although collegiality and community have a place in the formation of any frontier movement, that movement is led by individuals who dare to take the first steps when no else can or will. Frontier characters believe in themselves to the extent that they will not hesitate to step into the darkness, the void, because they believe there awaits a new platform on which to stand and take measure. If no one else will accompany them, they will still walk there. Frontier characters are *optimistic*.

The Spindletop character was both a *risk-taker* and at the same time preeminently *pragmatic*. They can be patient as patience is warranted, but more often exhibit a sense of impatience, wanting the discovery to take shape, make sense, make a difference. They are rarely satisfied arriving at any one point in thought or space or time: there is always a horizon. But their dreams or hopes or beliefs, however they might be called, must have a purpose. Frontier theorists seek to put ideas to work. In that sense frontier characters are often *materialistic*.

The Spindletop character was *enterprising* and therefore *innovative*. Again, there is a materialism existent here, whether it be clearing the Great Plains of the pestering bison herds by the railroads or the desperate resistance by the indigenous people whose societies survived interlocked with those same herds. The Iowa farmer and his wife came to the Midwest for land and a new future; the Hispanic cowboy found himself in Abilene for the same reason Joseph McCoy had started the town: to make money. So too the Chinese laborer and the Irishman on the other side of the Central Pacific tracks. The farmers came on the wagon of hope, and if it stopped raining, these people built irrigation ditches or diverted rivers. At Spindletop it was unprecedented wealth that beckoned. If moving was more practical than fighting, the people picked up and moved. If a tool or a weapon no longer functioned effectively, a new one was engineered to replace it. This character is by all accounts *adaptable*.

And the Spindletop persona was characterized by *energy* and by *faith*. The tough hide of frontier individuals does not cover a listless, conforming personality in order to protect it from whatever enemy may assault it; rather, that toughness is created by the constant efforts of individuals as they proactively engage whatever enemy stands in the way: weather, mountain ranges, reservations, limitless miles of track or trail, salt domes, or political sloth. An Owen Wister character declares, "We're building a country out here, and there's no place for weakness!"

And that is the character of the Spindletop experience, from Beaumont to Saratoga, and from Sour Lake to Batson Prairie to Humble. But how do we reach symbiosis with a Beaumont brick worker and an Austrian engineer, a twenty-two-year-old water well expert and a University of Texas geologist? When we add three brothers from the Corsicana fields, two Pennsylvania financiers, a bearded Baptist teetotaler, and a has-been Populist politician to the mix, does that bring us to the American frontier? Yes, it does. And into that strange, exotic mix of personalities add strong, self-reliant women, already wealthy and influential promoters— including a millionaire traveling salesman, and thousands more. The spirit and energy of the Spindletop experience belong right at the very crossroads of a frontier character striding into a new century.

The stories that follow are of men and women of differing backgrounds and ethnicity who touched the lodestone of the American frontier character, and for a brief moment in time took us down the trail of invention and faith and self-confidence. They were, mostly, particularly average folks if we measure people by education or intelligence quotients or wealth or political influence. Some were polished culturally, most were ragged and forthright and completely honest. They were self-reliant to a fault but knew exactly when and how to cooperate in the necessities of the moment. They were fiercely independent and democratic in their beliefs. Although many stayed, most were transient in their lifestyle, arriving with great expectations, working with compulsive diligence, and moving on—some without a trace—when a next horizon beckoned. One of them who came to Beaumont early on wrote later, "I decided that nothing should cause me to turn back, at least until I had seen whether or not what I had heard was true."

They came in all shapes and sizes—children, wives, and harlots, young men dreaming dreams and old men with vision. They brought hope and self-assurance, courage and perseverance with them, and little else. Most of them brought an attitude—that is the elusive frontier character we seek. They were cocky, and most of them could back up any boast they proffered. Some made fast friendships, and those who worked the rigs risked their lives for each other almost without exception. A few remained aloof and alone in the midst of the noisy throngs. Some melted into the high culture of Beaumont and Houston society, while others managed to offend almost everyone they met. One wag who stood in the midst of the throng of oil speculators and hopefuls observed that "not everybody here is an s.o.b., but every s.o.b. is here who could get here." And when many of them left, and most of them were gone in three years, they took little with them other than that same character, that same driving energy, that same faith.

This, then, is the story that they will tell, when the American frontier came through Spindletop.

THE TEXAS PIONEERS OF OIL COLLECTION

Following the fiftieth anniversary commemoration of the Spindletop gusher, interviewers spent the next three years speaking with the survivors from that brief period in American history. Nearly one hundred men and women spent countless hours reminiscing and responding to questions from the interviewers, whose written transcripts now form the Texas Pioneers of Oil Collection at the Center for American History, The University of Texas at Austin.

This valuable collection of eyewitness accounts provides the foundation for the book you are about to read, although there are many other primary and secondary sources contained herein. Scholarship on Spindletop's narrative history is indebted to those who first delved into these eyewitnesses' stories: Mody C. Boatright and William A. Owens, Michel T. Halbouty and James Clark. The story that unfolds here has taken their work to the next step by expanding both the history of the oil industry leading up through Spindletop and the anecdotes that have been retrieved from the collection.

Verbatim transcripts challenge the researcher to create a smooth flow to the myriad stories. Minor liberties have been taken by eliminating the interview questions and the "wells" and "you knows," and so forth. Rarely have any of the words or phrases or colloquialisms been altered, for that is where the flavor is. Forty of these women and men lived through the days that are the subject of this book. Their stories—here presented as a narrow "slice of life" sketch—are a rich treasure trove for reliving Spindletop.

Because this is *narrative,* or *anecdotal,* history, the stories of these women and men are recollections based on true events while at the same time filtered through time and social mores of another era. When the old-timer tells about "bodies thrown in the river every night," it does not mean that this was absolute fact: though not a regular occurrence, there *were* bodies found in the river many nights. The point of such stories is to relate the very real violence that existed in these frontier towns and fields.

The language of these reminiscences is often crude and inappropriate to culturally sensitive contemporary ears. But to ameliorate that would take much of the energy and reality from the stories. There are no apologies to be made here, because these folks, all now long-since deceased, would not likely retract their stories if given a second chance to do so. Perhaps it is simply "reader beware."

The social prejudices that emanate from many of the anecdotes that follow are again presented out of the world in which these men and women lived. It would be naïve for the author not to recognize the racial and religious biases that underlie much of the narrative; the reader would be mistaken to assume a blanket or even nominal acceptance of such prejudice. But to eliminate, or worse contemporize and therefore change, the stories to fit today's political and social sensitivities would be untenable. Changing history to make it palatable to different tastes in a different time is an exercise of inexcusable scholarship.

Rather, the *cumulative* effect of these entertaining if occasionally painful recollections is the objective here. These women and men, Anglo and African American, Protestant and Catholic and Jew together, *lived* the life they describe in these pages. And it is that life that the author wants to re-present through the stories that these eyewitnesses tell. If in so doing the reader gets a sense of what it might have been like to live in those Gladys City streets or to work on that salt dome hill in 1901 or 1904, warts and all, then this narrative has accomplished its goal.

1

Getting There

G W O'Bryan [*sic*] Esq, Beaumont

Dear "Pard"

It seemed to me that I heard Mr. Ingalls had sold his "Sour Lake." I want you to see the owner of that Sour Water tract of land and buy it for you and me. . . . If the tract is worth one thousand dollars give two or three thousand . . . If you manage this thing judiciously, there is a larger sum of gold dollars in it for us, than we have seen or heard of in our whole lives. . . . You must not breathe the subject of this letter to anyone.

The great excitement of this age is oil-petroleum, as it is termed. It promises to lay in the shade the great "South Sea Bubble" or any other bubble of any age. This region of Texas will be wild upon the subject within a few months. It don't matter to us whether there is a drop of oil within a thousand miles of the Ingalls Springs, we will make out fortune by selling before the fact is ascertained.

What is the use toiling and struggling with aching brains and weary bones for bread when gold so temptingly invites you to reach out and clutch it? I do like occasionally during these hard times to trust my imagination to a few millions in coin.

Let me hear from you immediately as to the prospects.

Yours Truly,

B. Trowell [1]

This letter to Captain George Washington O'Brien, one of the most upstanding citizens of Beaumont—and a national political figure as well—

contains many of the elements of excitement, speculation, greed, and hope that marked the Spindletop oil field experience. What makes this letter special is that it was written on September 15, *1865!*

O'Brien did in fact investigate the sour springs mound outside his city. An affidavit filed in papers some years later indicate that "after a heavy rain he [O'Brien] saw oozing or seeping with the water from the side of the inclined surface of said hill in a place bare of grass or other obstruction, and flowing over a sandy surface, an oily substance of bright or gilt color in the shining sun, which he suspected, but was not certain, was petroleum oil; and, from that fact . . . conceived the idea of purchasing the whole or part of said Veatch Survey."[2]

Aware of the search for oil in southeast Texas, B. T. Kavanaugh arrived in Beaumont in 1866 with the latest "oil divining" technology, a device invented by his brother. Some years later he wrote of his endeavor: "I found some fine veins, one passing under the sour wells some mile or two southwest of Beaumont. . . . Also I visited Sour Lake, where I found oil upon the surface in greater quantity than at any other point." Kavanaugh drilled to 142 feet before giving in to the quicksand beneath the surface. He reported some time later that a thin film of petroleum could be extracted from an underground mixture the locals called "sea wax"—bitumin and paraffin, but that the expense of such a procedure was prohibitive.[3]

The oil boom in Southeast Texas was still a generation away, but the first taste of the endeavor had made its impression.

THE DRAKE WELL

The history of drilling in the United States dates back to the beginning of the nineteenth century, in places like Pennsylvania and West Virginia. These early attempts mostly sought water deposits, although in the ensuing years salt and sulphur deposits were also objectives. In 1797 Elisha Brooks built a salt furnace in the Kanawha region of the Ohio valley, and "drilled" ten feet below the surface with hollowed gum tree limbs into the briny salt lick. By this method he managed to extract 150 pounds of brine daily.

In 1806 the Ruffner brothers, Joseph and David, also looking for salt deposits, sank a 20-foot oak log, converted into a three-and-a-half-inch "tube," into an Ohio river bed. By November of the next year, they had managed to drill to 28 feet, and to an unprecedented 58 feet by January 15, 1808. In the process they encountered, and solved, several problems that would haunt drillers for the next century: crevices and fissures that bent the drilling pipes, hard rock formations that shattered the drill bits, and the incessant quicksand. This, the first rock-bored salt well west of the Alleghenies, ultimately proved a financial success for the Ruffners' enterprise.

In 1831 Billy Morris extended the technology of well boring by adding the drill bit to the already helpful steam-powered drilling process. By this time, tin tubing had replaced hollowed limbs, and "seed bags," as they were called, formed water-tight joints around the drilling tubes. These bags were originally buckskin sacks filled with a combination of flaxseed and powdered gum tagacanth. The bags, inserted into the well, would inflate as they absorbed the water below the surface and form a tight protective outer skin to shut off the escaping pressure needed at the drilling point.[4]

The deliberate search for oil in North America begins with the familiar Drake well in Titusville, Pennsylvania. The year was 1859. Although oil had been found in many of the salt, water, and sulphur wells across the country by that time, it was generally considered—like gas—a nuisance if not a danger to the drilling. The use of oil for kerosene-based products, monopolized by Rockefeller's Standard Oil Company for most of the second half of the nineteenth century, required only an accessibility of the surface or near-surface shallow "seepage" pools of petroleum: drilling deep beneath the surface was hardly necessary. When Colonel Drake announced his plans to dig "as far as a thousand feet, if necessary, to find oil," most people scoffed at the needless expense and energy to do so.

But Drake was not to be deterred. On April 15, 1859, he began the drilling from a four-legged wooden derrick that stood forty feet in the air. The pipe hit bedrock around twenty feet on August 14, and the serious drilling began in earnest. Four days later the drill bit suddenly dropped six inches, indicating that the pipe had bored through the rock formation. At sixty-nine feet, driller "Uncle Billy" Smith watched as the hole filled with oil. The first true oil well had hit paydirt.[5]

Oil drilling spread across the Three Rivers region, and into West Virginia later in 1859. The Kanawha fields, where Brooks had experimented sixty years earlier, opened in 1860, and the Parkersburg "Volcano" fields in 1863. The Gale field opened in 1866. Several of these wells produced at the then unheard-of rate of 100 barrels a day. The fluctuating price of oil, however, kept the producers in a constant state of uncertainty. In 1859 the price of a barrel of oil was $20; in 1861 it was $0.10! Prices soared to $14 in

1864 but fell to $4 at the end of the Civil War. By 1870 oil prices had roller-coastered between $1.35 and $7.00, and stood in 1870 at a mere $2.70—hardly enough to encourage speculators.[6]

But continuing positive reports of successful drilling efforts in the Northeast may have been what spurred Texans like Trowell and O'Brien to seek oil in their own backyards, although the first recorded oil well drilling in Texas actually took place in Nacogdoches County. In 1859 a 106-foot-deep well was dug there that produced ten barrels of oil daily in the years that followed. This was the Skillern Tract well, the result of a steam-powered drilling operation using cypress casings and a rotating auger.[7]

In the 1870s and 1880s, exploratory oil wells were drilled in Bexar, Jefferson, and Hardin Counties. But at an average of ten barrels per day for most of these enterprises, and with still no great regional demand for petroleum other than for kerosene, lubricants, and questionable medicinal use, the oil "industry" in Texas lay dormant for another three decades until the 1890s and Corsicana.

CORSICANA

On June 9, 1894, rig workers on a water well operated by the American Well and Prospecting Company had just reached a depth past 1,000 feet. Instead of celebration, the crew's response turned to aggravation: oil was seeping into the hole. The artesian water for which they sought would soon be contaminated by the oil, thus rendering the well useless. The owners of the company, Elmer Akins, H. G. Johnson, and Charlie Rittersbacher, were called to the site. They decided to continue the drilling, but well beyond the mark they had just reached. Ultimately the crew drilled to over 2,400 feet, but oil continued to ruin the operation. Contracted by the Corsicana city leaders, the water well company knew they had wasted time and expense. But the people of Corsicana decided otherwise, and the "artesian well" became a curiosity for hundreds who came to see the oil bubbling to the surface. (Not everyone was impressed. In July the biggest news from Corsicana that made the Dallas paper was the death of a mule struck by a freight train.)[8]

Two of the locals decided, in fact, that an "oil strike" might be beneficial to Corsicana. Alexander Beaton and H. G. Damon retained the services of Pennsylvania oilman John Davidson late in that same summer of 1894, purchased an oil lease on the Bunert family property September 6, and incorporated the Corsicana Oil Development Company.

Davidson convinced two of the most famous oil financiers in the United States, fellow Pennsylvanians James M. Guffey and John H. Galey, to invest in the new company, while Beaton and Damon purchased the rights to other leases even within the city limits. Guffey and Galey would realize half of any profits from the five wells they contracted to subsidize.[9]

"Colonel" James McClurg Guffey was one of the most fascinating personalities in the petroleum industry, even though he personally knew next to nothing about the business from a geological or scientific point of view. A flamboyant character with a penchant for "making the sale," Guffey has been variously described as "a circuit-riding salesman" and a "Buffalo Bill look-alike." He was given to brightly colored vests and outrageously pleated shirts, Prince Albert coats worn year round, and a broad-brimmed black hat that sat atop his flowing white locks. His Windsor tie, poised just below a long white mustache, completed the remarkable picture. A British visitor to Pennsylvania had once remarked of him that he was "an example of the generally accepted type of an American," while an editor of an oil magazine had been somewhat less disingenuous: "Dash and push had characterized his [Guffey's] operations from the very first and he had not then, nor now, reached the point of life when he was content to travel by freight train if there was an express or flyer to be had." For all of his outlandish presentation, however, Guffey was a deal-maker of great prowess. In addition, his over-done stylization had not kept him from becoming deeply involved in the political world that he loved so dearly. In the early 1880s Guffey served as Democratic national chairman during President Chester Arthur's brief administration.[10]

The colonel's partner, John H. Galey, was, on the other hand, a pure oilman from Pittsburgh who had a special knack for knowing when petroleum was near and when the deal to obtain it was sweet. "Dr. Drill," as some Pennsylvania newspapermen knew him, was diminutive, quiet, and never given to the publicity that Guffey loved. But what Guffey lacked in knowledge, Galey possessed with a deep passion. For Galey, the hunt for oil was often as exciting and satisfying as the ultimate profit that the hunt made for him and his leasing company. Galey "smelled" the oil; Guffey swung the deal. They were a nationally known pair and had made themselves rich in the oil patches of Pennsylvania and Kansas. When word of oil came from Central Texas, John Galey went to Corsicana; when it would soon clarion from Beaumont, Galey would be one of the first Easterners on the train to southeast Texas.[11]

Drilling operations in Corsicana continued to use the rudimentary materials and tools that had their origins in Titusville, cable and rotary outfits. These included the Johnston rotary with Baker grip rings, first championed with the Chapman patent and used extensively in Illinois water wells; the Cameron and the Parker rotary machines and swivels; and hydraulic rotaries, which were rapidly replacing the antiquated percussion tools. In all of these patented rigs, the basic materials were similar: a hoist or drawworks consisting of a drum shaft, sprockets, and chains; rubber and canvas hose, pulley blocks, and ropes; a variety of floor tools; and pumps and bits of individual design. This equipment could deal with most of the obstacles beneath the surface, and at the relative depth required (although they would prove inadequate against the Spindletop sands).[12]

The first well, dug in 1895 to 1,030 feet, produced a "natural flow" of oil out of shale sand of less than three barrels daily, and the second well came up dry. But in May of 1896, a well drilled at Fourth and Collins Streets came in at 22 barrels a day, and the fourth and fifth wells drilled that summer produced at that same level. The Corsicana drilling had been considered successful.[13]

This now-seemingly miniscule production paid off in great dividends to the people of Corsicana, and to the oil promoters who soon arrived *en masse*, as derricks went up all over the city and "the boom" began. One of the first arrivals was Joseph Stephen Cullinan, a tall, handsome Pennsylvania oilman already well known in the industry. Cullinan had been an erstwhile partner with John D. Rockefeller's Standard Oil operations, and his presence in Texas surely raised concerned political eyebrows. Cullinan's impact in Corsicana—and in Beaumont—would be significant.

The Texas Petroleum Oil Company was organized in 1896, next the locally owned Southern Oil Company, and a handful more in the months that followed. Western Union opened its first telegraph office in the town, and Southwestern Telephone & Telegraph bought out the local Mutual Telephone Company. The Oil Man's Club, controversial because of its noticeably Irish Catholic flavor in the midst of a heavily Protestant town, opened its doors above the Freedman's Store on Beacon Street in 1899. It claimed sixty members.[14]

The entire east side of the city was pocked with wooden derricks, some crammed into spaces only a few feet from each other. Corrals, barns, and gardens were removed so drillers could bring in their machinery; locals signed off on leases on tiny lots in their backyards. Speculators and rig workers descended on the Central Texas town by the hundreds, coming by train from the Midwest and "back East." Hotels and saloons popped up on street corners. The city limits expanded, and every nook and cranny was either for sale or for rent: overcrowded streets, liveries, and boarding-houses were commonplace. Corsicana saw 350 new buildings built in 1899 alone.[15]

In 1897, fifty-seven wells were drilled in and around the city, and all but seven struck oil. That year, 66,000 barrels of oil were produced in Texas, over ninety percent from the Corsicana boom. By the end of the following year, oil production had quintupled, as another 287 successful wells were dug in Corsicana, and in 1899 oilmen prospered to the tune of $900,000. The composite area of the nearly 400 wells was only ten square miles! In addition, a dozen or more gas wells produced on the outskirts of town and as far away as Colonel W. J. McKie's farm seven miles from Corsicana. McKie, a business associate by now of Joseph Cullinan's, had been persuaded to lease mineral rights on his place in exchange for a small share of the profits everyone hoped would come.[16] Nearly every-one, including the speculators, gamblers, and wildcatters, profited. The people of Corsicana had gone "oil crazy."

OIL AND TEXAS POLITICS

In Corsicana, Joe Cullinan stood out in one of the now-myriad oil fields, staring with disgust as yet another successful drilling operation ended, literally, in flames. Gas pockets, numerous in the Texas oil patch, often flared during the drilling, and the lack of any process by which to control this event had resulted in the destruction of derricks, several injuries, and the closing down of what might have been profitable oil wells. Another problem, sometimes even more significant to the long-range success of a field, was the improper system used to "plug" abandoned wells. As water filled these abandoned holes, the oil deposit became contaminated, pres-sure beneath the surface changed, and a field's "life" could be irrevocably shortened.

Cullinan's experience back East enabled him to understand this prob-lem, but attempts to pass on the knowledge to these Texas operations proved futile and frustrating. Pennsylvania had initiated state-wide legis-lation to regulate compulsory well-plugging as early as 1878; New York, Ohio, and West Virginia had followed over the next thirteen years with similar regulations. Something had to be done in Corsicana. Cullinan wrote to a business associate: "In this country such legislation was essential where there are so many small holders, many of them wholly inexperienced and not likely to go to the expense of plugging wells unless compelled to do so."[17]

With local support for his ideas, Cullinan became a lobbyist to the Texas legislature in early 1899, and was successful in persuading Navarro County Congressman Robert E. Prince to introduce a bill "to regulate the drilling, operation, and abandonment of gas, oil, and mineral water wells and to prevent certain abuses connected therewith." House Bill 542 was referred to committee on February 14. Cullinan and other Corsicana businessmen spoke before the committee, which sent the bill to the floor on February 25. The House passed the bill March 6 and the Senate just seventeen days later, noting the critical time element "as surface water in wells now abandoned is calculated to ruin the oil field in Navarro County." Governor Joseph Sayers signed the new law on March 29. Among other provisions was a $100 penalty for violation of the new regulations for plugging abandoned wells in Texas. (Cullinan had hoped for a stiffer penalty, and warned his Texas oil colleagues that more stringent regulations would ultimately have to be considered. He was right.)[18]

Legislating Texas oil, however, had actually been a part of the highly charged, highly entertaining Texas political scene for several years leading up to Cullinan's efforts, and had been heretofore focused on two of the most powerful entities, and enemies, in the Populist era—Standard Oil of Ohio and Texas Governor James Stephen Hogg.

> Now in London all was ready,
> And arrangements were complete,
> Governor Hogg in all his glory,
> Great King Edward was to greet.
>
> The Ambassador was saying,
> "You must look your very best;
> In the regulation costume,
> At the court you must be dressed.
>
> "You must wear a sword and buckler,
> Breeches fastened at the knee."
> Hogg was filled with consternation,
> "Then a pretty sight I'd be."

He said, "Rigged in all these gewgaws,
I will not attend the ball,
I'll dress like an American,
Or I'll not appear at all."[19]

James Stephen Hogg did go to the ball, dressed to a fare thee well for the king. But for all the foolishness of the song, Hogg had gone to England for a serious purpose: to obtain investments for the Hogg-Swayne oil syndicate.

Seven years earlier, the recently retired Texas governor was embroiled in one of the most galling political fights of his remarkable public life, a fight over the monopolizing of the Texas oil fields. The ultimate outcome of that fight would in part determine the future of the oil industry in the Southwest, and whether it too would finally come under the massive controls of John Rockefeller and Standard Oil.

On an October afternoon in 1894, Governor Hogg stood on a small podium in Rockdale addressing friends and political allies with a farewell address. The atmosphere was celebratory: the Populist governor was leaving office after four challenging years. In part, he said: "The dark clouds that lowered over Texas and cast a gloom upon the hopes of the people two or three years ago have passed away, leaving the bright sunshine of content in the hearts of a reunited Democracy to shed its inspiring rays upon the feelings of every Texan. . . . Then why should we not all be happy? Why should not I be proud? Why should not my loyal, faithful supporters through so many hot, trying ordeals join in and share the glory that must crown our splendid State as a result of these magnificent laws? Texas," he declared with a flourish, "is safe!"[20]

James Stephen Hogg was referring to a series of reform laws that had passed during his administration, the most significant being those that tackled the incoming monopolies and trusts from outside the state, notably the railroad conglomerates and Standard Oil of Ohio. On July 6, 1889, the Waters-Pierce Oil Company, acting as a front to Rockefeller's elaborate petroleum trust, had been granted a charter to operate in Texas, this despite the efforts of then Attorney General Charles Culberson.

The Hogg administration had subsequently worked hard to overturn the ruling. By 1894 preliminary indictments had been brought against the chief officers of Waters-Pierce in a Waco court, including Rockefeller himself; Henry Clay Pierce, president; Vice President Arthur M. Finley, residing in Galveston; and Standard Oil's Henry C. Folger, a major player in the Texas operations. The business activities of Waters-Pierce, according to the court records, violated the spirit of both the Texas anti-trust laws (strengthened by Hogg himself while serving as attorney general) and the Sherman Anti-Trust Act passed by Congress in 1890. To put a dramatic exclamation point on the proceedings, extradition papers were filed against Rockefeller and Flagler to bring them to Texas. McClennan County Sheriff John W. Baker was ordered to retrieve the two and bring them to the Fifty-fourth State District Court.

Although the respective governors of New York and Florida refused to grant the extradition request on Constitutional grounds, and despite the public reference by Rockefeller's chief counsel Samuel C. T. Dodd that his boss was being harassed by "those crazy socialistic laws [in Texas]," Governor Hogg continued his attack against Waters-Pierce and Standard Oil. Shortly after Hogg left office in 1895, a division manager of Waters-Pierce in Denison, E. T. Hathaway, was convicted of being a party to "a conspiracy against trade" and fined $50! Hathaway refused to pay the fine, was put in a Texas jail, and subsequently released in June, 1896, by a criminal appeals judge.

Other cases circulated through the courts against Waters-Pierce division agents in 1895 and 1896, while the Texas legislature reinforced the state's anti-trust law with loophole-closing amendments. When one case appeared before the U.S. Fifth Circuit judge, as *John W. Baker, Sheriff v. William Grice,* it was sent on to the U.S. Supreme Court for a final showdown.[21]

Meanwhile, Texas Attorney General Martin M. Crane had begun additional proceedings against Waters-Pierce in an Austin courtroom. On June 15, 1897, the Texas court ruled against the oil trust, a judgment upheld the next March by the U.S. civil appeals court. Although Grice ultimately won his appeal in the highest court of the land, Waters-Pierce lost this one on March 19, 1900, when the justices upheld all three counts brought by the state of Texas. Eventually, all appeals exhausted, Standard Oil paid an unprecedented fine of $1.8 million to Texas for its violations. It was a monumental, and vindicating, moment for Hogg and his reformers, who had spent more than a decade fending off the outside monopolies that had threatened Texas business—this yet ten months before the Spindletop gusher would forever change the oil industry.[22]

The celebration may have been short-lived, for the Waters-Pierce Oil Company applied for a new charter to operate in Texas before the print had dried on the Supreme Court decision! And this next round, James Stephen Hogg would be only a citizen-warrior while his opponent would be tough and powerful Texas State Representative Joseph Bailey. The site of the heavyweight political fight was the State Democratic Convention in Waco August 8–10.

At a meeting of the State Bar Association earlier that summer, news of the granting of a new charter for Waters-Pierce had brought this electrical charge from Hogg, as he called the decision "a farce and a travesty upon justice, for the contracts were not changed, the agents were not changed . . . the company didn't even change the mules which were drawing its wagons." Hogg concluded, "If our trust laws are to be held under such precarious conditions as that we had as well wipe them out."[23]

The assault continued in Waco. State Representative Joseph W. Bailey waffled on the issue as he sought to salvage his political reputation. Bailey had done business with an officer of the Waters-Pierce Oil some time earlier, seemed to have supported the rechartering effort, and now backpedaled on the convention floor by declaring he had "warned" the oil company that it had better obey Texas trust laws or face the consequences. "He [Pierce] came here, took an oath he would uphold the majesty of our law, begging permission to conduct his business in conformity with the law," argued Bailey.

Citizen Hogg would have none of it. Rising to speak before the convention, he began by asking, "Shall Texas, or the trusts control?" Met by shouts and cheers, he blistered Bailey, Waters-Pierce, and Standard Oil, defending his own administration's struggles against the trusts: "We finally have a hold on the tail of the slimy serpent and they should not let it get hidden [again] in the tall grass." The *Dallas News* called it "the most acrimonious and bitter fight in the history of the Democratic party since the day when Richard Coke dethroned Edmund J. Davis," a bit hyperbolic, but respective of the debate's decibel level those hot August days. No specific action was taken by the convention on the issue, but another lively Texas debate had gone into the state's political annals, and many thought it had been one of the (numerous) great moments for Jim Hogg.

There was some irony, of course. First, the debate over oil trusts was taking place only days, literally, before the Lucas well would begin drilling outside of Beaumont on Big Hill. And second, Big Jim Hogg would soon be at the forefront of a prospering oil syndicate backed by Eastern money and raising concerns, though unwarranted, that he had "gone over to the other side" after Spindletop.

PATTILLO HIGGINS

I got the idea for starting up an oil company when I was working manufacturing bricks, looking for fuel and trying to save money. I studied the
oil business. They hadn't learned just yet how to refine oil, hadn't learned
how to develop oil. They just didn't know how to handle it.

Some of the class wanted to go down to Sour Springs—that's what we
called the area then—and they wanted me to take them on a trip down
there. There was a man who lived near me who owned a hack, a wagon
with a long body and a long seat on each side, carried twelve people. He
had two pretty gray horses and his little rig was nice. Charged me two
dollars.

That's when I noticed something peculiar about the five springs that
were out there. It was kind of dry time and the water was low. So when we
bailed out a little deeper, probably a foot or so, well, I noticed little clods.
Just a pile of little rock formations and different kinds, and I got to looking
at that. Well, I just decided then from looking at that that was an oil field—
those certain indications. You might say at the time it was theory, my
theory.

I organized the Gladys City Oil, Gas, and Manufacturing Company.
We got our charter on the 24th of August, 1892. I named the company
after Gladys Bingham, a little girl in my Sunday School class and the girl
whose picture was on my letterhead. I had a Baptist Sunday School. Her
parents were Episcopalian, but talking to other children in the class, she
wanted to join my class so I took her in.[24]

There was a sign on the north side of Big Hill that read: "This 1077
acres for sale—cheap." It had been placed there by agents of the James A.
Veatch survey. The asking price was $6 per acre. Pattillo Higgins knew he
had to have that land if he was ever going to get the opportunity to drill
for oil among the sour springs outside of Beaumont.

In the hot summer days of 1892, Higgins went practically door to door
selling his idea of oil near the town, almost always met with skepticism at
best, a scornful laugh more often. He sat in the drugstore and entertained customers with his vision—all for naught. He talked about the
salt dome formations across the country and the one near Beaumont and
the oil deposits sure to be found beneath. He described in painstaking
details the geological reasoning for this theory; he talked about anticline
pressure and sulphur and gas pockets. He drew sketches on café napkins

and accepted the mostly good-natured rebuffs he received from nearly everyone who would listen.[25]

But there were two men who did listen to Bud Higgins that summer, two men with the same Christian names—George Washington Carroll and George Washington O'Brien. Years earlier, as he made his peace with God and was baptized in a tributary of the Neches River one evening, Pattillo remembered being welcomed to the Christian fold by Mr. Carroll, an influential conservative Baptist and the president of the Beaumont Lumber Company. And "Cap'n" O'Brien, founder of Beaumont's Methodist Church, a Confederate war veteran and an able attorney, not only appreciated the effort of young Higgins to make something of himself, but had in fact held a curiosity for oil on Big Hill since the letter he had received thirty years earlier from a friend and fellow officer who had a similar vision. Both of these upstanding citizens saw something in Pattillo that no one else did, and both agreed to subsidize his latest endeavor. Besides, O'Brien owned land on Big Hill.[26]

At attorney O'Brien's suggestion, he, Carroll, Higgins, and J. F. Lanier, who owned 123 acres on the mound as well, incorporated the Gladys City Oil Company that summer, capitalized at $200,000. With Carroll's endorsement at the bank, Higgins swung a loan and purchased the Veatch survey for $5,000 on September 17, 1892. Higgins explained later, "Closed the deal right there. Went to Mr. Carroll and told him about it, took him out there and showed him the ground, and said, 'Now if it turns out like I believe it will, it'll be worth millions of dollars.'"[27]

"The Millionaire," as mocking citizens called Higgins in the weeks that followed, became increasingly frustrated when his company "directors" dragged their feet in the next step: drilling into the salt dome formation. "They put me in mind of a sea captain of a schooner I used to know," chided Higgins. "The captain would run his schooner into a port and unload. When he was through unloading he would wait for a fair wind to sail, and when the fair wind came, he would wait to see if it would hold before he sailed. He was always waiting to see how things would turn out and never got things done timely!"[28]

By early 1893 Higgins had extended his credit in the purchase or lease of other tracts around Big Hill, and finally convinced his company colleagues to drill. The oil company signed a contract with M. B. Looney of Dallas on February 17. Looney had been in Beaumont in 1889 drilling an 800-foot water well for the city adjacent to the town square when Higgins had first met him. This contract called for a well to be dug "to a depth not more than fifteen hundred feet" some three miles out of the city "for the purpose of ascertaining if there be oil, gas, sulphur or other valuable minerals in that vicinity, and if not, artesian water." The actual drilling was subcontracted out to twenty-two-year-old Walter B. Sharp, an unusually bright and industrious driller from Corsicana.[29]

The "Looney Project," as skeptical Beaumonters called it, fared poorly from the outset. Higgins immediately criticized the lightweight fishtail bit that Looney and Sharp wanted to use: the dome was too tough for this, argued Higgins to no avail. The drilling began late, not until March 22, and the going was slow from day one. The other directors scolded Higgins for his constant interfering with the drilling. Heavier than usual spring rains flooded the hill, and wind swept the small wooden derrick away at one point in the slow process. When they hit a gas pocket, the Gladys City Company placed a boiler tank at the site in hopes of at least realizing some benefit from the hole. But one of the crew climbed into the tank for an inspection and an ensuing explosion blew the man across the field. Finally, quicksand proved more than a match against Looney's flimsy equipment, and in July, at 418 feet, the drillers pulled out and abandoned the effort. In a moment of aggravation, Higgins ignited the "gasser" one summer day, and the flare that blew for the next two years became a beacon for "the millionaire's" broken dreams.[30]

Higgins's frustration was another man's prank. Young Clint Wood, who came to Beaumont in 1891 as a ten-year-old, recalled his earlier days. "Before Spindletop came in Walter and Jim Sharp were already there drilling. They got down to 400–500 feet and couldn't go any further because they didn't have the machinery. These wells would blow off every thirty minutes, gas wells. The gas would burn there for weeks and weeks until a storm would come along and put it out, then it'd just be a gasser. I used to go out there on Sundays on my bicycle and light the well up again. It'd make a whole lot of noise when you put a match to it. That was funny to me, to light that thing."[31]

In 1894 the nation's economy found itself strangling in one of the worst depressions in its centennial history. Commerce in southeast Texas ground to a halt as the economy worsened. Higgins had decided to return to the brick business, but there was no building in the Beaumont area that year, or the next, and little reason for Pattillo to do any more than keep plugging his now-tiring vision. His oil company was drying up as well, as Carroll and O'Brien—still "believers"—pulled back on all of their investments until better economic winds would blow: the Gladys City

Company was little more than a single dry hole and a fancy letterhead. Higgins even tried to shift his dream, and his company's business, to natural gas. He brought a sample of the combustible material in a wooden keg to George W. Carroll's office one day, and lit a match to ignite the gas from a spigot! It was a miracle that Higgins and Carroll and half the building didn't disintegrate: the flame went out, and with it Bud Higgins's last hope for a revival of his fortune's dream.[32]

But if he had little else, Pattillo had perseverance. In January, 1895, Higgins wrote E. T. Dimble, a state geologist in Austin, inviting him to Beaumont for a personal tour and assessment of the oil and gas potential there. Dimble sent an able assistant named William Kennedy, also a noted geologist, to see Higgins. Their initial visit in late February was cordial and both seemed optimistic at first, but as the "tour" wore on, Higgins began to feel that he was losing Kennedy. The geologist had agreed that there were potential problems to be overcome and that the current drilling process might be inadequate to the task, but Kennedy had a greater concern than that. Higgins recalled later the precise words that stunned him: "What I think, sir, is that you are wasting your time," concluded Kennedy, "and your money if you are looking for oil or gas here on the coastal prairie." The geologist explained there could be no oil deposits for miles in any direction based on the accepted geological data. "Rock," he said, "is necessary before you find oil," noting that a water well at 1,400 feet had been drilled in Beaumont where no rock formations had been found. "Your theories are without scientific basis."

Higgins was shocked and discouraged, but not nearly as much as he would be a month later, when an article written by Kennedy appeared in the *Beaumont Journal* bitterly criticizing Higgins's misplaced vision. Kennedy predicted that no substantial deposits of oil or gas would ever be found in the Beaumont area, and, as he wrote in a published article in April, "Instead of wasting money looking for the impossible, it would be much better for Beaumont to see to it that she obtain a good and sufficient supply of pure, wholesome, palatable water." As for Higgins, Kennedy wrote that his well "was dead and the money expended on it, a piece of extravagance only equaled by the foolishness of the advice under which it was taken. . . . There are hundreds of ways by which [prosperous drilling] can be done without frittering money away upon the idle dreams or insane notions of irresponsible parties on the vain outlook for either oil or useful gas."[33]

Pattillo Higgins was devastated, a laughingstock in his community, and a man of broken dreams. He would have his day of vindication, of course, and would even have the opportunity of confronting Kennedy after the Spindletop gusher came in. But now he was at his lowest moment.

But the one-armed Sunday School teacher had hardly a moment to sigh before another remarkable turn of events. That very spring, the West Virginia–based Savage Brothers Drilling Company arrived nearly at his doorstep. Attracted by the recent discovery of oil in Corsicana, the Easterners came to Sour Lake to investigate possible drilling sites, heard about Higgins in Beaumont, and paid him a visit. They offered to lease the myriad tracts around Big Hill in the Gladys City Company's name, and for a ten percent royalty drill for oil and gas. Higgins objected as soon as he saw the same flimsy drilling equipment—"coffee grinder rigs," he snorted—that Looney and Sharp had use two years earlier, but his partners, desperately in need of cash flow, signed a contract on May 27, 1895. Under the operations of the Texas Oil and Mineral Company, the Savage Brothers went to work. But at three hundred feet, the quicksand caught up with them as it had previously, and the West Virginians pulled out. Higgins had been correct, but that was little consolation to him or to his partners.[34]

Plummer Barfield was nine years old when he went to work for Pattillo on that drilling project around Big Hill.

> I was just kind of a sightseer, but my brother was driving an ox team for Mr. Higgins. My daddy had a portable steam boiler that Pattillo borrowed to pump water for his drilling rig. And my brother had the ox team and he started out with the boiler and he was crossing the T&NO railroad tracks down near Iron Bridge. It was summertime and there was a storm come up and lightning hit the rail lines somewhere up the line and it come right down the line and killed two of those oxen when they stepped on the rails.
>
> Well, I was sitting on the back of the wagon and I got scared and I ran ¾ of a mile back to the house and told Daddy that everybody had been killed. And we saddled up two horses and went out and saw my brother coming in with just two oxen and that wagon. Anyway, we finally moved that boiler from Willie Barr's rice farm over to the rig. Pattillo pumped water that was coming in from Roadeye Gulley southeast of there.
>
> I don't remember what the people thought of Pattillo then, but [they] never did insinuate that he was unrational, nothing like that.[35]

Shortly thereafter, the Savage Brothers succeeded in bringing in a shallow well near Sour Lake, at fifteen barrels a day. Carroll and O'Brien immediately renegotiated with the drilling company to return to Beaumont for another try. Ignored by his partners as he strenuously objected, Higgins resigned from his own company and sold his stock to George Carroll. He had given up on the company he created, but not on the vision. "I sold my interest in the company," he wrote, "and bought other land in the oil belt adjoining the company's lands."

Idled by frustration and no money to invest in land purchase or drilling, Pattillo Higgins spent the next two years in other ventures designed to distract him from his dream. He built strange and exotic machines to keep himself busy, wrote a commercial and industrial directory, *Deepwater Counties, a Special Directory of Southeast Texas,* which he marketed, and published a map of Jefferson County that he copyrighted and sold to the Beaumont Board of Trade. The map was crowned with a drawing of Edison's newfangled "light bulb" accompanied on each side by portraits of Gladys Bingham and Cecil Keith, another of his Sunday School students![36]

But he never entirely let his dream of oil gushers on Big Hill slip away. Higgins bought, and then sold, hundreds of acres of land around the mound. He was offered but was unable to buy $54,000 worth of the Gladys City Company tracts, yet he managed to hold on to what would be a significant 33 acres atop the hill. He even wrote John D. Rockefeller to invite him into a partnership. Rockefeller politely declined because of what he termed "adverse geological judgments" on that area: Kennedy's article continued to haunt.

July 9, 1896
Mr. Pattillo Higgins, Beaumont, Texas
Dear Sir: Again after a long absence I have returned and find yours of May 20th awaiting me. On careful reflection I do not think that I care to undertake the proposition that you submit. There is too much guesswork about it. I am however very greatly obliged to you for your kindness. Truly yours, F[lagler]. Rockefeller, Vice-President, Standard Oil Company[37]

In the winter of 1898–99, Higgins wrote an advertisement seeking an engineer who would be willing to invest in Higgins's idea, as he set it out in the article: a drilling operation in southeast Texas looking for oil, gas, or sulphur. The article was published in at least two national journals. In a letter dated May 4, 1899, one man answered, the only response to Higgins's published plea. That man was Captain Anthony F. Lucas of Washington, D.C. "Pardon me for writing you direct," the letter said in part, "yet I would say that as I have practically done all the explorations of salt deposits in Louisiana, I am naturally much interested to learn conditions of things of the sulphur deposits you are interested in near Beaumont."[38]

ANTHONY F. LUCAS

The Spindletop salt dome is actually a stalklike core of rock salt which has protruded up through the overlying beds of sands, shales and limestones, thus causing the pierced sedimentary beds to dip radially away from the salt core. The effect of the uplift of the salt on the dip of the overlying sediments can be illustrated by laying a flat, unwrinkled handkerchief on a table and gradually lifting the cloth with the fingers from the very center. This will show the radial effect of the plug forcing itself through the strata.

The Spindletop salt core is roughly circular in shape, about one mile in diameter. The uplift of the salt mass had an effect on the surface area overlying the dome, forming a mound or small hill, approximately the same diameter as the subsurface salt core, which is quite perceptible above the flat prairie lands of the Gulf Coast. This topographic feature is a characteristic surface expression of most of the piercement-type domes in the Gulf coastal plains. The mound at Spindletop rises barely fifteen feet above the general level of the plain, but this rise stands out against the very flat and gently sloping land.[39]

The only man to respond to Pattillo Higgins's advertisement was Austrian, born into the Luchich family of Dalmatia. Schooled in mining and engineering at Graz, Lucas joined the Austrian navy but left following a visit to an uncle in Michigan and moved to Macon, Georgia. Changing his name to the Americanized Lucas in 1887, he married Caroline Fitzgerald, daughter of a prominent Georgia physician, and applied for U.S. citizenship. The couple moved to the nation's capitol where Lucas began his career in engineering. With their one-year-old son Anthony in tow, the family moved to Louisiana in 1893 where the captain was employed in the operations of salt mines and wells. His valuable experience over the next six years in the fields at Jefferson Island, Petit Anse, and Anse LaButte, as well as occasional trips into Texas on business and pleasure, helped him form a base of knowledge regarding the mineral deposits and geological formations along the Gulf Coast. Similarities in the Big Hill salt dome with his Louisiana mines meant, for Lucas, the real potential for finding sulphur, his first objective in the pursuit. In Washington over that winter, Lucas had been more than just idly curious when he read about what this Beaumont brick maker had in mind.[40]

Captain Lucas arrived in Beaumont in mid-June, spent several days touring the area with Higgins, and on June 20 the two partners signed a deal for the lease-purchase of 663 acres on Big Hill, land owned by the Gladys City Oil, Gas, and Manufacturing Company! Within a month, additional contracts had guaranteed Lucas ninety percent of the mineral royalties, Higgins ten percent plus another ten percent offered by the grateful directors of the company Pattillo had created seven years before. Higgins hired his brother-in-law Tom Sugg, a road contractor, to prepare a site on Lot 44 atop the dome for drilling.

"I dreamed that I was in a small boat in a river," Higgins entered into his diary on June 28. "All at once the waves began to roll high and my boat was tossed high, back and forth. I studied whether to turn back or go ahead. I decided to trust God and go forward. . . . My boat soon passed over the waves and the water became still and smooth." He was pleased to share his dream with his Sunday School children and was encouraged by their optimistic response.[41]

The fourth well on Big Hill was spudded in in early July. Lucas and Higgins discussed at length the still-inadequate drilling rig that the captain had brought from Louisiana, but Lucas convinced his partner he could make a thousand feet with it as he had many times before. But by the end of the year, and at only 575 feet, Lucas began to experience irreconcilable problems with the deep sands under the salt dome. Although they had managed to draw up a small amount of heavy green crude oil, the anticlinal pressure was too much—the well-casing pipe collapsed just after New Years, 1900, and Lucas shut down the operation.[42]

Lucas and Higgins were down, but not out. Not yet. Higgins knew that the oil was much deeper than they had been able to drill thus far, and that a different drilling rig would ultimately be necessary for success. And Lucas agreed. Unable to persuade any locals to invest in their operation, Lucas ventured back East to Washington, Pennsylvania, and New York City. In a brief discussion with Pennsylvania U.S. Congressman Joseph

Crocker Sibley, himself an oil entrepreneur, Lucas was warned "against the dire consequences of unsubstantiated enthusiasm.... If you will assure me of several thousands of barrels of oil daily at Gladys City," said Sibley, "I'll go along with you." To which Lucas retorted on his way out the door, "If I could assure you of [that], I doubt that I would be here asking for your assistance." In New York he paid a visit to John D. Rockefeller's chief officer, Henry C. Folger, who was impressed enough by the Austrian American to at least send one of Standard Oil's own geologists to Beaumont to investigate.[43]

Calvin Payne arrived in Beaumont late in February, accompanied by Joseph S. Cullinan from Corsicana. For days the four men walked over the mound repeatedly, studied the sour springs, the crude that had been brought up in December, and Higgins's charts and maps. At first interested, Payne finally concluded that the evidence was insufficient to support Pattillo's theory, and therefore not worth the financial risk to Standard Oil.[44]

But Joseph Cullinan was not so sure, and not ready to abandon the enterprise just yet. Cullinan went to Port Arthur to meet with a man named Craig—agent for the Kansas City and Southern Railroad and a business associate of its owner, John "Bet a Million" Gates. "We want Gates," Cullinan admitted to the agent. "There's millions in this." Craig headed for Chicago on the next train, where he met with Gates and recommended Cullinan and Lucas on the basis of their reputations. The two discussed the advantage to themselves, including a pipeline to Port Arthur, refineries, and shipping. Gates went to Beaumont and found Cullinan. "Suppose you do find oil?" the wily Gates asked Cullinan. "What are you going to do, feed it to the longhorns? I got the railroad and I got the docks. You'll need a pipeline, and you'll need a refinery. They tell me, Cullinan, that you're the best damned refinery man in the business.... If we get oil, I'll finance you to build the best pipeline and refinery in the world. We'll build a fleet of boats. We'll sell more oil than John D. ever dreamed of." Cullinan made the deal.[45]

But back in Beaumont, when Dr. Willard Hayes, soon to be chief of the U.S. Geological Survey office, happened in for a look and concluded his review on yet another negative note, Lucas's proposed backers fled and so did, apparently, any last hope for resuming drilling on Big Hill.

"Captain Lucas," Higgins told his disheartened partner that spring, "those men should be asking you, not telling you. Your experience in

Louisiana makes you the greatest authority in the world—probably the only authority—on salt domes. . . . I know there is oil here in greater quantities than man has ever found before. I wish I could help you [more], but I can't. But for God's sake don't stop because ignorant men in high places say to stop!" Higgins added sardonically, "And get your backing before that man writes a letter to the Beaumont newspaper."[46]

In this moment of discouragement, one positive voice sounded through the gloom, that of University of Texas geologist and professor Dr. William Battle Phillips. Phillips had come to Beaumont to witness the spectacle that was making the news and, after speaking at length with Higgins and Lucas, believed that they *were* correct in their salt dome theory. His recommendation was for Lucas to make contact with yet another Easterner, the diminutive but sharp John Galey, currently working on operations in Corsicana. This single event may have changed the shape of the oil industry forever—a single assenting voice among so many others, and a contact with one of the few men whose curiosity, passion, and "sixth sense" about oil could, and would, make a difference.[47]

Lucas visited Galey in Corsicana, and soon the two men were off to Pittsburgh to make their pitch to Galey's partner, the flamboyant James Guffey. Impressed by a possible enterprise in southeast Texas, the trio now marched down the street to see Andrew Mellon at his bank, one of the wealthiest corporate ventures in the world. Mellon was sold on the idea and agreed to finance the drilling expedition outside of Beaumont. Lucas was to return there and buy up as many of the leases as he could, while Guffey and Galey worked the finances. Despite Lucas's protestations, the three Easterners were adamant that Bud Higgins was no longer to be a part of the picture: another partner diluted the profits, and besides, Higgins's contribution to the project—the salt dome theory itself—had long since been made.

Lucas returned to Beaumont in May, 1900, and leased fifty acres of the Chaison tract and the 5,300 acre Hebert tract south of the hill. He obtained leases from V. Weiss, W. K. Kyle, and W. P. H. McFaddin, and 3,800 acres on the McClure tract southwest of the hilltop. By mid-summer the captain had bought 15,000 acres of mineral rights, including another 2,500 acres from the Gladys City Oil Company, and by September 18 he had met the objectives of his "secret" partners. Lucas was cash-poor, having agreed in good faith to work without remuneration, but was counting on the small percentage of royalties sure to come. James Guffey was in Pittsburgh, preparing the financial paperwork at Andrew Mellon's bank. John Galey was back in Corsicana, talking to Al and Curt Hamill about a drilling operation near Beaumont.

And Pattillo Higgins was out save for his thirty-three acres. His only consolation, as he recollected years later: "My theory was right."[48]

2

Spindletop!

Isaac Cline stood on what had been a street corner at Twenty-sixth Street and stared across the jumble of broken buildings, wagons, crates, and the piles of swollen bodies. What had been the growing, bustling island city of Galveston, Texas, was now no more than a pile of rubble four miles long and fifty feet high. He would soon learn that some 6,000 friends and neighbors had died in the path of the September 8 hurricane. As a meteorologist, Cline had had the warning but not in time to save but a handful; no one could ever have imagined the level of destruction this storm would bring. The city, if it could ever stand again, would have to start over.

Jim Baker received a telegram on Monday morning, September 23, informing him of the death of Texas businessman William Marsh Rice in his New York City apartment the night before. An elderly man, Rice had apparently succumbed to the ravages of age. But the author of the message, a bank officer in New York, added that a man of unknown business relations to Rice had just that very same morning appeared to cash a $25,000 cash from the Rice estate; a peculiar sense of timing, thought Baker. Before the week was out, Baker was on his way to New York City to investigate what would soon turn out to be the sensational murder mystery of one of the richest men in America.

In September, 1900, these two newsmakers—the Galveston hurricane and the murder of William Marsh Rice—made the headlines around the country and the world.[1] On a small rise just south of Beaumont, a seemingly insignificant drilling operation was under way. Its impossible destination was more than a thousand feet below the surface, its object: an oil deposit that few believed existed there. Its name, Lucas Well No. 1. Its destiny, the Spindletop Gusher on January 10, 1901.

THE HAMILL BROTHERS

When we arrived in Beaumont, we had a four mule team and we had provisions for ourselves and hay and feed for the mules. We also had a black boy with us to do the cooking. On our way to Pearl Street one of the mules got down in the mud and we had to cut the tugs off the harness in order for the mule to get out from being drowned.

On arriving at our destination we found our little camp house had to be cleaned out and there was oodles of little white and green, different colored frogs all around the roof. And when we'd be eating our meals those little frogs would jump and land right on our table, sometimes in the butter. And we had no ice and everything was warm and sometimes the butter would slide all over the table.

Mosquitoes were bad, they were almost galanippers. Grass was as high as the fences and mosquitoes would rise out of the grass and we had lots of difficulties with them.[2]

Curt Hamill and his brothers, Jim and Al, would be instrumental in the very opening gambit of the Spindletop phenomenon, for they had been selected to do the drilling. Their company, which operated a cable tool drilling rig, had begun with Jim's work out of Pennsylvania as a tool dresser for Fowler & McGilvery. Jim established a reputation in the East, brought his brother Al into the business, and the two of them landed in Corsicana among the oil hubbub. Curt toiled as a dairyman and farmer until 1898 when his brothers persuaded him to come work for them. At a whopping $55 a month it took little persuading. Late in 1898 Jim and Al invested in a rotary drilling rig, replacing what they considered to be the outdated cable tool rig being used by most other companies in Texas. This forward-looking decision would put them in a position to gain the recognition necessary for the Beaumont project nearly two years later. For as John Galey observed the Corsicana fields in 1899 and 1900, it was his judgment that the Hamills had what it took to make the leap to the Big Hill: the right machinery and the right attitude.

Galey visited Beaumont in the fall of 1900 to assist in the decision of where and when to begin drilling with his partner Anthony Lucas. But

Lucas was not in town that day, and Caroline Lucas accompanied Galey out to the tract instead. As the story is told, Galey stared at the sour springs by a hog wallow where Mrs. Lucas pointed, even as Pattillo Higgins had stared in that identical spot eight years before, stepped fifty feet away until he stood on a bald alkali spot amidst the windswept autumn grass, and drove a stake a foot down into the ground. "Here is something different," he remarked to himself. "Mrs. Lucas, tell the Captain we will drill here."[3]

A short time later, when the captain had returned, he and Galey discussed the location and the depth of the well (three were contracted to be dug eventually). Lucas was worried that the cable tool rigs could not make the 1,000-foot depth he had anticipated, and past experiences bolstered that concern. But Galey had a solution. "Captain, I know a man who can drill that well to 1200 feet if it can be done at all. His name is Jim Hamill."

Curt Hamill tells the story of what happened next.

> We were setting up our rig one day in Corsicana when Jim brought a man out to look at the machinery. He introduced the man to me as Captain Anthony Lucas. Captain Lucas wanted Jim to go to Beaumont, Texas and drill three wells for him. Jim agreed.
>
> A little later Jim came to me and said the rig would be shipped to a location near Beaumont. I was night driller on the rig. Jim said the day driller didn't want to go to Beaumont because of his family. He said he had arranged with Henry McLeod, a derrick builder and driller, to go along, and that our brother Al would go as contractor, but would work as one of the crew. Peck Byrd would go as fireman.
>
> "Jim," I told him, "if you'll raise my salary to eighty dollars a month, I'll go."
>
> "I'll do that," Jim said, "and I'll give you room and board because you are going to stay in a camp."
>
> We arrived in Beaumont about the first day of October.[4]

When Al Hamill, the youngest brother, arrived to complete the paperwork with Lucas, he asked the captain about lumber for the derrick even before he stepped completely off the train at the Beaumont station. Lucas was impressed with the sense of urgency the young man displayed and his seriousness about getting to work. They went directly to George W. Carroll's lumber yard, where Carroll was pleased to sell the lumber but equally pleased to make this friendly wager: if their well brought in 5,000 barrels a day, offered Carroll, the derrick lumber would be free. It seemed a bit of a silly offer—*a 5,000-barrel well?*—but Lucas told Al as they headed back into town that he believed that the derrick would end up being free of charge after all was said and done.[5]

Next on the agenda would be unloading a freight car of pipe for the drilling operation. The rail car was available on a side track, and a house mover had been contacted to unload and transport the heavy materials; however, a delay of several days was now expected. Lucas was frustrated, so Al suggested they locate the freight right away. They found it on a spur not too far from Big Hill. As Lucas looked on in wonder, Al Hamill proceeded to scramble to the top of the stack of pipes, unchain the freight, toss two pieces of six-inch pipe over the side to act as guides, and slide the remaining pipe—2,600 feet of it—down to the ground where it could be stacked and transported by wagons to the drilling site.[6]

J. D. Brantly accumulated a list that most accurately reflects the inventory of the Lucas rig as it went up that October:

> 1 wooden derrick: 60 ft 20x20 base, 3x3 water table with 3 crown sheaves, 1 catline sheave, 1 sand line sheave
> 1 steam boiler: locomotive type, 100 psi working pressure, 25 hp
> 1 steam engine: 9½x12, slide valve, reversible, 18 hp, 175 rpm, maximum working speed, Oil Well Supply Company (Corsicana) engine
> 1 drawworks: drum shaft 3 ½" cold rolled steel, line shaft 3" same, drum 36" wide with 30" flanges, single brake rim 30" diameter with 6" face, unlined brake band
> 2 steam pumps: 8x4½x10, 108–180 gpm at 156 psi, at 40–65 rpm, on 100 psi steam, Smith-Vaile pumps
> 1 rotary table: grip ring, opening to pass 16" bit, Chapman
> 2 hydraulic swivels: 2"
> 1 swivel casing hook: 4"
> 1 traveling block: iron, three 16" sheaves with 2" manila rope grooves
> 4 crown sheaves: 16" diameter, 2" manila rope grooves, mounted on live oak beams
> 1 catline sheave: 12" diameter, 1½" manila rope groove
> 1 sand line sheave: 12" diameter, 1" manila rope sand line groove
> 1 casing line: 1,000' 2" manila hard lay

1 catline: 320' 1½" manila hard lay

drill pipe: 1,500' 4" 10.66 lb merchant pipe

casing: 100' 12" 35.75 lb

           500' 10" 23 lb

           900' 8" 20 lb

        1,200' 6" 17 lb

[drill pipe and casing were of lapweld construction with short
   couplings]

2 45' lengths of 2" mud hose

No. 4 (1240) chain for drawworks and engine to drawworks

No. 3 (1030) chain for drawworks shaft to table[7]

Curt Hamill recollects what happened the next day following their arrival in Beaumont:

I went with McLeod and Al in the buckboard to the spot where we were going to drill. The derrick sills Al had ordered in Beaumont were already there. Al told me to survey a nearby bayou and see if I could tell how much water was there for us to use and how much pipe it would take to build a water line from the bayou to the well.

While I was doing this, Al and McLeod drove to Beaumont for supplies. I finished my job and was sitting on the derrick sills at the location when a man drove up to the fence in a buggy. He came over to where I was sitting.

"Young fellow," he asked, "are you going to work on this well?"

I said yes and he said he was Pattillo Higgins.

"If you get this well down," he said, "you're going to bring in an oil well."

I asked, "What makes you think there is oil here, Mr. Higgins?"

"I had a vision and a dream about this hill," he said. "I dreamed I saw houses over this hill and it bothered me so much that the next morning I went down to the livery stable and got me a horse and a post auger and came out here and spent a whole day on the hill. I drilled six post-holes as deep as the auger would go and carried the information in to Mr. Carroll and told him of my dream. . . . The following night I had another dream. This time I saw derricks over this hill with fluid going high in the air. I awoke sitting up in bed."

The day after I had the talk with Pattillo Higgins, the balance of the derrick lumber was brought out and our crew began building the derrick.

[In Corsicana there were regular crews who would hire on to a drilling operation at the beginning and construct whatever size derrick the company wanted. In Beaumont there weren't any derrick crews.] We found that our derrick builder, Henry McLeod, didn't know any more about building a derrick than the rest of us. We knew what the foundation should be, and the height the derrick should reach, and the size the crown should be. So we made a pattern out of light lumber on the ground and the derrick was built from that pattern. [It was a perfect structure when raised.] When completed it was a stout derrick because we pulled with all the might of our machinery and never damaged it.

While we were building the derrick, Perry McFaddin, one of the land owners, drove up in a buckboard. He had a Negro driver, and in the back of the buckboard, chained so they could not jump out, were two hound dogs. Captain Lucas was on the derrick floor and McFaddin joined him. While we were talking, Captain Lucas looked out and saw the Negro by one of the sour spring boxes. He had the dogs by their collars and was dousing them up and down in the spring. Captain Lucas shouted, "Don't do that! My wife drinks that water!"

Mr. McFaddin said, "Captain, I have been bathing my dogs in those springs for more than a year to keep fleas off them."

Captain Lucas said, "My wife has been drinking it all this time. She thinks it's healthy mineral water."[8]

DRILLING LUCAS NO. I

October 26, 1900, *The Beaumont Journal:*

Captain A. F. Lucas has done considerable drilling near this city in the district known as Gladys City, but his research in that territory has been without results. He now purposes going into the matter with improved machinery and with facilities for better investigation. To this end he has erected an entirely new derrick about one-half mile south of the former operations and while he has not yet begun drilling the plant is nearly ready for operation. In speaking of this matter this morning, Mr. Lucas was of course unprepared to say what the results would be, but it is manifest that he thinks there is oil in the fields where he is going to operate or it would be useless for him to drill into the earth.

The work of such men as these cannot but result in great good to the town in its march of progress. . . . In speaking to a *Journal* reporter this morning Captain Lucas said he had heard that rumors were claiming that a large flow of oil had been discovered near this city and as he was the only one known to be investigating close to Beaumont supposed it referred to him, but he characterized the rumor as humorous to a degree easily appreciated when it is known that he has not yet started his drill into the earth.[9]

The Hamill brothers worked through most of October, raising the derrick above the spot where John Galey had sunk his stake. They dug a thirty-foot long, four-foot deep slush pit and used mules to soften the clay. They dug another pit to supply the boiler, eight feet long by six feet wide, and five feet deep. The clay would hold the water with little seepage. They laid water lines from the bayou, and bought a carload of slab from the Beaumont sawmill and cords of wood for fuel. Finally, they laid out the pipes in the field nearby, and set up the slush pumps, the drawworks, and the manila rope.

Early on the morning of October 27, 1900, they began the drilling of Lucas Well No. 1. They opened a fourteen-inch hole and got down to forty feet—two joints of pipe—before they got into trouble. The pipe stuck, and it took the rest of the day to extricate the pipe from the sand. The next morning they started again, but at thirty-two feet they hit sand that had sloughed into the hole, and stuck once more. By November 1 the problem had not been solved.

Jim Hamill decided to set ten-inch pipe instead. It went easily into the fourteen-inch hole but stuck at thirty-five feet. He and Curt grabbed a piece of cable drill stem, welded a ring on the top and tied a rope through the ring. They rigged the heavy stem and used it to hammer the ten-inch pipe deeper into the hole. When it was level to the ground, they took a smaller drill pipe and washed the sand out from inside the ten-inch. This was laborious work, and slow-going, and the extra labor exhausted the water in the slush pit, the holding ditch, and the bayou, and exhausted the drilling crew as well. It was too much for one: Henry McLeod quit. "I didn't come down here to shovel sand," were his parting words.

The Hamills drilled a water well at sixty feet almost directly under the derrick, which solved the water supply problem but not the quicksand. Now it was time to be creative. Curt Hamill explains: "We made a back-pressure valve. We whittled a piece of wood off a soap box with a pocket knife and trimmed it where it would go inside a 4-inch collar. We cut a hole in the middle of the piece of wood and made a flap out of the sole of a boot to cover the hole. We tacked the flap over the hole. We put the device at the top of the first joint of pipe above the drilling bit. We could pump water down the pipe and it would push aside the flap and go through the hole in the wood and then on down through the drill bit. But when the sand tried to get back up the pipe, it would simply push the flap firm over the hole. . . . This helped until we got down to about 200 feet."[10]

But their next "invention" may have been not only the most creative but one of the most significant in the oil drilling industry for decades to come. And it took a herd of cows to make it work, the Reverend Cheney's cows.

When they stuck again at 150 feet, the Hamills built a drive-block out of two six-by-eighteen-inch pieces of lumber bolted on either side of a six-by-six. On top of this trough-like piece they attached a round steel plate with a four-inch hole cut out of it, where the pipe would go through. Below the plate they attached a cast iron bushing that screwed into the drilling pipe. "When we lifted the drive block," Curt explains, "it would slide up the four-inch. When we dropped it, it would slide down the four-inch and slam into the plate across the top of the eight-inch." The drive-block was dropped from high in the air, and the rope slipped off the cathead and the drive block to release it each time. "We must have burned up several thousand feet of rope doing this," admitted Hamill.[11]

In the next twenty days they drilled to 400 feet, cleaned out and re-worked the pits, and went down another 240 feet. There the pipe stuck again in the sand, the water supply became inadequate, and the jet in the water well failed. Then they ran out of wood to fuel the boiler. It was nearly December and the drilling operation was in trouble again.

While Al headed into town to purchase more wood slab, Curt, Jim, and Peck set about trying to clean out the pits. Each time the clay pits had filled with sand and lost water, the Hamills had gone to see the Reverend J. C. Cheney who lived near Big Hill, three miles over on McFaddin Canal, and borrowed his mule team and wagon to help haul the sand and clean the pits. Willie Henry, McFaddin's skilled black teamster, often helped. On this visit, Curt remembers muttering in frustration, "I believe if we could get some *muddy* water we could stay on top of that sand [in the hole] and keep our pump running and get through the sand."

"Oh," replied Cheney, "I could furnish you all the muddy water you want. My corral fills with mud every time it rains because the livestock tromps around in it."

The next morning Cheney had his cattle herded from the corral nearby to the slush pit by the derrick on Big Hill. While the Hamills pumped water into the pit, the cattle wandered about in the mud for nearly four hours, "turning it into a muddy slush." A makeshift hose and nozzle was attached from the drill pumps to the pit to keep the mud wet. When Al returned with a new jet for the water well, the new system was ready to go. The mud pumped into the hole pushed the sand aside and allowed an easier drilling through the stuff that had stopped every previous attempt to penetrate the salt dome formation. "Drilling mud" became the key to future oil operations.[12]

One more drilling obstacle presented itself during the first week in December, and this time it was Captain Lucas who brought the solution. The counter-pressure at this depth, exerted by the pump, would slow the drilling and, despite the mud, allow sand to back up into the hole. In addition, gas pressure in the hole was making the situation worse. The crew had exhausted its creative juices. But Lucas awoke in the middle of the night, grabbed a pine box and a rubber belt from his woodshed, and rode out to the derrick where Al was on the night shift. When Curt and Peck arrived at dawn, the four of them rigged a "check valve" on the pump, using the perforated box and rubber belt placed between the couplings of the casings. The check valve counteracted the pressure from the pump, and the problem was solved.[13]

At 854 feet the drilling began to go exceptionally slowly and not because of any sand build-up that the crew could see in the hole. Lucas pored over the detritus from the hole, and realized that the small egg-shaped pieces of rock were likely limestone. "You have drilled into the dome structure proper," he announced to the excited crew. "This proves we are right."[14]

Then, at 870 feet, a new layer of very fine sand presented itself as a potential problem, while at the same time the crew noticed some oil on top of the mud ditch. A rumor quickly spread into Beaumont that oil was being pumped into the ditches on Big Hill, but Lucas patiently explained to over-excited observers that the oil-sand was nothing—yet—to be excited about. And John Galey had become so discouraged by the slow progress he now suggested that they abandon this well and move to a tract of land on the opposite side of the hill. It was Caroline Lucas who intervened this time. "Mr. Galey," she said, "the contract calls for drilling this well to 1200 feet. I feel that every effort should be made to carry this well [to that depth]. We need to know what is down that far." Even the tiniest hint of oil overcame the threat of the new sand, and the harder rock layer that they had passed through brought a new sense of optimism. Al Hamill stretched his imagination, optimistically telling Galey that he thought this well might bring in an unprecedented "fifty barrels of oil daily." The drilling would continue.[15]

December 21, 1900, *The Beaumont Journal:*

Captain A. F. Lucas Meets with Some Degree of Success

The question of whether there is oil underlying the lands of Jefferson County has in a manner been solved yet the solution itself contains a mystery or perplexity which may be more difficult to work out than was the original proposition.... [Captain Lucas's] well has shown signs of oil, faint at first, but sufficient to give hopes that the success he had wished for has come.... [But] the most disheartening feature of the well is the presence of salt water: if it were not for that there would be hope, but for reasons not pertinent to the story there is fear for the further expenditure of money here.

Capt. Lucas has not given up hope, however, the oil seems to be there and this new question of whether it can be extracted in paying quantities is yet to be determined. But it will require money and perseverance, patience and experience to develop the well further.[16]

From December 9 to Christmas Eve the crew now drilled around the clock, working twelve- and eighteen-hour shifts. On December 24 they reached 1,020 feet with six-inch pipe and relatively little trouble. Lucas's log of the drilling indicates what they had come through beneath the hill:

854 feet	hard rock, apparently limestone
856 feet	fine oil-sand, with hard layer toward bottom and heavy pressure
880 feet	hard clay
960 feet	calcareous concretions with layers of hard sandstone
1,010 feet	heavy gas pressure[17]

But the crew was utterly exhausted. They had been at it for fifty-nine days, half of that in twenty-four-hour shifts. They had overcome a world of obstacles and kept going. They had had a hint of gas and oil, and some corroboration of the Higgins-Lucas salt dome theory. But they were dog-tired. John Galey told them to go home, take a break, enjoy the holiday season. The Hamills went back to Corsicana. Captain Lucas went home to Caroline across the Big Hill. Peck Byrd volunteered to keep an eye on the derrick and stayed in the camp house.

Appearing in the January 2, 1901, edition of *The Beaumont Journal* was a delightful letter from Captain A. F. Lucas, a good-natured response to several inquiries and editorials from the previous weeks. In part it read:

My attention has been called to an article lately published in your journal entitled "Gladys City Mystery," in which it quotes that on the 28th instant Gladys City hill was brilliantly illuminated, some of the good citizens of this town attributing the illumination to the gas under exploration, others to prairie fires, and still others to a house on fire, or perhaps St. Elmo's fire, and by yourself as my desire to test the force of the gas discovered. [It was a prairie fire at some distance from the Lucas well site.] Besides these rumors much has been said about my secrecy and the refusal of my men to give information at large. As the above was all news to me I decided to become a good subscriber to your newsy journal so that I, at least, may be "en courant" of what I am doing on Gladys City hill, or rather under it.

Regarding the secrecy of me or my men, I would say that your informant was frightened off, perhaps, by some fetching signs conspicuously placed around the works stating, "Keep off the grass," "Move on," and "Ask no questions and we'll tell you no lies," etc.

The fact of the matter is that these signs were placed there in fair weather when idlers were in plenty in search of some exciting novelty. Now they are somewhat scarce, as the drive is damned by a chilly blast and water, and genuine Texas mud is spattered all around.

Gas? Yes, bless you, we have it in plenty. Enough to stock a book agent, or shall I say, a land agent, or light up a Beaumont crossing. Besides gas, we have lots of hard work and are dealing with nature's agencies, which I am sorry to say, are even worse than the most persistent book agent that ever lived. We are harnessing it up, however, and may in time reach a point where we could write a history of how it was done and who did it. When such a time does come, if it ever will, I would be most happy to invite the whole city of Beaumont and neighborhood to come and see the new gas works on top. I have no secrecy in the matter and would be happy to be the means of establishing a new and prosperous industry in this growing city.

For the present I can only say that I am pursuing a geological investigation of nature's laboratory, with the view of attaining commercial possibilities, but have no secrets in the matter. On the contrary, I am glad to have visitors of the right kind, and such that can appreciate my efforts. Respectfully yours.[18]

The crew returned to work on New Year's Day, 1901. They hit a pocket of gas around 1,050 feet that blew rock, sand, water, and mud out of the hole with a tremendous explosion. The blast carried on for ten minutes, a harbinger? Jim Hamill had just stepped down from a wagon when the hole blew out, and the ponies he had just tied jerked their reins off the fence and scampered back into town.

A few days later the men encountered two odd circumstances. The fishtail bit apparently had driven into a crevice that seemed to skew it sideways despite the crew's efforts to push downward. And a strange yellow substance began to appear, floating, in the pits. Curt and Peck put some in small buckets and showed them to Lucas. "Floating sand," he surmised incorrectly, not realizing the irony of his first look at Texas sulphur—the very substance that had brought him to Texas in the first place![19]

On the evening of January 9, Anthony and Caroline Lucas sat in their living room, talking quietly. Michel T. Halbouty tells the story:

> Suddenly, the hill seemed to light up with a fantastic glow, and then the great light seemed to gather into one large ball of flame and come to rest on the crown block of the derrick. The Hamills said it gave off a low hissing sound for a few minutes. It was the St. Elmo fire, which for centuries had visited the hill as if beckoning men to a great treasure. It was the last time the phenomenon would ever be seen on the hill. The Captain told Carrie what it was. "Doesn't that have a special meaning for men of the sea?" she asked. "Yes," Anthony Lucas replied, still gazing at the hill. "It means their ship will come safely into harbor."[20]

THE GUSHER, JANUARY 10, 1901

Halbouty's narrative about that January day continues:

> There wasn't a trace of a cloud in the sky. The weather was cold and invigorating and smoke was rising from every chimney in Beaumont. . . . Pattillo Higgins rode off into the north wind toward Hardin County to complete a deal that would get him out of debt. He had located a strip of timberland that Frank Keith would buy.
>
> Al Hamill was in the freight depot early to pick up the new fishtail bit

from Corsicana. It was barely daylight when he and Higgins, going separate ways, exchanged greetings as they passed each other on Park Street.

After a brief visit to the well, Captain Lucas returned to his home on
the way to town to tell Caroline he would be in Louie Mayer's store on
Crockett Street.

The morning *Daily Enterprise* gave its usual reports of the local, national and world events. The district attorney, who had been supported by
George Carroll in the recent election, would start a war on gambling. A
big diamond discovery was reported from Capitan near El Paso. Dr. Walter
Reed announced his famous discovery of the carrier of yellow fever. Old
Tom Sharkey was crying for another crack at Kid McCoy. William Jennings
Bryan was due to visit Houston, and Al G. Fields' minstrels and Sousa's
band were booked into the Goodhue Opera House. Mayor Wheat returned from Washington without selling the city's improvement bonds.
Governor Sayers was opening the new session of the state legislature in
Austin. Austin congressman David McFall rose to speak against the
relicensing of Waters-Pierce Oil Company in Texas, declaring it "a fraud
upon the state of Texas."

Beaumont was not prepared for the dramatic excitement that was now
only hours away. Its 9,000 inhabitants were satisfied with conditions as
they were. Beaumont had a chamber of commerce, solid citizens, culture
and magnolias. It was as cosmopolitan as any city in the South. A fourth
of its citizens were Negroes. Many of its successful merchants were Jews.
Almost every other white man and most of the Negroes spoke a Louisiana
patois. It had a healthy immigrant population, particularly Italians. There
was a Dutch settlement just south of town called Nederland. Beaumont
was more southern than southwestern, but it did have a few cowpokes. It
was a pleasant place to live.[21]

Outside the city toward Big Hill sat a real-estate development that
had been named Spindletop Heights. It was long and narrow and extended right up onto the hill itself. Several legends circulated to identify
the source of that name. One said that, seen from the Heights, high-
masted sailboats on the nearby Neches River showed only the tops of
their sails over the trees that crowded the banks. Another story claimed
that the Big Thicket evergreens themselves, with their often spindly tops
waving high in the air, had given someone the idea for the name. Many
remembered that there had been one particular tree that had stood for
many years adjacent to Big Hill, its quirky growth producing an upside-

down cone shape peculiar enough to be noticed and named. Soon, that name of mysterious origins would become known from downtown Beaumont to downtown London, from New York City to San Francisco. The names of "Big Hill" and "Gladys City" would fade; "Spindletop's oil" would carry on in epic proportions.

Back on Big Hill that Friday morning, Curt and Al Hamill worked alongside Peck Byrd installing the just-delivered fishtail bit. It was 10:30 A.M. They lowered the drill stem back into the hole and sunk it to around 700 feet, some 400 feet short of its destination. As Curt steered the pipe from atop the wooden derrick, he felt a tremor shudder up to the double boards and through his legs. Before he could even react, mud flew from the hole, splattered the rotary table and derrick floor, and squirted the forty feet onto his overalls. The tremor increased; Curt leaped for the ladder and began to make his way down, the mud covering him from head to toe as he descended. Al and Peck backed away from the derrick, waited for Curt to join them, and took off running. The ground they raced across shook as if a small earthquake had raked it from below. With a massive burst, loud enough to cause all three men to look back over their shoulders, the mud drove the 700 feet of pipe up and out of the hole, shooting it like a missile up through the shivering derrick and out the crown block into the air. The twenty-foot sections of four-inch pipe, now four tons of scrap metal, broke off in mid-air and fell in odd, tumbling patterns to the ground, driving into the muddied clay like arrows shot from some Greek god's bow. Rocks the size of five-gallon buckets showered down like meteorites, imbedding themselves back into the earth. Even as the last pipe plummeted from the sky, the tremor ceased. The mud became just a trickle spilling onto the derrick floor, and the whole world seemed to go silent.

The three men stared at one another for what seemed like an eternity. Curt Hamill was drenched in the muddy gunk that had spewed from the hole without warning. Nothing like this had ever happened in Corsicana. They walked slowly back to the edge of the derrick to survey the damage. Curt climbed gingerly onto a rung of the ladder he had come sliding down only moments before. Al picked up a muddied shovel and took aim at a pile of rock and sludge at his feet. Peck Byrd muttered to no one in particular, "What the hell are we going to do with the damn thing now?"

And in that instant the Lucas oil well blew in. The men recalled later that the first sound was as if a cannon had just gone off right in their ears. Mud and rock sprayed out of the hole and in every direction. Then gas exploded from the well, sending a powerful force of energy into the morning sky. It blew Peck Byrd into the slush pit; it jammed Curt Hamill against the ladder he now clung to for dear life. Al started running.

Then came the oil, green and heavy, in a six-inch diameter funnel that shot straight for the heavens, with more than enough force to blow the crown block from the derrick top, and another hundred feet beyond. It surged from the ground with a power that seemed to bring the gusher to life, angry and venting a million years of pent-up frustration, taking out its wrath on everything that stood or cowered or grew on Big Hill.

Al shouted instructions to Peck, who rousted himself from the slush pit and headed for Lucas's house to tell him the news. As he turned back toward the weaving derrick, Al saw his brother slipping and falling from the ladder to the floor. Curt related:

> I could hear him calling me to get off and get into the clear. But I could see that the clutch was still in gear on the drum. The machinery was still running and I could see the traveling block was going toward the top of the derrick. I knew it would bring the derrick crashing down. I made my way across the derrick floor and kicked the clutch out. My eyes were full of oil and I couldn't see, but Al kept hollering at me. I got off the floor somehow, guided by his voice calling me. The well was making such a roaring noise I could barely hear him.
>
> I remembered the boiler. A big fire was in it. "We've got to get that fire out!" I shouted. The smoke stack had been knocked off the boiler by the crown block which had been blown off the top of the derrick. Oil was falling on it and all around it. We grabbed buckets and dipped water out of the boiler pit and threw it in the fire box. We put the fire out. It was a miracle that well didn't catch on fire from that boiler.[22]

Meanwhile, Peck Byrd had reached the vicinity of the Lucas home a thousand yards north of the well, close enough to be heard by Caroline as he shouted across her yard. "It looks like oil!" he was screaming. "Hurry! Hurry!" Mrs. Lucas ran out onto the porch. Byrd had already turned and headed back for the derrick. She looked past him and to the horizon, and gasped as she saw the huge oil spout rising into the sky, a black storm cloud against the cold blue that silhouetted it.

Caroline Lucas ran inside and grabbed the telephone, nearly wrenching it from the wall in her excitement. She rang up Louie Mayer's store in town and shouted for her husband, who was at the phone in an instant. "Hurry, Anthony," she blurted, "something awful has happened. The well is spouting."

The Captain dropped the receiver and left it dangling to the floor as he dashed to his carriage. Leaping to the floor board and snapping reins in the same motion, he jolted down Crockett and then Park Street, up Highland Avenue and out of the town. He never paused or looked aside as he rode pell-mell past his own home, Caroline standing waving at him as he went by in a blur. As he passed his house he could see what she had seen only minutes earlier: a veritable geyser of what looked like mud or oil. Later the captain would write, "The well was only a mile from our home which was in plain view. There my wife stood in the door watching the display, and it was a heap of satisfaction to see her there. She soon came hurrying over to the gusher, and the look of joy which illuminated her countenance was reward sufficient for all the worry and work I had gone through."

At the edge of Big Hill the ponies slowed a bit as they started up the rise, too slow now for their driver. Lucas jumped from the gig and tried to land on his feet running. Instead, he tumbled in an awkward somersault hard onto the ground.

Al Hamill saw the Captain hit the ground and roll, and started toward him in a dead run. But Lucas was on his feet an instant later and shouting as he closed the distance to the well, "Al! Al! What is it?"

"It's oil, Captain," Hamill responded, "every drop of it."

Lucas grabbed Al as they met and swung him off his feet. "Thank God, thank God," he cried. "You've done it! You've done it!"[23]

Thirteen-year-old Plummer Barfield was in the woods by the marsh, not far from the gusher. He and several friends had gone duck hunting. "Ducks'd come in there and feed on acorns in the woods," he recollected. "And we were down there and we heard all this commotion, well we heard the roar, and it was a clear day and we could see the spray. We saddled our horses and went out. Then everybody went out."[24]

A few hundred yards away, twelve-year-old Wilbur Gilbert sat on his nervous pony. Riding in the vicinity, he had steered his mount toward the terrible thundering noise he had heard coming from the hill. He stared, motionless, at what he saw before him. "I just sat there and watched it," he remembered, "gushing 150 feet into the air like black snow. It was roaring considerably and it was discoloring the houses, and then the town, and even the silver in my pocket. Nobody around here had ever seen anything like it," he still bubbled years later, "or practically anybody in the whole world."[25]

FEVER IN THE EARTH

By noon, more oil had spewed from the Spindletop gusher than all the oil produced in the first fifty years of the state's history.

By the next morning its hourly flow matched the entire Corsicana field's production for all of 1897.

In all but the most conservative estimates that day, it was blasting the green-black crude into the air at the rate of a barrel every second.

And Al Hamill's overly optimistic statement to John Galey that the well would produce fifty barrels a day was now pouring true . . . every minute.

That afternoon, among the multitudes who had heard about or seen the explosive gusher, including trainloads who now filled the Beaumont station every hour, Frank J. Trost arrived from Port Arthur. The veteran news photographer lugged his tripod and camera equipment out onto Big Hill and set it up some 250 feet away from the black geyser. The smarmy oil spray had already pervaded the air for thousands of square yards, and Trost struggled with the slippery goo on his camera and especially on the lens. The wind had picked up by late afternoon, and gusts disturbed his concentration. At a moment since frozen in time, Trost captured the gusher in all of its glory as it grew up out of the wooden derrick and blossomed in the sky high above. At the base of the derrick and just to the right stood Captain Anthony F. Lucas, no more than a speck, it seemed to Trost, in the picture he had just framed. Trost closed up his equipment, took the next train home, worked through that Friday night in his darkroom producing 130 copies of the most famous photograph ever made of Spindletop, and returned to Big Hill to sell them to eager observers for fifty cents each. By March 1 he had sold over 45,000 copies and made his own oil "fortune."[26]

At the same time Trost walked toward Big Hill from town, Pattillo Higgins arrived in the vicinity, on the other side of Beaumont, unaware of the excitement he had caused with his curious "theory." "I was on my way back from Orange County," he says, "where I'd been looking for some timber land. It was about four o'clock and I was riding on the road right down through town from the north side. I was just riding along on my old horse. Jim Collier was coming along the road on the sidewalk, and he hollered at me as I got opposite him. 'Mr. Higgins,' he hollered. 'What?' I said. 'Did you know you were the wisest man in the world?' That's how I learned about the well coming in." Pattillo rode on, thinking to himself, "They didn't bring that well in. It brought itself in." He didn't bother going out to Gladys City that evening.[27]

BEATING A PATH TO BEAUMONT

An enterprising local named King who owned a cleaner and dyer shop penned the following doggerel and handed it out in flyers on the hill:

> When the oil is aspoutin'
> And the Beaumont folks is shoutin'
> > And Lucas has realized his dream,
> Just remember, I'm still workin'
> And my business I'm not shirkin',
> > So bring me all your siled clothes to clean.
> And if you ventured near the geyser
> When you should have been much wiser
> > And your clothes got full of Lucas grease,
> The spots I'll remove and
> Press them slick and smooth
> > An' in your pants I'll put the proper crease.
> And by patronizing me, you Help the town you see—
> > And that's been the tried and proper caper,
> And in one year from this date
> Bradstreet us high will rate
> > And I will build a 90-story scraper.
> So Speculator, Grafter,
> And the gang that follows after,
> > Your star of luck is looming up on high.
> While you are carrying off the money
> Please don't forget, ma honey,
> > The King that does the expert clean and dye.[28]

According to a legend reminiscent of Paul Revere's midnight ride, Charley Ingalls, a Beaumont native, watched excitedly as the Lucas gusher filled the sky. He raced his horse into town and was one of the first to shout the news of the oil discovery. But his message was one of doom not fortune! Afraid that his livestock would drown in the flood of oil, Ingalls announced his willingness to sell his seven acres and get out of the way. Four eager Beaumonters offered $4,000 cash, so the story is told, but Ingalls's wife hesitated. When they threw in a buggy and a sorrel mare, she accepted on her husband's behalf. In May, 1901, the seven acres was sold again for $5 million![29]

For a world where communications still tended to be laboriously slow and inexact, the word of Lucas's gusher spread like a Texas prairie wildfire. Telegraph and telephone operators kept busy through the day and night passing the startling message along. Before dusk that Friday, men were boarding trains or hitching carriages in Corsicana and Port Arthur, New Orleans and Fort Worth. The word spread to St. Louis and Pittsburgh, then reached both coasts.

The first train from Corsicana hit town well before sundown. Hundreds of the curious, many who had had to stand in the aisles of the passenger cars the entire 200 miles, tumbled out on to the platform station, hollering for nonexistent luggage carriers and anxious hacks. Throwing wads of dollar bills at the black drivers, they piled into the wagons a dozen at a time as each carriage bolted for Big Hill. Many just ran alongside; others swapped dollars for reins of horses posted on the streets of Beaumont, shouting promises to return the mount later.

One of the first to climb down from the Corsicana train was Joseph S. Cullinan. Right behind him came T. J. Wood, another oilman, and their guest who had been touring the Central Texas oil field. Samuel "Golden Rule" Jones marveled at the chaos he witnessed that evening, in contrast to the long-since settled business atmosphere in Corsicana. Jones was mayor of Toledo, Ohio, a popular reform politician who had just implemented a controversial plan to provide city-funded free kindergarten classes at the workplace. Likewise interested in the petroleum industry for fueling city utilities, he spoke to a reporter soon after, expressing both dubious and far-sighted first impressions: "It is fortunate for the oil trade that [the Spindletop oil] is not illuminating oil. If it were, it would paralyze the whole industry. Its advent, however, means that liquid fuel is to be the fuel of the twentieth century. . . . I believe this is the real beginning of the era of liquid fuel in the United States." In fact, the oil sample Dr. R. W. Raymond sent that week to A. R. Ledoux, a petroleum engineer in New York City, tested at a gravity of 21.5 degrees Baume, "higher than other oils that had yielded notable quantities of illuminants," Ledoux concluded.[30]

Others flocked to Beaumont, a thousand or more jammed against a nearby fence by the end of the day, men, women, and children, wiping the oily film repeatedly from their eyes, some cheering, most silent as they watched the gusher show off its power. At one point about fifty of the more obstinate had clambered over the fence to get a closer look at the spout. Lucas, furious that they would not heed his warnings to stay away, remarked to Curt Hamill that a guard with a shotgun might be necessary.

The multitudes remained until the darkness hid all but the incessant roaring noise of the geyser, but before dawn on Saturday they were back, and a thousand more. The city of 9,000 was scattered across Big Hill, with thousands of strangers pouring in from every road, leaping from the trains coming in, crawling up the river banks of the Neches to catch a glimpse of the phenomenon at Gladys City. The transient population would double the size of the Gulf plains town that week, and double it again soon after.

Walter Sharp arrived early Saturday from Corsicana, still feeling the effects of an illness that had kept him bedridden for several days. He made his way through the crowds to Big Hill, and mused about his own experience drilling there years before. The old drill pipe that had failed at 418 feet still looked out from the hole only yards from Lucas's derrick. What might have been, he thought to himself, with better equipment. Sharp and his brother Jim were destined to be major players on this hill, however, and their names would become synonymous with the Beaumont oil patch.

From Galveston, where he had heard the report while standing in a newspaper office, David R. Beatty came to the site before sunup. A well-known railroad and real estate promoter, Beatty had lost nearly all of his possessions in the hurricane four months earlier. Now he sensed the importance of the telegram that would soon be headline news, and was aboard the special train that left the island that evening. He brought no luggage, had only $20 in his pocket, and did not bother to sleep that night nor look for accommodations upon his arrival. Beatty would soon be one of the richest oilmen in Texas.[31]

Captain Lucas walked out to the derrick early Saturday morning, accepting shouts of congratulations with a quiet nod. A reporter for the local *Journal* caught up with him in the field and asked for an estimate of the gusher's flow. "Six thousand barrels a day," Lucas replied, coming up with the largest possible number he could imagine since no well in North

America had ever produced even half that in a month. Lucas was be-
mused some weeks later when the more accurate estimates made by two
Standard Oil engineers indicated that his first guess had been short by
sixty-six thousand barrels![32]

At breakfast that morning, Anthony and Caroline and their son Tony
were joined by Al Hamill. To everyone's amusement the Captain related
the story of a local Italian grocer who had leased his land for $5,000 only
hours after the gusher came in. On the previous Wednesday the grocer
had politely refused to sell a bag of produce to Lucas "on credit." Now
overjoyed and feeling a bit guilty, he had sought out the Captain that
evening and presented him with two heads of cabbage—no charge!—
proclaiming, "You have made me a very reech man. Bless you, Captain!"

As breakfast ended, a knock at their door brought the Lucases face
to face with Cullinan, Wood, and Toledo's Mayor Jones, who had come
by to pay their respects and ask the Captain to escort them to his well.
Caroline insisted that they eat, and at the table Cullinan asked Al Hamill
at what depth the well had come in. Lucas spoke up. "1160 feet," he said.
In all of the years that would pass from that moment, Al Hamill never
inquired of the Captain why he had given that figure. Al had measured
the hole at 1020 feet earlier Friday morning where a crevice had
corkscrewed the bit the day before. The new bit they inserted Friday had
not made it back to that level when the well exploded. Lucas's own journal of well No. 1 indicates a "calcareous layer of sand between 1050 and
1160 feet," and in later interviews the Austrian American used the deeper
figure again. (It appears on the historical marker at the well site.) Since
that breakfast conversation, the two disparate figures have shown up in
papers and textbooks and stories told.

After breakfast, Captain Lucas and Al Hamill took their distinguished
guests out to the field. Lucas was somewhat surprised to see that the
gusher was flowing as powerfully as it had twenty-four hours earlier, for
he had expected an inevitable weakening after the initial blast. He was
more surprised with Peck Byrd's report. "Captain," the night shift driller
said, "she started getting weaker earlier this morning, then I'll be damned
if she didn't stop altogether for almost a minute. I figured the show was
over and was walking up to kiss her goodbye when the old fool blasted
out again like the *Maine* blowing up. That stream started up and she's
been shooting stronger and higher than before."[33]

A thousand miles away in a Pittsburgh office, James M. Guffey grabbed
his partner in a bear hug and shouted at the news Galey had just deliv-

ered. "You lucky old oil hound," he exclaimed. "Now get yourself back to Beaumont and find out exactly what this thing is. If it is what it sounds like, those Mellon brothers are going to get a chance to finance an oil company that'll make old John D. sick." Galey made his way to Beaumont by train, collecting newspapers at every stop along the way to read about Lucas No. 1. Upon his arrival, John Galey met with Captain Lucas and Jim Hamill, gratefully acknowledged the faith that Caroline Lucas had had that kept the drilling going, and offered to treat the men to a stiff drink and a fine cigar. The straight-laced Captain politely declined. "Well, I'll be damned," Hamill remembers Galey responding to that. "The Captain doesn't swear, either," Jim said good-naturedly. "Well," Galey thought for a moment, "I guess I can forgive him his character, since he can damn sure find oil!"[34]

On Sunday, January 12, just before noon, the Lucases sat at the dinner table, the sound of the gusher quite audible from their doorstep. Thousands of people continued to line the muddy road from the town to the hill that ran past their home. Thousands more stood in a huge undulating circle around the hilltop, staring and pointing and speculating. The oil covered the fields and filled the ditches, some 150,000 barrels having spread itself everywhere already. The crowds stepped in puddles and ponds of it, scraped it off leggings and wagon hitches, rubbed it off ponies and cattle and yelping dogs, and generally ignored the otherwise discomfort of the black shower that still poured down on them.

And then someone tossed a match onto the ground.

Curt Hamill recalled that first crisis.

We'd had a heavy frost, and it was really cold, and Peck and myself had on slicker suits over our other clothes. . . . There were five or six hundred people gathered in the little pasture near the well when the fire started toward it. Everybody ran, got out just as quick as they could. They was afraid everything would blow up.

And Peck and myself went to fighting this fire. We was about a hundred yards apart at the time the blaze started, and I was the closer. I got to the fire first, and I pulled off my slicker coat, and I went to fighting the fire with it. Directly Peck got there and he pulled off his slicker coat and we both fought the fire all we could. We burned our slicker coats up. We then pulled off our jumpers; we burned them up. And we pulled off our shirts, too.

By this time, some of the men had begun to return. They saw it wasn't going to blow, and so we had about twenty men to help us fight the fire. And some of them brought saddle blankets to throw on the fire, but they burned up real fast. There was a barn not too far away, and we put the men to carrying boards from the barn, sixteen and twenty feet long some of them. They'd throw the boards over the fence, and Peck and myself would throw them on the fire [to suffocate it]. The fire was narrow and spreading all the time, but we'd put out sixteen or twenty feet of it each time.

We used possible fifty or seventy-five boards this way, sometimes throwing two on the same place, and the fire burned over an acre of ground before we got it out. No one was hurt other than the two of us—our faces were blistered, hands were blistered.[35]

The billowing smoke could be seen all the way back in town, and the Lucases' cook had screamed when she saw it, sending the Captain in a mad dash to the site. Al Hamill was just riding up when the fire started. He remembers his brother "all smoked up, and his clothes were all dirty, and coat was ruined, and he was out of breath. . . . If [the fire] had ever gotten to the well, I don't know what we'd have done with it."[36] Signal thoughts, because the fires that would reach these gushers in the weeks and months ahead became the most dangerous single element on the oil patch.

"O CHRISTMAS TREE"

Mike Welker, ace reporter of the *Beaumont Daily Enterprise,* managed a curt interview with John Galey on Monday, January 13, the morning after the oilman arrived in Beaumont. "We must demonstrate the permanency of supply and accumulate stocks," Galey was quoted as saying, "to be able to contract with fuel users for fifteen or twenty years before we can expect them to change their boilers over from coal to oil. This will mean the investment of millions of dollars. It will mean that this well, the most wonderful thing I have ever seen in my life, must prove itself.

"Right now, however, our problem is to get the flow under control. This waste can't go on."[37]

The night before, in a room at the Crosby House—the only hotel in Beaumont at that time and overflowing with boarders—Al and Jim Hamill, Captain Lucas, and John Galey sat around a table discussing the events of the previous sixty hours. One of the conversation topics was capping, or shutting off and controlling, the well. Several options were discussed, and suggestions made as to whom—in Corsicana or Neosha or Pittsburgh—might be the best for the operation. Joseph Cullinan stopped in and made several suggestions of his own of Standard Oil men who might be considered. But Jim Hamill, who had been the contractor up to this point at the well, interjected at several points that because he and his brothers had brought it in, they should be given the first shot at capping it. Finally, John Galey turned to Jim and said point-blank, "You think you can do it?" "I think we can, Mr. Galey," Jim responded. "All right," the Pennsylvanian nodded, "Go to it."[38]

For two days Jim and his brothers toyed with a myriad of possible solutions. This was uncharted territory for everyone, including the best the country could have offered from back East, because there had never been a well of this magnitude, which exacerbated the task of controlling it. Jim came up with the basics of what would be the successful solution, and on Tuesday night he shared it with Curt, Peck Byrd, and Elmer Dobbins, a driller whom Jim had sent down from Corsicana the week before to help. Peck's father, an engineer, had taught his son about mechanics, and Byrd was a good one with whom to explore these ideas. Curt and Peck sat out on the porch that night, discussing Jim's basic idea while Byrd doodled on a brown paper bag. He showed the sketch to Curt, and then got Jim's approval: the capping mechanism might just work.

The crew met Al Hamill at the well Wednesday morning where, although the differing stories over the years have muddied what happened next, it seems that Dobbins told Al the solution was his and that he would "sell" it to the Hamills for $500. Al in turn contracted with John Galey to cap Lucas No. 1 for $1,000, to which Galey readily agreed. Dobbins got his $500, made little additional contribution to the operation, and soon fell out with the Hamills and went to work as a contractor for Scott Heywood. The three brothers would eventually split the remaining $500, although each considered the capping to have been part of the original drilling contract and would have gone through with it anyway.[39]

The two biggest challenges to the capping operation were equipment and the force of the gusher itself. The moveable carriage and gate valve mechanism required supplies that for the most part could not be obtained in the Beaumont area. And even when the parts were assembled, no one knew for sure that the well would not disintegrate the entire thing once it was laid over the coursing six-inch stream of oil. Parts were ordered from Corsicana and even St. Louis, rushed by train to Big Hill on

Thursday, Friday, and Saturday. The Hamills and Peck Byrd set about assembling what additional supplies they could find in the vicinity.

In Jim Hamill's plan and Peck Byrd's sketches, a gate valve made up of eight-inch pipe with tees and nipples would be swung over the gusher by a carriage on runners using ropes and pulleys to put it in place. This required building a platform on the derrick floor, reinforcing it against the massive force that would try to rip the mechanism to pieces, and building a kind of rail to pull the gate valve over and onto the oil stream. Once—if—the gate valve was managed over the flow so that it now blew through the eight-inch pipe, the oil would be diverted through a horizontal valve and then slowly stemmed and cut off. Ditches would be dug to take the horizontal flow until the pipe was closed off.[40]

The liabilities were many. The equipment could very likely be blown into a million parts all over Big Hill. The construction of the carriage and the actual moving of the gate valve over the flow would be against the deafening roar of the well and in literally blinding conditions that close to the gusher. Any crisis that occurred during the delicate operation would have to be dealt with then and there: there would be one shot at this.

Each man went to work on his part of the operation. Jim Hamill ordered the parts from all over the country. John Galey assisted and put up the funds as they went along. Captain Lucas supervised the security around the gusher while his crew prepared to cap it. Peck Byrd and Curt Hamill fine-tuned the mechanism on paper. Al Hamill collected local supplies and had them delivered to the site. Mr. Carroll's lumber company supplied a stack of lumber including long, heavy four-by-twelves to be bolted to the derrick floor as the carriage platform. With no one around to see, Al "borrowed" two long railroad irons from the Beaumont station yard— "they were light little irons out there on the Southern Pacific's switch track," he confessed years later—and hauled them to the derrick.[41]

By Saturday the parts had come in and been assembled to create this gate valve. The platform had been screwed onto the derrick floor, a second layer of heavy lumber attached to the derrick wall four feet above the floor, and the entire framework reinforced, all connected to five lines of block and tackle, with a windlass some twenty feet away and entrenched into the ground. The gate valve mechanism itself was pulled into place on the runners with the ropes and pulleys until it sat only twelve inches from the oil stream.

In the original plan it was not necessary for any of the crew to be anywhere near the dangerous framework itself, because the whole mechanism could be pulled into place from a safe distance away from the derrick. However, during the original drilling operations in December the crew had riveted a protector plate on the drilling pipe to keep it from deteriorating each time the pipe was sunk in and pulled out: this protector plate was now an obstacle to the gate valve's moving smoothly over the flow. It could not be screwed off: someone would have to cut it off. Al remarked later, "So as I was the unmarried one, why, I took the responsibility to go in there.

"Before I started this, I went into town and got me a pair of goggles and got adhesive tape and taped all around those goggles and my eyes. I had a hat on, of course, a slicker hat, and a slicker suit." John Galey retrieved some sponges from a local store, cut them into small pieces, soaked them in glycerin, and had Al secure them over his mouth and nose to keep from breathing in the oily air. "I got diamond points and a hack saw and one thing and another," Al continued, "and just went to work in there." *In there* was sitting astraddle the platform framework constructed for the gate valve mechanism, less than two feet away from the oil stream, sawing at the protector plate "through the afternoon"! Joseph Cullinan, an interested observer, turned to Jim Hamill and said, "You watch that kid. He's in great danger. If he hits a spark there, why, he just—well it will be impossible for him to get out."

Al Hamill hacked the protector plate away from the drill pipe, and all was ready to move the gate valve contraption a foot more and over the gusher. Al admitted later that he was essentially blind and deaf for several hours during and after the harrowing experience. It was also one of the singular heroic efforts of the entire operation.

One other problem presented itself and delayed the actual operation another day. At unpredictable intervals ever since the well had come in, now a whole week before, chunks of rock would explode from the hole and fly out into the air. Clearly, a large rock moving at that force would destroy the gate valve in an instant, and all the work would be for naught. The crew decided to wait until there appeared to be no recurrence of this damaging possibility. Although they had been ready early Saturday to move the gate valve, the delay moved the capping to Sunday, January 19, after more than twenty-four hours without any rocks thrown from the well.

On the tenth day since the gusher came in, and an estimated 700,000 barrels of oil later, Captain Lucas's crew moved the gate valve over the last twelve inches. Curt Hamill describes the final moments:

The rope on the block and fall was wrapped several times around the 4-inch pipe, or windlass. We turned this pipe with chain tongs. As the rope wound around the pipe, the assembly moved slowly over the well and the oil shot through the gate valve. We were almost through.

The clamps holding the gate valve to the assembly were loosened and it slipped down into the casing collar. We screwed it up without any trouble. An 8x6-inch nipple was screwed into an 8-inch tee on the big valve and a 6-inch joint of pipe screwed into the 6-inch end of the swedge nipple. This pipe was horizontal to the ground and extended out from the well. [The gate valve sat on the end of that pipe.]

When we closed the gate on the big valve, the oil started shooting out the 6-inch pipe. [The big valve had been clamped down with a one-inch rod attached to 12x12 timbers] to keep it from getting away.

Then we closed the gate valve on the horizontal pipe.

The well was capped.[42]

As the first oil field "Christmas tree" assembly, as it would forever be known, slid into place a great cheer went up from hundreds of curious onlookers who had gathered during the suspenseful moment, the sound replacing the deafening roar that had pervaded the Texas countryside for the last 250 hours. Then it was eerily silent on Big Hill.

Captain Lucas quickly organized a clean-up crew to wash down or dig over the oil that lay for acres in every direction. While that was going on, sand, soil, and clay was shoveled and hauled to the derrick and heaped on and around the well inside and outside a large steel drum that the crew brought. This was not just to prevent a fire from reaching the capped well: Lucas hoped the huge mound would keep the crowds off the mechanism as well. It helped some. Over-anxious observers, including women and children, continued to sneak through the security to climb all over the derrick. Still, Lucas hoped in vain, the silenced gusher might lose its pestering audience now.

How wrong he was.

3

The World Gone Mad

The dirtiest, noisiest, busiest and most interesting town!

The crowds continued to arrive unabated in Beaumont and make their chaotic, undisciplined way to "Spindletop." So harried the situation, so confused the little lumber town, that in the Friday, January 17, edition of its paper was this front page assessment: "Beaumont is becoming both accustomed to *and tired of* the oil excitement, which has been kept up here now for six days. The intensity of the strain has exhausted everybody. Beaumont has been fearfully wrought up. There is no denying that frenzy has penetrated every mind and the blood has coursed like fire through the veins of everyone who owned a bit of land somewhere in creation." The newspaper editor had no way of knowing what frenzy still lay ahead. Not too long after, *Harper's Weekly* broadly declared that "the dirtiest, noisiest, busiest, and most interesting town on the continent today is Beaumont, Texas."[1]

Frank Redman rode into Beaumont on January 10, 1901.

> The mud was everywhere good God Almighty everywhere. . . . A man would come out there with a boiler and all his lumber to build his derrick and his engine and everything and unload it. Just pile it up there against another fellow's. And a fellow wanting to build a derrick would just get anybody's he could. It didn't make no difference. Just go ahead and get it. They had a 16th of an acre of ground for $10,000, that's what they sold it

for. Just put in your derrick, engine and boiler, sludge pit, too. And right over a half block away the Beaumont Palestine Oil Company brought in a wild gusher and killed three men. If only we'd known then what we know now. Could've saved them. Artificial respiration. They just dragged them out of there away from that gas, got a diver from Galveston to go in there and he didn't know nothing about [capping it]. Just unscrewed the pipe and let it drop back in the well and then closed the valve. God, there was oil everywhere. Went to breakfast one morning down to Cook's Boarding House, just a big old shed. And the oil was knee deep in the dining room, in the kitchen, everywhere. Everybody was gone. We didn't get no breakfast that morning.[2]

In the first week of the Spindletop gusher, and still before the Hamill Brothers Drilling Company capped Lucas Well No. 1, three men who would change the oil industry in Texas were making their way to Beaumont in search of personal fortune.

David R. Beatty came to Gladys City on the first train out of Galveston after the news hit that devastated island city. After spending the morning hours out in the field with thousands of other observers, the promoter went looking for a place to stay. As he wandered through the milling crowds he overheard a young man saying something about his home just over the hill. Not wanting to seem eager, Beatty waited until the man headed for home, and followed him the half-mile there. He introduced himself as they neared the house, and Lige Adams greeted the stranger and invited him in. Mrs. Adams and the couple's baby girl were home, and the ever-friendly Beatty quickly ingratiated himself to the three.

The Adamses were recently moved from Port Arthur where Lige had worked as a millwright. They had paid $200 for a ten-acre farm, but their first winter was going poorly so far. Beatty offered to lease the mineral rights to the Adams farm, on credit as the Galvestonian had no money with him, and agreed to give Adams one-eighth of any profits realized from a successful well. Lige knew nothing about drilling but accepted the offer on the single condition that Beatty would hire him on as camp cook once the operation was under way. Beatty left with the deal made.

The promoter was back in less than two weeks, having traveled from Galveston to Corsicana to obtain the backing he needed as well as hire the services of Wes Sturm and his brother Jim, the best-known drilling team in Texas at that time. Beatty had until February 11 to begin drilling, else Adams would be free to accept another, and, by that time, much more lucrative, offer from others. Equipment problems and shipping deadlines proved difficult, but the Sturm Brothers "spudded in" the well on February 10.

After myriad challenges had been overcome, Beatty's well came in on March 26 with a terrifying blast of gas that knocked Jim Sturm unconscious from the rig and overcame Lige Adams nearby in the cook shed. Moments later the oil shot through the crown block and nearly as far into the sky as Lucas's well had ten weeks earlier. Beatty's well, the second gusher on Big Hill, only confirmed what most folks knew by then: there was oil aplenty under this salt dome.

David Beatty sold the well to New Yorker C. D. Pullen for $1.25 million, of which he kept $250,000 for his share minus the $10,000 he had put in three months before. His reputation secured, the promoter from Galveston never looked back, buying and selling leases, negotiating multimillion dollar deals for clients, and making a fortune for himself along the way.[3]

A Spindletop rig worker named Ray Sittig recalled years later that "there was a road show that would come through there at Beaumont called the Heywood Brothers Road Show, and it would play at the Opera House here in town. The actors' names were O. W. and Alba Heywood." There were two other brothers as well, Dewey and Scott. All of them would eventually profit from Spindletop oil, but W. Scott Heywood put his own particular mark on that moment of Texas history.

Scott Heywood was an adventurer all of his life, a Hollywood actor and a road show vaudevillian with his brothers, a gold miner in the Klondike, and, in early 1901, a promoter in California. Reading the headlines of the *San Francisco Examiner* one January morning while sipping coffee in a San Francisco café, Heywood noticed the article about an oil strike in Texas, where crude was flowing at the rate of 30,000 barrels a day, a conservative estimate as it turned out. "I immediately made up my mind to see the strike and try to get in on the ground floor," wrote Heywood later. "I purchased a round-trip ticket to Beaumont and left at once. I wired my brothers, who were still in the concert business, telling them I was going to Beaumont, and asked that one of them meet me there."

Heywood stepped off the train at Beaumont around noon on Sunday, January 19, the very hour the Lucas well was being capped. "I put my grips in a grocery store across the street from the depot and engaged a hack to take me out to the well at once. I found the well shut in and a wire cable put up some distance around the well. A man on horseback was there to keep people away." But Heywood caught the attention of Elmer Dobbins, the crew member cleaning up at the well, and managed to talk his way past the security man and into Dobbins's trust. "Knowing the weakness of drillers to eventually become contractors, I asked Dobbins how he would like to contract to drill a well for me. Of course this was just what he wanted."

Heywood plied information out of Dobbins and spent some additional time surveying the ground around the well. He noticed the oil-sand and the rocks as well as the crude itself still sitting in puddles. He applied this information to what expertise he had already gained about oil and drilling, and knew he could make a fortune here on Big Hill. Now he needed his brothers, and he needed land to lease.

Dewey Heywood finally arrived several days after his brother had expected him, having taking a remarkably circuitous route because Scott had failed to specify the Beaumont in Texas rather than the one in California! Dewey still had no idea that oil had been discovered here until he got off the train. The brothers made two valiant attempts to lease tracts over the next week, but both times were foiled by a man named Beatty who continued to work one step ahead of them. But John C. Ward pointed to a small fifteen-acre tract up on the hill not a thousand feet from the Lucas well. That lease was owned by Pattillo Higgins's newly formed Higgins Oil Company, and Scott Heywood this time beat Beatty to the punch, securing the deal with a $2,500 cash bonus plus royalties.

Now Scott needed the money. He found two resources in time to begin his drilling operations by the first of March. One came from his two vaudeville brothers, who sent a message with the funds: "Don't bother about the details. You are on the ground. Play ball. Be careful at first base, but play ball." The other came from Captain W. C. Tyrell, who had just arrived in Beaumont himself from Port Arthur, looking to invest in a well. The negotiations went quickly: both men were eager to drill Spindletop. Tyrell put up $9,000, and Heywood had enough to begin. Dobbins signed on as the contractor.

While Scott Heywood returned for a brief business visit to California to tie up loose ends, Dewey and Dobbins began the operation. A rotary drilling outfit came from Corsicana, the lumber from Beaumont, and the crew from a swelling mob of fortune-seekers jammed into the vicinity. Heywood No. 1 blew up at 800 feet when a gas pocket caught fire and destroyed the wooden derrick and the drill stem. But Heywood No. 2, drilled from May 1 to May 25, came in with the ferocity of Lucas's well in

January, and more. Its spray was calculated at over 217 feet, some 60 feet higher than the Captain's, and its eventually controlled flow produced nearly 150,000 barrels daily by the end of 1901.

Heywood No. 2 was the sixth and last of the first round of Big Hill gushers, with Higgins No. 1 and Guffey & Galey's two coming in in April between Beatty and the Californians. This last spout, the biggest of the gushers, renewed what had nearly become lagging interest at Spindletop: another rush was soon under way.[4]

O. B. Colquitt was at home when he heard about Spindletop. The Dallas area businessman—his home was in Terrell—who had made sound investments in Corsicana caught a train immediately for the coast, arriving by Sunday morning to gape at the Lucas gusher along with thousands of others. Colquitt stayed in Beaumont until Wednesday, and purchased a small tract of land near the hilltop. He caught a train to Austin where he hoped to persuade some business associates there to invest in his new oil deal. Twenty years later he remembered that day in Austin: "Going up Congress Avenue to Billy Wolf's barber shop, I met [James S.] Hogg standing at the foot of the steps leading to his office which was upstairs in the same building. I stopped and chatted with him and he asked me where I had come from and I told him about the wonderful oil gusher and the chance to make some money by getting down there early . . . and I urged him to go. But he said he was practicing law and didn't have any money to risk in such a venture."

Colquitt tried once more that day to convince Hogg to go take a look, and then went on home to Terrell, where he remained for a week before heading back to Beaumont. "On my return there as I went to the hotel from the train I found Gov. Hogg sitting on the porch of the old Crosby House. He saw me coming and got up and walked to meet me and told me he had no idea it was as big a thing as it was even after I had told him. . . . He told me he had bought him some leases and made some good profits."

James Stephen Hogg had come to Spindletop, where he too would make an indelible mark on the oil industry that began there. By February, having finished up his political business in Austin, the ex-governor was hooked on the oil venture. His former political ally, State Representative James Swayne of Fort Worth, had agreed to go into business with him, and by a handshake the Hogg-Swayne Syndicate was born. Three others—Judge Robert E. Brooks, A. S. Fisher, and William T. Campbell— joined up as well and put together $40,000 to start. Their cash flow increased dramatically right out of the gate when Hogg sold 2 ½ acres of his first tract for $200,000![5]

The Hogg-Swayne Syndicate land eventually became one of three tracts where derricks lined up side by side and numbered in the hundreds. Along with Keith-Ward and Yellowpine, dense drilling leases that came along later in 1901, Hogg-Swayne at one point numbered 120 wells on just fifteen acres, more than half of all the active wells on Big Hill at that time. Many of the so-called oil companies that drilled there operated on pieces of land no more than 1/16 and 1/32 of an acre. (In Yellowpine they called it the "Shoestring District," where platforms were connected by planks of lumber enabling rig workers to walk the length of the field and never touch the ground.) The effect of this dense drilling also caused Big Hill to "dry up" more quickly than it might have otherwise because of the loss of pressure below the ground.

During his successful years in the Spindletop oil venture, Hogg managed to make a comfortable living, although he certainly was not considered a multimillionaire. The old Populist and anti-trust warrior also stayed just a step away from feeling occasionally guilty about his being on the other side, the corporate syndicate. But as he toed his own ethical and political line, Hogg indirectly kept those very trusts, notably Standard Oil, at bay just by his presence in the oil patch. James Guffey once remarked that "Northern men were not very well respected in Texas. . . . Governor Hogg was a power down there and I wanted him on my side because I was going to spend a lot of money."[6]

Men like Beatty, Heywood, and Hogg, alongside Walter Sharp and Anthony Lucas, John Galey, Joseph Cullinan, J. Edgar Pew, and others, represented the vanguard of oil men who would bring that certain "character" to the oil fields, put Texas on the industrial world map, and give John D. Rockefeller, quite literally, a run for his money.

The Lucas Gusher March

Let me tell you of the greatest town the world has ever seen,
I know you'll not believe me, it does seem like a dream,
When I tell you of the geyser that spouted up green oil,
But it's right down here in Texas, in good old Beaumont soil.
Ten thousand barrels of greasy goods came spouting out the pipe,
The railroads brought a million in to see the wonder sight.
The oil it spouted up so high you could not see the Sun,
It flowed in rivers, lakes and streams, you ought to see it run.

The streets were filled with happy folks who left their daily toil.
The news was passed from mouth to mouth that Lucas had struck
  oil.
The millionaires came pouring in the wonder for to see,
And the farmer who owned the land, his heart was full of glee.
They all grabbed Lucas by the hand and shook it until sore,
They tried to lease the Public Square for more oil to bore,
The happy owners of the land, this lucky Beaumont soil,
Had to carry a gun to keep the gang from boring them for oil.

The Standard they came quickly in with millions at the back,
Old "Golden Rule" of Toledo fame brought his money in a sack,
The Crosby got so full of folks with four men in a bed,
And before the rush was over they stood them on their head.
You talk about your Klondike rush and gold in frozen soil,
But it don't compare with Beaumont rush when Lucas he struck oil.
So if you want a lease for oil you must be an early riser
To get a whack at our Cracker Jack, The Famous Beaumont Geyser.[7]

"FIRE IN THE LAND"

Curt Hamill knew there was danger in that oil lake. But with the spring rains coming almost every day it seemed, and the work that was going on all across Big Hill, he had little time to tend to the potential disaster awaiting Spindletop Heights. "Our old slush pond was covered with oil, and the ground everywhere was oil-soaked. The oil all went into the flatlands in that section, and during this time, while the well was flowing, the oil was washed away with the water, a great deal of it. The railroad had shipped several carloads of sand or clay into a culvert, a bridge, that was on the downside of the country, with hopes of holding the oil. And that place filled up. That whole section of the country filled up with oil."[8]

By March 3, after over seven weeks of drilling on the hill, the culverts and the low ground had formed a lake of oil. The railroad ran alongside this growing lake. About midday a coal-burning switch engine belched a warning that it was coming into the railyard outside of Beaumont. Trains had been traversing these rails almost constantly since the Lucas well had come in; today didn't seem any different. But it was.

A spark glanced from beneath the engine, perhaps from the coal stove or off the steel wheels' friction against the rails themselves. No one ever knew for sure. But the spark survived its fall from the rails into the culvert below, and it ignited a small fire in the oil-filled ditch. The fire spread slowly at first, struggling against the mud and water that diluted the crude. It made its way down the culvert toward the oil lake, and when it struck a stream of purer oil it leaped into towering flames, dashing away from the rails, leaving a growing smoke trail behind.

When it hit the flats down from the hill, it exploded into a ball of fire and raced across the lake. The smoke column could now be seen for miles in every direction. People raced to the fire and away from it, depending on their own sense of urgency. As it flew around the edge of the lake it struck the Guffey & Galey camp head-on. Some of its eighty occupants were sleeping in the longhouse, while the rest worked in the oil patch. The alarm went out ahead of the flames and all of the men managed to get out in time. But the camp houses were swallowed whole by the conflagration.

The fire destroyed the Daugherty boarding house nearby, and the McFaddin tract suffered the loss of one of its wooden derricks, which looked like a funeral pyre burning through that night. Walter Sharp, who was contractor on the derrick, shook his fist and cursed as the fire went by, leaving nothing behind. Back on a side track where it had first ignited, a secondary fire crawled up out of the culvert and enveloped three rail cars filled with lumber and pipe. Closer to town, the heavy smoke and searing heat drove families out of their homes and to the north end of Beaumont. When they returned late that night, the paint had peeled off the houses and gritty residue covered every item inside, even in closed drawers and cabinets.

At the edge of Big Hill, rig workers joined in the effort to divert the flames that licked at their equipment. Derricks of the wells that would soon be the next to spout—Higgins and Heywood and Beatty—managed to elude the danger. Incredibly, no one was killed, and only a few suffered smoke inhalation.

Cap Forney, the superintendent of the two Guffey & Galey wells, and Captain Lucas saw the flames coming and then watched as they headed for the oil lake to the east of the hill. As the fire reached the lake proper, the flames shot up hundreds of feet into the sky, and the smoke blocked out the noonday sun. Forney and Lucas both knew the fire could last for days if nothing were done to quell it. Shouting instructions to his crews as he raced for his buckboard, Forney rode his horses hard around the edge of the lake and to the opposite side away from the fire. He watched for several minutes as the flames headed in his direction, then lit a fire on the surface where he stood. Instantly the new fire reached out around the shore, building to a dramatic wall of orange and black as it surged toward the middle of the green-black lake.

The two giant walls of fire now moved inexorably toward a great confrontation near the middle of the flats. Observers reported that the vacuum the holocaust created would send whole deposits of oil flailing upward in front of one fire or the other, where it would explode as if a bomb had detonated in mid-air. Over and over the noise of the explosions sent its own shock waves across the countryside: people reported hearing the popping sounds miles away. Men in the field compared the sight to fireworks. After what seemed an interminable period but was actually less than four hours altogether, the two fires converged at a single line across the lake and devoured one another in one final rending explosion. By evening, the fire was out.[9]

The worst fire Jefferson County had ever witnessed brought both bad and good news to the people of Beaumont and the thousands of roughnecks now making the town their home. City fathers and church leaders met to protest the uncontrolled, undisciplined drilling that was going on at Big Hill. Some families simply packed their belongings and moved away. The smoke damage could still be seen at the edge of town months later. Preachers railed from the pulpits in March; the press had a field day with the "disaster"; and drilling crews wondered aloud about their own safety.

On the other hand, the fire had taught a valuable lesson to the oil patch without any loss of life. There was a need for better controls, especially of the waste fuels that were being dumped so carelessly. Most crews agreed shortly after the fire to haul the waste oil to a nearby bayou every Sunday, where it was burned under a controlled watch. And, the oil lake had been forever destroyed and would no longer pose a threat to the hill: had the fire come along in late May with six producing wells including the Heywood gusher, the toll would have been exponentially higher. Finally, several of the more responsible companies instituted safety rules for their crews, including alarm signals, protective clothing, and ready access to water or sand piles for dousing a fire. Although these measures did not eliminate the fire as a danger on Spindletop, for another fire would ultimately destroy hundreds of wooden derricks at Yellowpine, the March 3 experience had made a lasting impression on Big Hill.

"WILD WITH THE OIL CRAZE"

The scenes about the Crosby House in this city, where it seems headquarters for everything has been established, have a tendency to fill the air with excitement. Men jostle and crowd about in an excited condition, as though this thing was going to end in a short time and that they only had a few minutes left in which to accumulate a million dollars or two. It is safe to say that three-fifths of the people moving about have no destination. Someone suddenly becomes impressed with the idea he wants to see somebody and he tears about through the streets like a house was a fire. And when he finds his man he probably asks him what he knows, then asks himself what he really was after.[10]

And they just kept coming. Holland S. Reavis arrived on one of the first trains from Missouri as a reporter for the *Saint Louis Republic* newspaper. His editor had rushed him to Texas to scoop the Midwest competitors, and Reavis quickly immersed himself in the everyday activities in Beaumont and out on Big Hill. So interested and invested finally in the swirling new world around him, Reavis quit his reporter's job, bought a home in the city, and soon founded his own publication, *The Oil Investor's Journal*. His first seven volumes became the last word in the Texas petroleum industry. Beginning with the eighth volume and continuing to the present, Reavis's *Oil and Gas Journal* represented for millions the voice of the Southwest oil patch.[11]

In the unlikely town of Laredo, Texas, on April 19, Weetman Pearson stood at the railway station and fumed. He had missed his connection to Mexico City and would have to wait nine hours in the hot, dusty border town. Stranded, he checked in at the boardinghouse and then with the telegraph office, where he sent word to his business associates of the Mexican Eagle Company in Tabasco that he would be late arriving. The next morning at breakfast, everyone was talking about oil and Beaumont "wild with the oil craze," he recalled. Learning as much as he could in the last hours before the next train would send him on his way, Pearson cabled his station manager to "move sharply to acquire prospective lands in and around Beaumont. And be sure," he warned, "that we are dealing with principals." His most recent project, the Tehuantepec Railway operation, would need fuel: Texas oil would have to be less expensive than shipping it to Mexico from the East. The manager was making those connections before Pearson left Laredo.

But this was no ordinary promoter. In nine hours, an *Englishman* in a Texas border town had started up an oil company of his own. For Weetman Pearson, *Lord Cowdray* his title, an international investor and engineer who had worked for years with the difficult Diaz regime on major construction projects across Mexico, had proven once again that he richly deserved his reputation for having "the Pearson Touch."[12]

In Toledo, Ohio, Joseph Newton Pew read about Spindletop when the telegram message flashed back East on January 11. An acquaintance of Mayor Jones, who already was making his way to Beaumont from his Corsicana stay, Pew owned and operated Sun Oil Company there after successful ventures already in Pennsylvania. Pew's small but substantial company, no match against Rockefeller but a player nonetheless with Ohio fields and the Toledo refinery, was in its tenth year. Pew sent his nephew to Beaumont immediately. There, Robert Pew quickly assessed the situation amidst the confusion, reporting to his uncle that despite some skeptics he was sure that Spindletop would be the future for the oil industry in Texas and beyond.

Now the president of Sun Oil sent Robert's younger brother, J. Edgar, to replace Robert in Beaumont as an investor and observer. J. Edgar had proven himself in the Corsicana fields two years before, and headed back to Texas to repeat his performance. A last warning from his brother about the conditions in Beaumont suggested that he be prepared for the violence there: J. Edgar Pew stepped off the train soon after, a .41 caliber pistol strapped to his side.

Meanwhile back in Pennsylvania his uncle was procuring eighty-two acres of land on the Delaware River at Marcus Hook, where a refinery would soon be built. J. Edgar's optimistic confirmation after the first Beatty well came in spurred Sun Oil to prepare investments in shipping, pipelines, and storage facilities across the country.[13]

J. Edgar Pew remained in Beaumont, where he eventually became one of the most popular and successful oilmen in those early days, although Clint Wood remembers that the Easterner had to be "initiated" properly:

> The Sun Company come in there, and they were building some big earthen tanks, filling them with this cheap oil. They had to have this 3x8 decking to line them with. So Ed Pew, he came in to the Beaumont lumber yard and placed an order for a big lot of that stuff. It all had to be cut just right, go through the dry kiln, the planing mill and be worked up because it wasn't regular stock.

So Pew shows up with his team and wagons to go hauling that stuff. And I said, "Mr. Pew, that stuff has to be cut special by blueprint, sorted out, and it'll take some time, maybe three or four days, anyhow." Mr. Pew said, "I'll tell you, I've been down here in the South may be three weeks and I haven't seen one son of a bitch in the South who can do anything." Well, I climbed up on his back and gave him an awful licking. Made him take his damned order and get out of there.

He went to the other saw mills around there and they wouldn't touch it either. Mr. Gilbert asked me to take the order after awhile, and I said I wouldn't fool with that man, but I did and Mr. Pew come down and we were the best of friends that ever was from then on. Not a better man lived than Ed Pew, he'd just gotten off on the wrong foot.[14]

W. S. Farish and Lee Blaffer literally bumped into each other one day in the streets of Beaumont. Farish was a lawyer from Natchez and Blaffer a New Orleans man who worked in his family's coal and coke business. Their chance encounter turned into a fast friendship and then a business partnership. Before long they put their collective talents together with Walter Sharp and Ed Prather in a Beaumont boarding house parley, pouring themselves into the Spindletop venture in those first months, borrowing and buying, leasing and drilling with the same fever that had made Beatty, Heywood, and Cullinan so successful. Their investments would soon spread out from Spindletop and in 1904 be incorporated as Humble Oil, and their future would continue to be one of growth and prosperity as one of America's largest petroleum interests.[15]

Two of the first men to set their sights on Spindletop, Joseph Cullinan and James Guffey, also would put their mark on the national oil industry. On March 28, 1901, Cullinan organized the Texas Fuel Company with his brother Michael and fellow investor H. L. Scales. The ancestor of Texaco, Cullinan's enterprise was built with intense energy and business savvy, including hiring men like Walter Sharp and Howard Hughes, Sr.[16] "Buckskin Joe" took a $50,000 investment and made it into an international corporation.

James Guffey, for all of his interest and financial wizardry in support of the Lucas well and two of the next five gushers on Big Hill, only came to Beaumont once in his life, leaving the office and banks of Pittsburgh to make an appearance on May 16, 1901. Before he had left, the J. M. Guffey Petroleum Company—eventually reorganized as Gulf Refining Company by William Mellon—was born. In June Guffey began to arrange a massive international deal with the London-based Shell Transport and Trading Company. The result was yet another of the first truly successful oil companies now in serious competition with Rockefeller and each other.

The Texas Company (Texaco today), Sun Oil (Sunoco), Humble (Exxon), Gulf (Chevron), Magnolia (Mobil)—the rebirth of the petroleum industry at Spindletop in 1901 still carries with it the weight of these visionaries a century after.

> "Once I was a farmer man who owned a piece of ground
> Where taters, corn and sich like grew that I peddled over town.
> But now I'm rich and money have and live in bang-up style,
> And it came about without a doubt cause Lucas he struck ile.
>
> I done bought my wife a diamond ring to wear upon her hand,
> My daughter Sal a peane grand—she plays to beat the band.
> We're going to hire a Pullman car to travel East in style,
> And it comes about without a doubt cause Lucas he struck ile.
>
> And when we get to big New York the people they will stare,
> And shout "Hurray! There goes the Jay, the oily millionaire."
> We'll show the Gotham folks just how to put on Beaumont style,
> And it comes about without a doubt cause Lucas he struck ile.
>
> We'll hire old Sousa and his band at a thousand plunks a day,
> To follow us 'round the streets of York and rag-time music play.
> We'll buy our kids an automobile, dress in the latest style,
> And it comes about without a doubt cause Lucas he struck ile."[17]

SWINDLETOP

Millions and millions—and they were scheming to make it tens of millions. It was a game, marvelous, irresistible; everybody was playing it.[18]

Mrs. Sullivan was approached by an oil promoter one bright, chilly day in the early spring of 1901. He had crisscrossed Big Hill in search of a small lease where he could drill for his fortune, and had spotted her dilapidated shack. The tract was on a line that matched up well with Lucas No. 1 and the Beatty operation. When he first approached the house he had noticed two things right away: the place was a pig farm, and the smell—not just from the pigs—was plenty of competition with the sour springs and the odor of oil in that area! And Mrs. Sullivan was not home. When he went into Beaumont and inquired about the pig farm owner's whereabouts, several citizens who knew her pointed down the street. The object in that direction was a small woman, bent over at a muddy curb, shoving trash into a bag. The speculator watched with horror and amusement as she tossed the piles into a wretched buckboard that leaned far to one side.

Mrs. Sullivan was more than pleased to visit with the "nice young man" who escorted her back to her hovel. He kept his distance as they sat on the wagon's bench for the ride to Big Hill. He refused the offer of refreshments, and talked to her about mineral leases. Confused at first, she certainly understood enough to accept his deal of $35,000 for her property. "Mrs. Slop," as the newspaper reporters called her when they added her story to the others, became nationally known as the garbage lady of Beaumont who sold her pig farm for an oil fortune.[19]

An adjacent piece of property had recently been surveyed and evaluated at $8.00 an acre, not any different than the price the owner had paid for it some years before. On one particular day that spring, the owner sold it for considerably more, that speculator turned it around for his own quick profit, and the lease changed hands a half-dozen times by dusk. The final offer taken that night was $30,000!

A stranger stepped down off the train just into Beaumont from Missouri, surveyed the crowded melee around him, pushed his way across the station platform and hired a hack to take him to Spindletop. He had little more than $20 in pocket, the result of a failed career back in the Midwest. Here would be his next chance, he believed. He wandered out to the edge of Big Hill and by mid-morning had purchased an acre of nondescript land, far off the beaten path, with all of the money he had on him. When he sat down for supper that evening at the Crosby House, he no longer owned that acre, but his newly purchased money belt bulged against his coat. He returned the next day to Missouri a wealthy "oilman."[20]

"One of the most interesting things to me was the fact that the Western Union had its office in the lobby of the Crosby House," notes H. P. Nichols. "Anyone familiar with Morse Code could easily ascertain the prices quoted by competitors, and underbid a penny a barrel to get the next contract coming in!"[21]

Clint Wood remembers the crowds, and the bank. "The people came from everywhere. They came from New York, Chicago, Kansas City. None of 'em knew a thing about the oil business or the value of it. Hell, land sold for $500 an acre *ten miles away*," he declared. "And there was just one little bank there in Beaumont, the First National, and they just shipped money in there by the sackfuls. Got where the bank wouldn't accept deposits, because they had it piled up in sacks around the lobby. Just a little bitty 25 foot space, 'til you couldn't get in or out. Full of money. Piled up in sacks."[22]

At the end of 1900 the bank in Beaumont boasted deposits of nearly $900,000. By July, 1901, that bank and two brand new ones estimated— the money was rolling in so fast and back out again that the number changed every minute—a composite total of deposits at $3,370,000. That number would double again by the end of the year.

The *Beaumont Daily Enterprise,* April 10, 1901:

> Thousands of strangers are here. It is impossible to describe the state of mind of the strangers for they all have the oil fever of the most virulent type. There were thirteen coaches loaded to the platforms from Galveston and Houston. Probably more than ten thousand people came. All the livery stable rigs were engaged several days in advance and constant streams of people were disappointed. "Give me a dog cart, saddle horse, wagon or any old thing," they would plead, but they were not there to give.[23]

"A couple of fellows come down there from back east," says Clint Wood, "and couldn't get out to Spindletop because of the crowds. So they bought a team and wagon from an old soup peddler. Unloaded it, drove it out there, drove it back, turned the team loose there in town, and just walked away."[24]

A black citizen of Beaumont whose home stood near Big Hill was approached by a speculator waving papers in his hands as the man walked through town. He had been with relatives who lived on a small farm north of the city and now was headed back for his wife, children, and home. He had no idea about the oil wells and their importance, and had never given it a thought. Now this stranger was talking to him real smoothly, and mentioning amounts of money that turned the man's head. When the promoter offered him $20,000 for his farm, right then, right there where they stood, it took no time to decide. "Sure," he said. They stopped outside a building at the edge of Beaumont and the bewildered farmer signed the papers laid out on a flat board in front of him.

The deal struck, the man headed on home with a quicker step than before—he and his family were rich beyond their dreams. As he walked up to the porch of his home, his wife stood there with another stranger, a broad smile on her face. She spoke before he could tell her his good news. "This man has offered us money for our place," she exclaimed delightedly. "$50,000!" Her husband stood there as if struck dumb by the news. His promoter acquaintance did not. He handed the papers to the man on the porch, made the deal as the couple watched, and walked away with a $20,000 profit made in less than a half hour![25]

A commissary clerk in Beaumont had saved his meager salary for months to a grand total of $60. An opportunity arose in 1900 for him to buy four acres of land south of town for only $15 an acre, and he couldn't resist what he considered an "important investment in land." When the Lucas gusher hit and the first speculators hit town, the clerk was approached by a line of customers-turned-oilmen, and took the best offer for his property: $100,000.[26]

Money changed hands every minute of every hour of every day through the spring of 1901, millions of dollars, most in cash, some "on paper." A Beaumont banker figured conservatively that $4.4 million had been invested in oil leases by mid-summer.

Two men from St. Louis, one a reporter, arrived into the midst of the Beaumont chaos like most everyone else, at the train station. The first off the train was immediately approached to invest in one of the oil tracts at Spindletop. He politely declined, but the Missourian behind him agreed to the terms. They arranged to meet later for lunch. There, the investor had good news and bad news already. Two hours after their arrival he had sold his lease for $5,000, a clean 500 percent profit; that same lease had gone for $20,000 an hour later.

A railway employee got in on the act himself after watching the passengers reap the unbelievable profits, some before they had left the station. He took his break and headed out to Big Hill. The people were selling off the land now by *quarter-acre lots,* and the railroad brakeman plopped down a quick dollar for his part in a lease deal. He quickly arranged a second deal whereby he would head up an oil company, established a lucrative partnership with other investors, prepared the paperwork, gave himself a $10,000-a-month salary, and retired from the railway business a wealthy man![27]

Not everyone came out well. Michel T. Halbouty records the fate of one Beaumont family whose fortune was made with a $50,000 offer for their small farm. The money came so quickly and easily that the head of that household couldn't handle the excitement or the responsibility: he went mad in the weeks that followed, and his insanity destroyed the family.[28]

Others made their money through hard work, taking advantage of the boom town that was birthing along the Neches that spring. Hiram Sloop was just eleven when his family moved to Spindletop.

I got into the grocery business shortly after, but the main means of gain at first was our mule teams hauling people and supplies all over. We'd make $500 hauling equipment from Wichita Falls to the oil field.

Most mornings we'd go into Beaumont about three o'clock to some of the wholesale houses and packing companies. We'd load up the wagons with meat or groceries and haul it out to the Hill from four until six. There was always trouble when it was wet, and we'd drive off the roads and through the fields and back sometimes. Saw some mule teams drown in the mud it was so bad sometimes.

And we had a store on the east side of the Hill near the middle of it. Didn't have a street address or anything then. Every morning we had 55-gallon tanks of [kerosene] delivered to the store, and my job was to dispense that to the various kinds of lights, kerosene lamps—there were three or four hundred of those to fill every morning. We'd fill them and they'd take them back out to the oil field. That was their only lights out there.[29]

The *Beaumont Daily Enterprise*, April 3, 1901:

Operators were again surprised. Carroll and O'Brien land. It's a Guffey well. W. B. Sharp the lucky driller. Treat in store for the curious. Notes from the field. W. B. Sharp's well, the J. M. Guffey Company No. 3 came in rather unexpectedly last evening while preparations were being made to drill through the rock. . . . Mr. Sharp said this morning that he was compelled to put the oil saver on the pipe on account of the danger from fire. The J. M. Guffey Company have a number of oil tanks near the well and it is feared that if the oil is permitted to flow on the prairie it will saturate the grass around these tanks and they will be in great danger of fire. When the cable drill pierces the rock, however, the well will spout until the cable is withdrawn and the valve closed.[30]

Bud Coyle boarded at Mrs. Klein's when he first arrived in Beaumont that spring. "Good meals," he remembers, "plenty of good garden stuff, and chickens." He was working on the Guffey well for Walter Sharp when a pipe came loose and smashed his fingers on one hand. He explains:

> We were going to blow the well with air, and we were setting up an air machine and letting it down on the foundation. I saw it beginning to stick, put my fingers under there to move a bolt. So it hit and the doggone pipe slipped out of the thing and fell on my hand.
>
> Now old Doc Cunningham was in Beaumont, and Walter Sharp and Ed Prather put me in a wagon. Walter had a team, the fastest in the country. And he was flying into town. They could race like a sonofagun. And I says, "You're gonna kill them horses!" And Mr. Sharp shouted back over his shoulder, "We can buy more horses but we can't buy you another hand!"[31]

MR. WALTER SHARP AND HIS BROTHER JIM

The New Crosby Hotel, Beaumont, Texas, January 18, 1901—"Dear Mrs. Sharp, Have just returned from the country where I have been looking after deals. I have about closed for 90 acres of oil land for $200.00 per acre that it may be oil land. It is about one mile from the big well. I stayed in Sour Lake yesterday. Saw Mrs. Newton.... Mr. Savage came in today. Jimmie and his outfit will land here tomorrow. My Dallas rig will be here Monday.... People are wild here and the hotels are full. Rooms are rented for ten dollars per night, sounds like the Klondike, doesn't it? [signed] Walter Sharp"[32]

There are hardly two more significant personalities in the days of Spindletop than the Tennessee-born brothers Walter and Jim Sharp. They brought distinctive character to Big Hill, Sour Lake, and Batson in those early years, and would be remembered for decades thereafter. Their skills, innate sense of the oil fields, and general optimism pervaded the crowds where they walked and the crews who respected them. Their stories became legend, and their contribution to the Spindletop phenomenon immeasurable. Walter was forever known as "Mr. Walter Sharp"; his brother, always "Jim."

Walter Benona Sharp was born on December 12, 1870. He and his younger brother Jim came with their widowed father to Texas as children. By age sixteen Walter was on his own, working jobs across Central Texas. In 1888 he was in Dallas drilling water wells and using a prototype rig that would eventually become the rotary drilling process. His 1893 frustration on Spindletop drilling for Pattillo Higgins did not discourage him, although his exhaustion of funds did necessitate his *walking* from Beaumont back home to Dallas. Walter practiced his drilling methods on shallow fields around Sour Lake for two years, and then hit stride in the Corsicana fields after 1897.

In Corsicana, Walter Sharp brought Jim on board with the drilling operations, continued to develop better methods for deeper and more efficient drilling, and befriended the ex–Standard Oil man, Joseph Cullinan. Walter married Estelle Boughton in 1897; they would raise three children in Corsicana and Beaumont. When the Lucas gusher came in, Sharp arrived on Big Hill twenty-four hours later. He brought his Dallas colleague Ed Prather, then his brother Jim, and these men along with Cullinan soon made their significant mark on the Spindletop oil fields. "Mr. Walter always had the welfare of his men at heart," an old roughneck remembered. It would also be Walter Sharp in association with Howard Hughes, Sr., who would organize the Moonshine Oil Company, develop the next generation of drill bits, and organize the company that marketed them. The Sharp-Hughes Company ultimately became much more world-famous as the Hughes Tool Company after Sharp's untimely death in 1912 at the age of forty-one.[33]

While Walter provided the brains, the methodology, and the supervision of the wells that were brought in under his guidance, his brother Jim provided the brawn, the entertainment, and the model for the roughnecks who would emerge in the oil patch. He coordinated security at his brother's well sites, looked after the needs of the crew members he hired on, and gained a reputation as one of the most colorful men in Texas. Years after this era, memories served well of Mr. Walter and Jim Sharp.

Beaumont lawyer and judge Edgar Eggleston Townes recalls,

> Mr. Walter Sharp was a large, rather raw-boned, sandy-haired man, a very forceful character, and physically forceful. He gave his business his personal attention and knew what was going on. He paid little attention to correspondence, however. I represented him in a case in court and wrote him several times asking for names of witnesses and to come by my Beaumont office for conference. I got no response. Finally his right hand man Bill Lyons came by my office and told me there wasn't any use writing Walter, Walter wouldn't answer the letter, wouldn't read it; that to write to him, Lyons, and he would talk to Walter and answer me.
>
> It reminded me of Napoleon who was said never to read a letter but to

throw it aside and say, "If it is of importance I'll hear from it again; if not why waste time reading it?" This however made the handling of Mr. Sharp's business in those early days rather difficult.

He was rather nervous, never liked to wait to see anyone. He usually carried in his pockets some little gadget with which to while away the time. He had a watch with a glass back on it. There were grooves inside and a shot, and he would amuse himself shaking that watch and trying to get the shot into the hole, bringing it around the grooves.

Or he would play crackaloo: you flip a coin and let it fall to the floor to see if it will fall in a crack. And if there are two people playing, then the one whose nickel or dollar or whatever gets closest to the crack wins the bet.[34]

Walter Cline has his memories of Mr. Walter.

I was in his office one day visiting with him. He said, "Walter, did you know that people are just as honest as you make them believe that you think they are? People will do anything if they get the idea that you expect them to do it. They'll never lie to you, never double-cross you, never steal from you." And he walked to his front office window, and across the street there was a little boy selling newspapers, and he told his secretary to go down on the street and tell the boy he would buy ten newspapers from him if he'd come up to the office. Well, of course the boy came right up.

When he came into the office, Mr. Sharp took a twenty dollar bill out of his pocket and said, "Now Son, take this down to the bank and get me some change. I want ten dollars in dollar bills and ten dollars in fifty-cent pieces." And the boy left and Mr. Sharp turned to me and said, "Do you think he's coming back?" And I said, "I don't know." He said, "Well, I've never seen that boy before, but I know he's coming back, because I expect him to come back, and he knows that I expect him to come back." The boy came back with Mr. Sharp's change.

He'd trust anybody. Made lots of jawbone trades. And I don't think he ever got double-crossed.

Mr. Sharp sent me to Liberty to lease some land. Well, I didn't know anything about leasing land and I told him so. "Nobody else does, either," he assured me. "Now take these blank forms, catch this afternoon's train and get on over to Liberty and start leasing land." "But Mr. Sharp," I protested, "what should I pay for the land?" "Hell," he said, "if I knew that there wouldn't be much need in sending you. Pay whatever it takes."[35]

"Mr. Walter Sharp would do anything in the world for you," says Sam Webb. "If you got fired, he'd give you another chance, he'd go talk to whoever it was that fired you and speak to them, and you always got another chance. But if you ever got out again with Walter Sharp, you'd be out for all time to come. He wouldn't pick you up anymore."[36]

"Jim Sharp was quite a boxer and fighter," recalls Clint Wood. "He'd taken boxing lessons and gone to Chicago several times and went through the clubs there. Was real proud of himself. But one time there was a Black man from New Orleans brought a bunch of mule teams and was doing the hauling around the oil field. Something happened he didn't do what Jim wanted him to do, so Jim jumped him right out in front of the Crosby House. Well, that man whipped the hell of Jim. So Jim went back to get his gun. Someone told the man he'd better get out of town, because Jim'd kill him. So he took off."[37]

Sam Webb tells this story:

The Sharps had a mighty nice camp up on that Hill, right next to where the first well was ever dug there. The pipe was sticking up where that first well had been dug [by Walter Sharp]. I've seen Jim Sharp come in there with his pistols and shoot the doorknobs off. He never drank or anything like that, he was just one of those go-getters. Walter wasn't; Walter all he ever done was chew on those cigars. Never seen him smoke one; always had them in his pocket. Take one out and chew on it.

I got in a fight one time, gone over to Houston to put some money in the bank there. I was playing pool one day at the Rice Hotel with some young fellow. And I put down my cue and went after him for something that came up. House detective came right up and marched us off down to the jail. I stopped by at the bank to get some money to pay my fine, and Jim Sharp was there. He came with me and said he'd pay my fine.

Walter Sharp went five miles over to Vivian and there was a woman there named Mrs. Thorn running a boarding house, and Walter got a barber, set him up out there, and men could go to that barber and it wouldn't cost a thing. They'd go to the cook shack for coffee and sandwiches, didn't cost a cent. And many nights when it was cool weather, I'd see Mr. Walter Sharp go round at night, had blankets there for men to sleep on and cover up with. He'd cover up the men who were sleeping without a blanket; that was Walter Sharp, looked after his men.

Jim Sharp, he went to Shreveport one time and bought a cannon, brought it down to the oil field to shoot the connections coming across his property. Walter made him stop. . . . But one time we were going to lay some pipeline connections across the Gulf Oil property. And Jim told us to watch out for the sheriff and not let him catch us in there. Well we got in there and we were laying connections and some Gulf people showed up with 30-30s in their hand: they weren't gonna let us lay that pipe. But Jim Sharp showed up and he was armed and we did lay that pipe then. Nobody fired a shot. Just saw Jim Sharp with his rifle. He could shoot them rifles and pistols.

In Batson Jim Sharp brought us all up to the tool house, and when we got there he had us sign up to vote and he paid for the poll tax so we could vote.[38]

Jim Kinnear remembers it a little differently. "The electioneers would get a hold of you and say, "Come on in here to vote. Right here on this ballot is where you want to make your mark." They had the political situation pretty well in hand.[39]

Well, not completely. When the oil promoters ran Iowa lawyer H. B. Betty for Jefferson County judge in 1904, the Beaumont press and citizens balked at an outsider who had "drifted into the county since the boom." On September 21, the *Journal* wondered aloud about "the leeches on this community, where they came from and why they were forced to leave their last roosting place." Betty lost.[40]

Bud Coyle remembers living in the Sharps' camp.

They had an A Number One camp," he says. "Had tents to sleep in. Had a dining room and a kitchen in a wooden building [the one that burned in the first Hill fire]. Had a row of shelves with every kind of canned fruit, peaches, pears, everything. You'd just ask for it, they'd give it to you. Maybe 40 or 50 of us living there. Mr. Walter Sharp had six rigs running day and night at one time. Had good cooks. . . . And Mrs. [Estelle] Sharp was a crack cook. She'd broil this steak and we'd eat half a bull.

At another camp we had no bath, just a Chick Sale [an open-air outhouse with just a bench]. Old Jim Sharp he'd shoot a hole in that Chick Sale and go to enlarging it until by gosh it'd get too big! Jim got mad at me when I had a carpenter come out and fix a new one. 'You just gotta stop shooting at that,' I said to him.

A newsboy came by the well one day and he had three dollars in his pocket and he was looking down the well and the silver dollars fell out of his pocket into the well. And the kid was gonna crawl down in that hole and get his dollars, but some gas come up and knocked him out down in there. And they were all hollering and Jim Sharp run and got down there and jerked him out of the hole. Boy would've died if it weren't for Jim Sharp. Just pumped the life right back into that boy.[41]

RULES FOR THE OIL PATCH

By the end of the summer of 1901, as the number of wells swelled to over sixty and as the population of Beaumont and Big Hill jumped to more than 30,000, the need for safety increased to a critical level. There were fourteen producing wells, and fifteen more being drilled. Eighteen new rigs were being constructed in preparation for drilling as soon as possible, and three had already been abandoned. There were more than 1,000 crew members in the fields at any one time, and twenty-four hours a day. Several roughnecks had already died on rigs because of fires, falls, or gas explosions.

W. M. Hudson worked on Spindletop in the spring of 1901. "I experienced several boiler explosions while I was there. One time, the center boiler of a battery of five exploded and the fireman was standing on the boiler for some reason. It may have been a dry boiler and he must have turned some water through the stop cock. Well, they found one of his legs about forty feet up the derrick hanging there. It just scattered him all over the countryside.

"Another time," Hudson continues in gory detail, "a boiler exploded and the whole thing jumped about a hundred feet toward a nearby house. The flues came out of the boiler like spears and went diagonally through the door of that house, didn't even splinter the wood. It just made a hole clean through the door. And an old man was sitting at his table and the flue went right through one eye, and his brains dropped out at the end of the flue."[42]

On June 24 one of the Guffey wells blew out. The pressure of the gas obliterated the wooden derrick and lifted the whole drilling rig right off its moorings. Four hundred feet of pipe shot out of the hole and witnesses claimed some of the pipe flew two thousand feet straight up, coming down like deadly javelins. The crew lay all over the field, knocked unconscious by the gas, although miraculously no one died. The well blew for seven hours but never caught fire.

Sometimes, "marketing" Spindletop got the best of everyone. When three capped gushers were "turned on" to demonstrate the oil pressure and impress a group of New York newspaper reporters who had come down, the ensuing spray ignited when it hit a boiler, and the newsmen had a story and an unforgettable picture to go with it. A courageous roughneck managed to devise a long-handled wrench and shut down the well.

Lightning was a constant problem on Big Hill, and innumerable stories relate the dangers of passing storm clouds to the oil field. When a bolt struck the tank of one of Scott Heywood's wells in August, the flame that erupted the venting gas atop the adjacent derrick shot straight up into the air. Only luck and the hard work of the crews kept the entire field from disintegrating.

Deaths in the city were on the increase as well, with the violent crowds that roamed the towns at night and the unsavory characters who were beginning to show up—typical parasites at the edge of bustling, prospering cities. A whole attitude pervaded the area like seeping gas; a mean streak had invaded Big Hill. Even horseplay around the derricks became a dangerous game, sometimes in a peculiar way. A new, unproven derrick worker was known as a "boll weevil." He regularly endured the initiation rites of the roughneck. Making the boy ride the rotary was one form of entertainment, usually resulting in the initiate becoming nauseous and dizzy. When a German boy from the Texas Hill Country injured his back on his ride, he returned to the rig with a loaded pistol, and ordered the rig's driller onto the rotary at gunpoint. It was time to end the insanity.[43]

The obvious need to bring some control to the drinking, brawling, and unsafe working conditions came to a head that first summer. A dozen of the most influential oilmen on Big Hill, including Jim Sharp, Wes Sturm, George Washington Carroll, and Jim Swayne, got together in August, put aside their competitive spirit for one night and agreed to a dozen rules designed to establish a safe area across the oil fields now scattered all around the land south of Beaumont. These first rules for Big Hill were posted on August 30. They would serve their purpose in the months to come, and would in many ways provide a fitting end to the first phase of the wild days of Spindletop, the days of the Lucas Gusher of January 10, 1901.

1. No lodging house, boarding house, restaurant, nor cooking stove in use shall be permitted to remain within a distance of 150 feet of any drilling or producing well, and all such shall be removable to a distance of 500 feet, at the discretion of the Executive Committee.

2. No smoking shall be done within 100 feet of any producing well or pool of oil.

3. No lantern, torch or candle shall be taken within 20 feet of any open tank.

4. Watchmen appointed by the Committee shall wear a conspicuous uniform or badge.

5. The inspector and watchmen shall always be notified two hours in advance of the spouting of any well.

6. No well shall be permitted to flow unnecessarily nor except for substantial reasons, and then only so long as is necessary.

7. Drillers and contractors, operators and others, shall extinguish all fires in their boilers or other places or have a man in readiness to do so at a moment's notice, when any well within a radius of 300 feet is about to come, is being bailed or agitated.

8. All contractors shall require that no workman carry matches while at work in the field.

9. All sluice tanks shall be filled or leveled by the owner on ceasing to be used for drilling.

10. All land owners whose property abuts on the ditches to be cut for safety drainage shall take the utmost precaution to keep same open and unobstructed.

11. All wells shall be safely cased or bricked in promptly after the well is brought in.

12. No land owner shall permit any saloon to be conducted on his land within 1000 feet of any oil well, nor shall any saloon in the vicinity sell liquor more intoxicating than beer.[44]

"A HUNDRED MILLION DOLLARS"

In a retrospective of those first boom days, R. T. Hill published a report on "The Beaumont Oil Field, with Notes on Other Oil Fields of the Texas Region" in the *Journal of the Franklin Institute.* In his summary paragraph, he wrote, "Thousands of acres of this land 150 miles from Beaumont have sold for as much as $1,000 per acre. Land within the proved field has sold for nearly $1,000,000 an acre; $900,000 having recently been paid for one acre. No sales were made for less than $200,000 per acre. Spindletop today may be justly assessed at a valuation of $500,000 an acre, or $100,000,000."[45]

Swathed in hyperbole, although a Sour Lake field would later be purchased for an astounding $999,999, and other accountants claimed the *capitalization* at Spindletop had reached the $200 million mark, Hill's report at least captured the excitement of the Big Hill fever, and for that matter caused a fever all its own when promoters and speculators read his figures as fact. One thing was beyond question: the oil craze in southeast Texas was real, and it was just beginning.

And so the American petroleum industry had begun all over again, this time in southeast Texas rather than western Pennsylvania. Its impact on the lives of the women and men who congregated in and around Beaumont proved to be sensational. The city of Beaumont itself also withstood the social and economic blow that the Lucas well delivered on that January morning. In many ways the city launched itself into the twentieth century. Prosperity was welcomed with open arms. But the harder side of this oil boom—violence, overcrowded streets, drunkenness and carousing from saloon door to brothel bedroom—took its toll as well. The world along the lower Neches River was changing, for good and ill.

Pattillo Higgins.
Courtesy Texas
Energy Museum,
Beaumont, Texas.

Anthony F. Lucas.
Courtesy Texas Energy
Museum, Beaumont,
Texas.

Gladys City Oil, Gas & Manufacturing Co. Share Stock. Courtesy Texas Energy Museum, Beaumont, Texas.

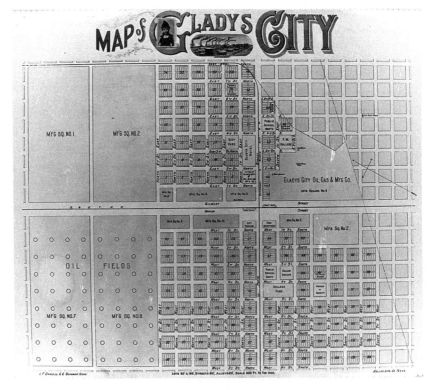

Map of Gladys City. Courtesy Texas Energy Museum, Beaumont, Texas.

Lucas gusher, 1901. Photograph by Frank Trost. Courtesy Texas Energy
Museum, Beaumont, Texas.

Although this photo is marked with "first rotary drilling job, Spindletop," it may have been misidentified. Courtesy Texas Energy Museum, Beaumont, Texas.

Drilling crew, Spindletop. Courtesy Texas Energy Museum, Beaumont, Texas.

McFaddin No. 10, Guffey & Galey, 1902. Courtesy Texas Energy Museum, Beaumont, Texas.

Visitors at well site, Spindletop. Photograph by Carl Liddell. Courtesy Texas Energy Museum, Beaumont, Texas.

Woman on derrick floor, Spindletop. Courtesy Texas Energy Museum, Beaumont, Texas.

Campsite at Spindletop. Courtesy Texas Energy Museum, Beaumont, Texas.

Oil field fire at Spindletop. Courtesy Texas Energy Museum, Beaumont, Texas.

Forty hours after the fire started. Photograph by H. L. Edgerton. Courtesy
Texas Energy Museum, Beaumont, Texas.

Boiler Avenue, Spindletop, 1903. Photograph by H. L. Edgerton. Courtesy Texas Energy Museum, Beaumont, Texas.

Gladys City. Courtesy Texas Energy Museum, Beaumont, Texas.

Gladys City Rooming House. Courtesy Texas Energy Museum, Beaumont, Texas.

Pear Street Grocery, Beaumont. Courtesy General Photographic Archives, Tyrrell Historical Library.

P. A. Looney Grocery. Courtesy Texas Energy Museum, Beaumont, Texas.

Maschek & Cameron Blacksmiths. Notice the derrick in the background and the shadow on the wall at right. Courtesy Texas Energy Museum, Beaumont, Texas.

Beaumont train station. Photograph by Frank Trost. Courtesy Texas Energy Museum, Beaumont, Texas.

Crosby Hotel, Beaumont. Courtesy Texas Energy Museum, Beaumont, Texas.

Fish market, Beaumont. Courtesy Texas Energy Museum, Beaumont, Texas.

The *Laura* on the Neches River. Courtesy John H. Walker Collection, Tyrrell Historical Library.

4

Queen of the Neches

The fame of the Lucas gusher is not to stop at its wonderful oil producing capacity. It has had a cigar named after it and is now on sale at S. Lederer's who complimented The Enterprise force with a box and the boys unite in saying that they are all right.
— The Beaumont Daily Enterprise, *April 3, 1901*

Bill Owens felt both exhaustion and exhilaration at the same time. In the aftermath of the fiftieth anniversary celebration, he tracked down dozens of the participants to interview them. The last of the Spindletop folks had given him hundreds of pages of material, anecdotes and old jokes, poignant reminiscences and hilarious recollections. Most were still lucid and their memories vividly clear; others had stumbled or needed a spouse or child to help them through the story. But, no doubt, he now held a treasure.

Now Owens looked at the manuscript before him, a novel based on the very stories he had collected for three years. *Fever in the Earth,* he had named it. He hoped it would bring those years back to life for readers two generations since, capture the emotions and the atmosphere he had gleaned from the interviews. One chapter, entitled "Boom Town Night," described the city of Beaumont after the Lucas gusher had come in, with milling crowds and odd characters, and his own fictional protagonist, Hale Carrington, in the middle of it all. . . .

The Rattlesnake and the Bird

A caravan of work wagons, sightseers' buckboards, hacks, returning from Spindletop, crawled through Pearl Street, mules and horses straining through the mud, drivers and passengers swearing at the slow progress. Hale and the preacher made better time walking.

They drifted back to the Crosby House and station. Crowds were larger, and increasing with every hack load from Spindletop. Trains waited on track and siding to take them west. Well-dressed businessmen and a few women, excursionists, strolled back and forth beside the trains, waiting for the call "All aboard." Men in work clothes, tired-looking and unshaven, sat on the rails, their shoulders sagging, their boots resting on ties above the mud.

Along the street there were other buildings, other saloons. Carrie Nation would have found a month's work here—but she was on trial in Topeka for smashing saloons.

Ahead on Crockett Street and on side streets other buildings were going up, two-story hotel-like structures, and between them cribs each big enough for one woman.

A barker maneuvered his buckboard to the middle of the street between the station and the Crosby House. He stood up and shouted attention.

"Free show. Come see the free show. See the rattlesnake charm the bird. Biggest attraction in Beaumont. Come one. Come all. A free show for everybody at the Gusher Saloon. Ladies and gents invited."

He clucked to his horse.

"Follow me. It's close enough to walk."

"You seen it?" Carrington asked the man beside him.

"I did. It's the cruelest damn thing I ever saw. Hanrahan's a nervy one."

"What about the excursion?" a passenger yelled to the barker.

"We just got word it'd be delayed long enough for the show."

"That cost Hanrahan," the man said to Carrington. "But he's got it to spend, I reckon."

The barker turned his buckboard around and like a wave the crowd followed him our Crockett Street. He stopped before a low building with an awning extending over dirty board walks. A sign with the picture and the words Gusher Saloon hung from the awning.

A peddler moved through the crowd shouting, "Lucas ties. Get your Lucas tie here. Gusher hand-painted on silk. Latest thing in neckwear."

Two white-jacketed bartenders brought out a glass and wire mesh cage and set it on a stand on the sidewalk. Crowds on foot jammed close together—derby-hatted men from the trains, oil field hands in their work clothes, women from the reservation farther out Deep Crockett, painted, gaudily dressed, jeering, jibing, inviting. Buggies, hacks, buckboards, some with women passengers from the trains, blocked off the street. Carrington was absorbed by the rattlesnake coiled in the cage, his eyes black and hard, his rattles buzzing, his black forked tongue licking out slowly and dropping down over the hard bone of his jaw.

The barker stood on a bar stool and leaned his elbow on the cage. He drummed the mesh enough to keep the head darting. A faint musky snake smell mingled with the smell of mud and cheap perfume.

"Ain't he a dandy?" he said, his voice pitched to the fringe of the crowd. "We just got him from San Antone this morning. They don't grow much bigger in West Texas. Observe the diamonds on his back. Every one perfect. Look how ga'nt he is. He ain't et in a long time."

Men and women looked and shuddered. The barker rapped the cage harder and the rattling increased. The head darted back and forth and then struck out, bone against glass.

"Look out," a woman screamed.

Men laughed at her nervously, themselves on edge.

The crowd shifted. Carrington found himself close to an open window, looking straight into the eyes of a young woman. Her eyes, dark and frightened, seemed held by the snake. A feverish flush heightened the color of her throat and cheeks. Her hands whitened in their grip on the window sill.

"Hey, Mr. Hanrahan," a bartender called.

Hanrahan, in black suit, white shirt, black derby, came from the saloon and stood beside the cage.

"My friends," the barker shouted. "Your host, Jim Hanrahan."

Hanrahan bowed. Carrington caught a flash in his eyes. They were blue, cold, hard.

"In a moment," Hanrahan said, "you are going to be treated to a great show—the most exciting that nature has to offer. It is on the house and won't cost you a red cent." He bowed to the burst of applause. "After the show is over, after we have watched the rattler gorge himself, you may want a drink. Nearest place is right through these open doors—good whiskey fifteen cents, squirrel a dime, beer a nickel. Feel a thirst coming on?"

"Yeah!"

"Among our guests are trainmen from both trains. They guarantee not to pull out before you get your refreshments."

"Heah, man!"

"I want to announce another attraction unequaled in all Beaumont. Everybody that's been here a half a day knows about her. I'll have to explain to the newcomers."

He bowed to the ripple of laughter.

"Her name is Loretta Lee. She is beautiful, accomplished, gracious— the finest singer in the South. She sings and plays the latest songs. When my act's over, step inside."

"No variety?" a man called.

Hanrahan regarded him sternly.

"Go to the Reservation if you want variety," he said.

A bartender brought a sparrow in his hands. It fluttered a bit as Hanrahan took it.

"Pity the poor bird," a woman whispered.

"You will notice, ladies and gentlemen, that to release the bird in the cage, I must put my hand in striking distance of the deadly reptile."

Men and women leaned back, as if to escape danger.

"Now watch." His face was stern, his hand steady. "The trick is to get the bird in without disturbing the rattler."

With his left hand he lifted a trap door in the top of the cage. He stroked the bird's feathers again. Then he slowly put his hand inside the cage.

For a moment the bird rested quietly in his open palm. The snake stirred uneasily and licked his tongue in and out slowly. The rattling increased to a steady whirr.

With a flick of his thumb Hanrahan brushed the bird free and withdrew his hand from the cage. Quietly he dropped the trap door, leaving the bird fluttering inside. Again the crowd pressed forward.

The rattler, quiet again, tightened his muscles and licked out his tongue. The bird flew, back and forth, back and forth, crashing against glass and mesh. Finding no perch, he kept his wings beating to keep out of reach.

The rattler was in no hurry. His head moved slightly from side to side, his eyes following the bird. For the watchers all sense of time and place were suspended until the horror would be over.

The bird, weary and bruised from the beating, circled the cage.

"He's in for it now," the bartender whispered. "He's under the spell."

The wing rhythm grew slower and slower, the circle smaller and smaller. Each moment of flight brought the rattler's head nearer.

"Watch out," a man yelled.

With a dart almost invisible in its quickness the snake lashed out. The hard boning of his jaws struck the bird and knocked it down. Slowly, deliberately, the jaws extended wide, unhinged, and took the bird in, head first, fluttering. The crowd, breathless, pressed closer together.

"I cain't watch the lump," a woman wailed and shoved her way out.

Carrington turned to the woman in the open window. Tears stood on her eyelashes and cheeks. Her lips trembled.

"It's only a sparrer, ma'am," he said gently.

For a moment her eyes were on him, and he seemed to be seeing more of her than of anyone he had ever seen before.

"I know," she replied, and turned swiftly from the window.

A man broke the tension of the crowd by yelling, "That's enough to give a feller the Beaumonts."

Hanrahan bowed to his audience and stepped inside. Two Negro boys took the cage and hustled it out of sight. The barker stood before the door.

"Right this way, gentlemen. Quench your thirst. See the show inside. Hear Loretta Lee."

Hacks with women passengers turned back toward the Crosby House. Women from Deep Crockett walked away with the men they had latched onto. There were still enough men to pack the Gusher Saloon, and have some left over.

Carrington and Preacher watched the people depart.

"You going in?" Carrington asked.

"Not me. I'd be et up like that bird was. I seen enough of evil in Eden to last me awhile. . . ."[1]

BEAUMONT

Nancy and Noah Tevis knelt together along the banks of the Neches River, their heads bowed in prayer. It was Christmas Day, 1824. They asked God's blessings on their homestead, for a safe winter, and a good planting season come spring. They prayed for their family and for the neighbors who might soon be putting up cabins nearby. Noah had named their place "Tevis Bluff." Surely it would have a prosperous and abundant future; they had come to Texas with those hopes and assurances. Little did they know that seventy-seven years later their little farm would be trampled by tens of thousands of fortune seekers, promoters, speculators, and oil field workers. Nor could they have known that the city built around their old homestead, Beaumont, would suffer the pangs of overnight growth and uncontrollable confusion—a boom town like Texas had never seen.[2]

The *Beaumont Daily Enterprise* of April 4, 1901, noted: "This morning's Southern Pacific train from the west showed no falling off in the number of visitors coming into the city and the number of strangers here now will probably exceed the first excitement [in January]. They will be better cared for, however. Different oil companies send representatives to the fields. The business for livery stables is not decreasing for the newcomers must see the field."[3]

The Beaumont presses came to a screeching halt one week early in the boom days, or at least so goes the story. A gambler with a pyramid scheme convinced enough of the local editors to invest with him until they had all shut down their offices to enjoy their imminent fortunes. When nothing came of it except chagrin and the loss of some $30,000, the editors cranked the presses back up, a lesson learned.[4]

The *Beaumont Daily Enterprise,* April 5, 1901—"George W. Carroll has set a good example by sprinkling the street in front of his residence with oil. All streets should be thus sprinkled to keep the mud off the paved streets. Other cities do this for $1.00 a barrel and it is quite possible that our city could get it for almost nothing."[5]

Frank Redman remembered his arrival in chaotic Beaumont.

Got out of a boxcar right by Fuller's Restaurant on Pearl Street, at four o'clock in the morning. I'd never been in a restaurant, you know, to order anything. I was nineteen years old. I went in a French restaurant up there and saw some sardines setting up there. I said, "Give me a box of them sardines." I only had a quarter in my pocket. That's all I had left. And he set them out and I give him a quarter to give me the change and he said, "They're two bits a box." I said, "Good God Almighty!"

And I walked there to Spindletop, five miles or six. And Park Street was dust about six inches deep and they'd spread that oil on it to keep the dust down. And then I got sick. I got out there at Noon and went to work at one o'clock without any dinner. Just had them sardines for breakfast, you see. And I stayed there for two years.[6]

Bud Coyle had a similar awakening at a Beaumont eating establishment upon his arrival to the boom town. "An old fellow Daugherty had a boarding house. He was from back East somewhere. It was a regular flophouse. He was a tough old Irishman, had Bowery Boys as waiters. One fellow called one of them over one day and says, 'Hey, I got a fly in my soup!' The waiter says, 'What the hell you *want* in there, ants?'"[7]

Will Armstrong, the son of an Irishman, came to Beaumont from Temple, Texas, where he had served on the city's police force.

I met a bunch of my railroad friends there, and they begged me to go down and see the mayor to see if I could get on the police force there. I went down the street and met the old gentleman and told him my business. And he says, All right where can I find you? So in about ten days I got a message to show up at the police station. I went in there and went to work.

They put me down on Pearl Street on Ogden Corner, what they called it. There was a saloon there. I worked four nights and the police chief walked up to me one day and says, How you doing there? You new here, aren't you? And I says Yes. And he says, Well let's go in and have a drink. And I says, No thank you. I don't drink. Well, a cigar, he says. I don't smoke. How about a wine? No sir. A beer? No sir. Well, he says, You're a hell of a policeman! And I says, Maybe I am. He come back later that night and says, I see they haven't run you off yet. I says, Cap'n, I didn't come here to be run off.

Armstrong recalls some of Beaumont in those early days. "The Crosby House was an old wooden building. Over near there was the Edison Hotel, and there was a little brick house there. And then you'd come up to the corner where Dunlap's drugstore was, and there was a little house near there, too. And across the street was the old Cobweb Saloon. They called it that 'cause there was cobwebs hanging from the ceiling plum down to your head. The boys liked to drink there 'cause they got a schooner of beer that'd hold about a quart. And the Italians all lived down a street in wooden buildings. And there was a Chinaman's restaurant there in a tin house. And there was the old Mississippi Store, and the Santa Fe depot. I went to Buffalo Bill's show there once."[8]

James A. Clark explains that the Crosby House was "the center for all the madness. It was an old frame building with two great galleries where men gathered day and night. The bar and the café became twenty-four-hour operations along with the remainder of the hotel. Even Old Jonas, the candy man who had held forth in the Crosby lobby for years, had to give way to progress and the madness. It was here that most of the traders chose to assemble. They would stand on tables and chairs and offer to buy or sell leases. One night a man stood on a chair in the center of the lobby waving a hundred $100 bills, which he was offering for a single acre in proven territory. The crowd laughed. That was the price a *twenty-foot lot* would bring."[9]

"There was three big oak trees in front of the Crosby House," says Frank Redman, "and the Southern Pacific train come in night and day and them limbs would rub on the top of the coaches when she'd go by." The trees didn't last: the space was too valuable, and they were soon replaced with small lots that sold for a camping place or an "outdoor" office. Promoters and traders just laid claim to some part of the garden or the front lawn, and someone would always be available to sell them that spot![10]

"The saloons were numerous," recalls Daniel Walter Davis, one of the first doctors to hang a shingle after the boom hit Beaumont. "One on Pearl Street, and around the corner two more. A block down was another one and across the Sunset Court were two. One on Orleans and one in between there. Outside of town all the grocery stores sold beer and wine without a license. All the suburbs had saloons. Some were not well ordered, and the Sunday proposition [blue law], well, they were selling whiskey on Sundays and there was quite a bit of trouble about that. In fact, one man was killed on account of it on Sunset Court. There was a bartender stepped out of the back of a saloon there, and a man was walking there and he just killed him as he passed by."[11]

Over on Highland Avenue there was another string of saloons. One of the proprietors, a man named Mosso, succumbed to the public pressure to obey the Sunday blue laws, and then did the city one better. He would clear out his bar at dawn every Sunday and invite a local Sunday School class to hold its meetings there! The boomers would start lining up at the door just before noon, their faces pressed against the glass windows, and rush to the bar the moment the last child was escorted out.

Several records indicate that half the whiskey imbibed in Texas in 1901 and 1902 was drunk in Beaumont. The only dry day was January 11, 1901, the day after the Lucas well came in: the town emptied, and no saloon patrons were left behind to toast the moment. That changed. In 1900 Beaumont "boasted" twelve saloons. By the end of 1902 there were thirty-six. In 1904 there were eighty-nine.[12]

"There was a drug store out near Spindletop that handled groceries, too," says Harry Paramore, "one butcher shop, one restaurant, and three saloons. There was the Old Log Cabin and there was the Alamo, and another one owned by the Smiths. They sold beer and whiskey, and they would sell Jamaica Ginger. Some would drink lemon extract with the liquor, and the lemon always run out first." Strong stuff, too, from the sound of Bill Philp's recollection: "You could take that whiskey and put it on two brickbats and they'd jump up and go to fighting each other right there. That's about the way Spindletop was, just a saloon here—and all around over it."[13]

Saloon keepers, marketing their place in the intense competition, often took the doors completely off their front entrances—because they would be open twenty-four hours anyway, and named drinks to fit the special occasion of the gusher field. A thirsty customer could order a Gusher Punch or an Oilette, and try a Geyser Julip or a Spouting Fluid. One establishment boasted "a Madman's Treat and other fascinating, thirst-destroying concoctions."[14]

Curt Hamill tells about one of the first new stores to come to Beaumont with the boom. "Three Jewish boys put up a little shack and sold handkerchiefs and socks and suspenders. And then added work clothes. Something went wrong between them, though, and two of the boys took the third one out into the field one day and whipped him near to death with a wet rope. There was awful yelling, and he'd get away from them and they'd catch him and hit him with that rope again, and he finally ran off and we never heard of him again. . . . Then there were just the two Jews running the store."[15]

Judge E. E. Townes summarizes those early boom days. "Beaumont was in a crowded state of confusion. Probably just before oil was discovered Beaumont had between one thousand and 1,500 people, with just the ordinary facilities and utilities. With the coming in of the Lucas Gusher there was dumped into this little neighborhood crossroads town, interested up to that time principally in lumber and cattle, thousands and thousands of people for who there were no houses, lodgings, and practically no conveniences. Health conditions were terrible. And you can imagine what the law enforcement situation was. A percentage of the people who rushed in were gamblers and disreputable people of various kinds— camp followers. And they were all strangers."[16]

H. P. Nichols had a difficult time even finding a place to bed down, and he wasn't looking for much at that.

My first three nights in Beaumont left an indelible impression on my mind. I paid three dollars per night to sleep in the loft of Broussard's livery barn. The bed consisted of a limited amount of straw, covered with a tarpaulin. It was a democratic bunch of men that roosted in Broussard's stable. Millionaires and working men tried to get a few hours of sleep.

I'm certain I never heard a more wonderful exhibition of snoring. The voices covered the entire range from basso profundo to coloratura soprano. There wasn't any designated footage that a man could use up in the loft, and as I recall it, the fellow next to me, who did not take his shoes off, kicked me a time or two in the stomach. Sleeping next to him was not very pleasant. I changed places the following night.[17]

The liveliest place, according to many of the storytellers, was the Oaks, a hostel and gathering place. Jim Hogg was often seen there, along with his good friend the enigmatic, always popular Englishman James Roche. They swapped stories and lies to the great enjoyment of their vast audience, made up often of the Beaumont ladies who had an eye for the handsome and debonair Roche. As he told the tale, he had been ranching in North Dakota when an Indian raid wiped out several of his ranch hands while he was away. Upon returning he found his own name etched on a tombstone in the local cemetery. Considering it a sign to move on, he placed a wreath at his own grave and headed for Texas. At least his flare for a tall tale had found a home.[18]

Building in Beaumont soon was under way as retailers and entrepreneurs tried gamely to keep up with the boom crowds and the myriad oil companies looking for office space. A local blacksmith named Hyman Asher Perlstein contracted for the building of a six-story "skyscraper." Over along Alamo Street a row of new buildings went up under the supervision of James Weed and his partners. Oil magnates built structures with their own names over the grandiose entrances: Gilbert, Keith, Wiess, and others. Frank Keith built a showplace mansion outside of town with his newfound fortunes. Back in the city on Calder Avenue, where the "old money" resided, Sam McNeeley sold four of his lots for drilling and others were preparing to do the same before an ordinance was passed prohibiting oil wells within the city limits.

Wes Kyle opened an opera house in Beaumont unparalleled in the South at that time, and drew some of the greatest national attractions to be had—traveling troupes, singers, and orators. The touring companies that came through Beaumont feted the citizens and the occasional driller to popular plays such as "The School for Scandal," "The Prisoner of Zenda," and "When Knighthood Was In Flower" starring the dazzling beauty Miss Rosell Knot. Kyle hired the Floradora Sextette to sing for the crowds when the troupes were not in town.

Local proprietors tried to stay up with the frantic pace. The town barber, Robert E. Lee, expanded his shop to twenty chairs to take the on-slaught of roughnecks and millionaires as well as his regular clientele. His barbers made hundreds of dollars every week on tips alone; the shops were forced to open at dawn and remained busy into the nights. Several blocks away, a woman who called herself Madame La Monte set up a fortuneteller booth in the Cordova Hotel lobby. At a reasonable $10 per prophecy, the diviner was one of the *nouveau riche* by the end of the month and used her profits to buy the entire hotel and the block on which it sat! (As the prophecies petered out, the madam was last seen at the train station with two bulging suitcases of cash, on her way to the next oppor-tunity.)[19]

Beaumont Mayor D. P. Wheat called a series of "emergency meetings" that spring and summer to respond to the masses that had invaded his city. The old city auditorium soon became a city shelter with hundreds of cots rented out at a dollar for every six-hour sleep shift. There was usually no time even to wash out the cots between shifts, but no one seemed to mind. A local church sent its ladies guild to designated areas with coffee and sandwiches to sell to the hungry, exhausted field workers. The Beau-mont chapter of the Women's Christian Temperance Union reacted with its usual aplomb upon hearing that local doctors had recommended that the crowds drink whiskey rather than the now-unpotable city water: they boiled copious amounts of water and handed it out at what became known as "watering corners."[20]

"The old part of town was over on the river," recalls Dr. Daniel W. Davis.

> It covered not more than about two blocks in any one direction before the boom. The Kirby Lumber Company had two old wooden buildings there. The town gradually moved on over and down Pearl Street, mostly north, and then gradually over to Orleans Street. Both Park Street and High-land Avenue extended south, toward Gladys City and Big Hill. These were the main avenues for those who would make their way to the oil fields.
>
> My wife and I were walking down Pearl Street one day, and I saw Ralph Landry, the sheriff, standing with his gun out and this fellow was kind of standing up in a buggy in the middle of the street and Ralph was talking to him. I said to my wife, "I believe I'll go over there. Ralph may be in trouble." So I went over there—my wife tried to get me not to go—and Ralph said, "This fellow says he's gonna get out of the buggy and whip the hell out of me and I said that he was gonna have to go to jail." I said, "Well,

do you want any help?" Ralph said yes and I said to the man, "All right boy come on down." Well, he jumped out of the wagon and was going to tear me to pieces. He made a pass for me and I just caught hold of his arm, threw my hand behind his elbow and stuck my foot under his foot, and threw him down on the sidewalk.

Ralph told me to take the man up Pearl Street to the city jail, but I didn't want any part of Pearl Street up that way, and I said I'd take him over by Main Street instead. The city jail was at the foot of Crockett just a block off of Main. So I took the man over to Main Street and there were five or six policemen watching me from the railroad tracks as I headed for the jail. Every time this man would start cutting up I'd just flip him over on his face again. Believe me, that gave me a reputation I never wanted in this town. It haunted me for years. They really thought I was some tough hombre because I did that.[21]

Advertisement in the *Beaumont Daily Journal:*

Drs. D. W. and Grace Davis, Osteopathic Physicians. The osteopathic method of treating disease, chronic and otherwise, has come to be regarded as the most rational method, and is fast gaining headway in the affections of the public, because it means "cures without drugs." Doctors D. W. and Grace Davis are the pioneer exponents [*sic*] of this wonderful system of healing in Beaumont, and the success which has attended their ministrations, and the cures they have accomplished in this city, are extremely gratifying, not only to their patients, but to the doctors also. Doctor D. W. Davis is a native of Illinois, and had charge there of the Lincoln Infirmary. Mrs. Doctor Davis comes from Missouri. . . .[22]

Hiram Sloop, who was twelve when the boom hit his town, got into the hauling and grocery business with his family soon after. "There was a school in Beaumont," he muses, "and we went there some. It wasn't compulsory. . . ." He continues,

We had big long shelves in our store, and we'd just sell right out of the boxes. Just set the big boxes on the shelves and tear out the side of the cartons and dispense the food that way. And we sold sacks of beans and potatoes, onions and what not. We took orders around to the boarding houses for awhile, until the French Market came to town. They took up a lot of business in the bigger boarding houses.

We'd make deliveries around the Hill from six o'clock until Noon, then we'd go into Beaumont and load up those big old wagons and bring the stuff back for the next morning. Used mostly the two-horse wagons, the big Studebaker wagons. We could put tons of food in those wagons, half a store full in one haul from Beaumont. We had a little one-horse wagon for the other deliveries.

And we delivered gasoline to the saloons. They had maybe 300 gasoline lights. We'd go to the saloon and we'd have big tanks in the wagons, and one of the men would come out with ten or twelve gasoline lamps and we'd fill them from the wagon. The lamps would last about six hours so they had to be filled every day.

Sometimes it was dangerous just to be sitting around. Recalls Sloop, "One time I was sitting in the window at the store not doing much, just reading or studying a little bit, not much going on. And there was a little cloud came up in the sky. It didn't look like much, just a long cloud looked like a telephone pole across the sky. All of a sudden there was a big clap of thunder and a streak of lightning came out of that little cloud and hit right in front of the store. There was an ice wagon standing there and the lightning hit it and killed the two mules and tore up the wagon, scattered three or four tons of ice all over the street. It knocked me right off my seat in the window and out onto the porch. Created a lot of excitement."[23]

Hiram Sloop remembered another doctor, named Cox, who ran a clinic in downtown Beaumont. When things got slow at the office, the citizens enjoyed watching old Doc Cox take his wagon and race it from one end of the city to the other, as fast as his pony would take him, "Old Lee and the little horse blowing to beat hell," until, worn from the trek, the wagon would halt and the physician would disappear back inside his place "like he had big business waiting for him."

Beaumont grew by the proverbial leaps and bounds in the months that followed Lucas Well No. 1. Whereas in 1900 there had been at most only one of the following, or none at all, by December of 1902 the burgeoning city claimed four lumber mills, three factories, three brickyards, three of the largest rice mills in the United States, two iron foundries, an electric plant and a refrigerating plant, a flour mill, and five printing offices. At the edge of town twenty-five manufacturing plants of all sorts and kinds employed over five thousand workers at an annual payroll of $4 million.

The post office added on in 1902, extending one wall out to meet the press of business. Between January and August of 1901 alone, the station mailed out 20,000 registered letters, and received another 16,000!

In 1901 Beaumont claimed two banks, the First National and Beaumont National. With bags of money literally piled on their floors, and signs posted on their doors imploring investors to "please come during business hours and not after Midnight," the two financial institutions soon found themselves in competition with four more: the American National Bank, Citizens National Bank, Shepherd's Savings & Loan, and the Beaumont Trust Company. The Beaumont Oil Exchange, established in the fall of 1901, brought some semblance of order to the purchase, sale, and trade of stocks for the myriad oil companies that seemed to organize hourly.[24]

Hotel accommodations increased rapidly, but not nearly fast enough to prevent creative sleeping arrangements all over the city and Big Hill. Crosby House manager C. A. Hageman expanded his place and depended on Captain George W. Kidd to operate the always busy Acme Bar & Lounge. F. A. Lynch and J. W. Ennis managed the New Enloe Hotel, which stood opposite the opera house and its popular Sazarac Bar. By the end of 1902 the city directory listed the K. C. House, the New City Hotel, the Cordova, the Oaks at Calder and Oakland (managed by George Hart), the Fields Hotel, Hamilton's, Dutton's, and the Gowling.[25]

Boardinghouses increased from twenty-three in 1901 to forty-eight by the end of that year. One of the more successful, run by the McGlauns, almost didn't get off the ground. When their farm flooded following the Great Storm of 1900, Jimmy McGlaun left Lavaca County and went looking for work. After roughnecking on Big Hill for several months he sent for his wife and children. Caught in late fall rains on their way, one child was nearly swept away in the Trinity River, and a wagon and team was lost. It took the family two months to travel the 245 miles to their new home.[26]

Mamie Perlstein anguished, "Strangers would knock on our door and ask to please let them sleep in the hallways. Of course I was afraid to let strangers in, and I regretted it but I could not accommodate them." Mamie Ward recalls, on the other hand, that "the young girls at that time had a marvelous time with all the attractive young men who came to Beaumont." Allen Hamill disagrees. "The women of Beaumont," as he recalls, "didn't seem to pay much attention to the Spindletop boom. In fact all the time we were drilling the old Lucas well we boys felt kinda badly that none of the girls ever showed up out there. When we was on wildcats out in other places, why, the whole country'd turn out and come see us, especially on Sundays. Guess the Beaumont girls didn't think much of us. Took me almost nine years," he added, "before I could convince one of them that maybe an oil man wasn't such a bad one to live with."[27]

Besides the French Restaurant, the hungry could eat at the Palace, the Creamery, the Oil City Café—which served 700 meals *daily*—Duke's Café, and Pizzini's French Café, which listed boiled water on its menu. The Longe Tea & Coffee Company opened in 1902 for upscale consumers.

Hodges Dry Goods and Speers Dry Goods joined J. J. Nathan's in the retail district. Nathan had been the only worker in his store when he opened it before the boom; by 1903 he had twenty-six employees and had added three floors to the building. Helen Weber remembers that "it was lovely. The store was first class. It was really an old-fashioned store, from one department to the next. The jewelry was up in front to catch the people's eye, and the facial creams and things, too. Combs, we used a lot of them, were by the jewelry. In the back were the piece goods and the shoe department, and the men's wear was over in another part of the store. . . . Nathan's always wrapped their packages."

E. L. Wilson had a hardware store, while T. S. Reed and W. C. Gosling ran groceries. For ladies wear, besides the dry goods stores there was Hecht's, Wiess-Martin's, Deutser's, the expensive Rosenthal's, and the elaborate White House, which catered to the wealthy wives from Calder Avenue. Seamstresses included Nora Berwick, Emily Fuller, Ida Griffin, Addie Lay, and Nellie Wakefield, a list that rivaled any in Houston or New Orleans.[28]

From the pages of the *Pittsburgh (Pennsylvania) Leader,* May, 1901:

> Lo, Texas doffs her broad-brimmed hat and strikes a grateful attitude
> Which coupled with a pleasant smile implies the deepest gratitude,
> To Guffey—gallant Colonel Jim—it tenders with sincerity
> Profoundest thanks because of him it owes its new prosperity.
>
> The Colonel, in that barren land where nature is penurious,
> When scouting with his magic wand—to test things he was curious,
> He smote the arid, sandy soil—and (who'd expect as much from him)
> There came a gush of fuel oil, responsive to the touch of him.
>
> Beaumont—that's where the strike was made—at once leaped into
> prominence;

All rival places in the shade were laid by its predominance.
Prospectors came in numbers vast, with infinite long greenery,
And derricks sprang up thick and fast—athwart the desert scenery.

The farmers all for miles around came prancing forth delightedly
And marketed their bits of ground and took the cash excitedly.
They scrupled not to screw a pinch; hard-heartedly and greedy
They asked at least one plunk an inch and got the money speedily.

While others played these fevered pranks, resolved to rip and tear
    away,
The Colonel built gigantic tanks and pipes, the oil to bear away;
And then he made the land resound with this announcement
    thunderous:
"An ample market we have found and no one can come under us."

So Texas cracks its broadest grin and says, "Where Colonel Guffey is
The coin, for sure, comes rolling in, the hottest kind of stuff
    he is."
The Lone Star now may brightly flash; and why should it not
    "respline" a bit
When every Texan rolls in cash and gets a chance to spend a bit?[29]

OIL FIELD MEDICO

George Parker Stoker was born in 1877, attended Virginia Medical College, and made his way to the Beaumont boom in 1903 as a twenty-six-
year-old doctor. Writing under the pseudonym of George Parker, the
adventurous physician published a wonderful narrative of his escapades in
southeast Texas, entitled *Oil Field Medico*. In chapter 1 Stoker tells of his
arrival into a city deep in mud and high in raucous energy. His delightful
description gives the reader a real taste of those days around Big Hill.

    A slow drizzling rain was falling as I stepped out of the Pullman and
took my bag from the porter's hand. A narrow, muddy street ran in front
of the station. Men in high boots were swinging and cracking long whips
over the backs of mule teams, wallowing in mud up to their bellies, straining to pull the wagons laden with heavy pipe and other oil well supplies,
plunging, falling into the mud, getting up to lunge again, as the singing

whips tore at their backs, and the raw curses of the mule-skinners filled the air. A wave of distaste and excitement swept over me as I viewed the scene. But I had left my growing practice of medicine with all its bright prospects for the very thing I was looking at, and had set out with high heart on this adventure, lured by the thrilling tales of the Croesus-like fortunes being made in the black gold flowing from Texas' first oil gushers. I decided that no fastidiousness of mine should cause me to turn back, at least until I had seen whether or not what I heard was true.

The Crosby House stood like an old scow pushed up against the banks of a river. I gingerly picked my way through the mud to the uninteresting, ramshackle, one-story frame building with an apparent afterthought of an extra story in the rear. The lower story, one room wide, running out like an extended invitation, had a roof as steep and pointed as an Alpine mountaineer's hat. Around the entrance ran a wide gallery which had been divided into narrow stall-like places by planks nailed to the wall of the building and the banister of the gallery. Over the unfinished boards of the walls were tacked blueprints of the Great Spindle-Top Oil Field.

An intense air of excitement pervaded the place. Men and women, gesticulating wildly, ran from one stall to another. Stacks of greenbacks stood out in vivid contrast against the blue of the maps. I had never seen so much money. I stood and watched with amazement as hundreds of thousands of dollars were exchanged for future oil wells in Texas' first gusher field.

I crossed the narrow place boarded off on the gallery and entered the hotel lobby. A roar of noise burst upon my ears. The high-pitched, strained voices of women, mingled with the coarser voices of men; oaths and curses exploded through a haze of cigarette, cigar, and pipe smoke which hung over the lobby. A milling throng of humanity of every type moved in groups or alone. Well-dressed, prosperous businessmen stood talking to the roughneck in high boot and slicker suit. Disheveled, hard-faced women screamed at each other above the din. The one theme of all was oil leases.

I stepped up to the desk, which was made of rough planks nailed together and painted a bilious-looking brown. A sallow-faced clerk, his dark hair plastered back from his narrow forehead, looked at me with bored, indifferent eyes. I told him I should like to engage a room, but he informed me all rooms were occupied. When I asked him if he did not have a cot he might give me to sleep on in a hall, he grew a bit more eloquent and informed me that all space in the halls was at present occupied with cots. Then waving his hand toward the uncomfortable-looking chairs in the lobby, he told me he could not even rent me a seat, for they had all been rented for months every night. Not because of lack of money, he said; for the people who occupied those chairs in the lobby at night often carried in their pockets a hundred thousand dollars in currency. That left me in an uncertain mood.

My introduction to the oil field was diverting, to say the least; just off the train, no room to sleep in, on all sides of me persons, to all appearances, lunatics, who would chatter about only one thing, and that one thing, oil.

Without exception the old-timers all remembered the mud of the Beaumont streets and how the quagmire seemed to wallow endlessly all the way out to Big Hill. Only Pearl Street was paved. For some it was a year-round presence, and ever a nuisance. When spread across the surface with oil or the occasional winter film of ice, it went from merely sticky to dangerously slick.[30] "One road had been graded up several feet and covered with shell," writes Stoker, "so the wagons hauling the heavy oil-field machinery would not sink down out of sight into the mud holes. Sometimes there would be a stretch of fifty yards without a mud hole, and again, the horses would strain through a slippery, sliding mass of water and mud, almost up to their bellies. The rain which had not abated since I stepped off the train pattered on the hotel roof."

George Stoker walked out of the Crosby and hailed a hack to take him out to Spindletop, although he was encouraged neither by the look of the driver nor his two horses. Nervously astride the "lumpy, sagging, springless seat," the Easterner held on for dear life for the ride that followed.

Down the street we galloped, mud and water making merry with the passersby, until the burst of speed that each crack of the whip put into the sad-looking nags exhausted itself, and we settled down to a more prudent pace.

The streets were checkerboards of mud and deep holes, made by the wagons carrying pipe and heavy machinery for the oil field. These holes were filled with water. If the horses made a misstep into one of these, the old hack would lurch and list from side to side, as if it were on a stormy sea. But the hackie told me to hold to my seat and assured me that we would neither flounder nor sink. The rough sailing was made more bearable by the beauty of the stately magnolias and cape jasmine trees, which lined the mud holes that Beaumont called streets.

The hack finally reached the edge of the city and moved on to the shell road that headed across the wide open fields toward Big Hill. The rain continued to come down, and the driver kept up a constant stream of talk of his own, pausing "only when he shifted his cud of tobacco from one side of his jaw to the other, or when he tried to overflow a mudhole with a stream of tobacco juice as he discharged it with amazing accuracy at some object in the road." The derricks began to come into view, and the driver kept a running information tour for each one they passed. Stoker slid back deeper into his seat, "for by now my burning desire was to catch a train out of that mudhole and go back home." The hack pulled up in the midst of a line of shacks, many of them up on stilts and out of the mud and oil—Gladys City. The driver motioned for Stoker to get out there, there being a hotel, of sorts. Stoker was stunned.

> I paid him, took my bag, and stepped down. A fountain of mud, oil, and water burst forth to greet my shoes and the lower part of my pants. Two jumps and I had landed on a boardwalk in front of the larger shack. My pants and shoes were dripping a black, greasy substance, mud and water mixed with Spindle-Top oil. Mud and water was sloshing in my socks as I walked and words were sloshing in my mind about Spindle-Top and her streets.
>
> There were men all around, some laughing, others singing, and some were swearing. I felt like joining the last group. I walked into the "hotel."

There was a room available in this hovel, and the weary guest made his way through the loud drunken lobby crowd, following a "tough-looking Negro" to the room.

> I closed the door and looked around. A musty, damp smell pervaded the room. It was small and bare, made out of the same unpainted lumber as the lobby. A half-sized, sagging bed covered with dirty linen, which had been used by many former guests without recourse to the laundry, stood in one corner. Through an unwashed window, which could boast only a few cobwebs for a curtain, streamed the gray light. A broken mirror hung over the wash-stand on which stood a bowl with a dark-looking rim, a mute reminder of the previous washings of many oily hands. A used, dirty towel

was thrown in a discouraged way over the stained water pitcher. One broken chair leaned rakishly against the wall.

I went over to the small table on which were a small pitcher and an unwashed tumbler. The pitcher was filled with water. Being thirsty, I poured out a glass of water and raised it to my lips. One swallow and I set the glass down. If that was Spindle-Top's drinking water, I knew why I had seen so many drunks in the hotel lobby!

In one final soiree back through the lobby and into the dining room, Stoker describes the meal that was presented him, on a table cloth where elbows, knives and forks had left "the whiteness a dingy gray, with odd patterns of coffee stain, polka dots of egg yolk, and gray splashes of gravy. Thick, white, cracked platters held half-cooked beans and a mass of smeary rice. Soggy, water-logged potatoes winked slyly at one with eyes which the cook had forgotten to remove. And what appeared to be steak floated in a weak-looking gravy, adorned with chunks of grease."[31]

"THE BEAUMONTS"

Although there are plenty of anecdotes to corroborate one another, perhaps H. P. Nichols tells about the Beaumont water with the most vivid word painting, including the dreaded consequences of drinking it. "The city water of Beaumont back in those days was soupy. Its odor clearly indicated the presence of alligators, bullfrogs, and fish. Everyone soon learned if the water was used for drinking purposes that it caused severe stomach cramps, or what was locally known as 'the Beaumonts.' Toilet facilities being limited, a bad case of the Beaumonts called for biddings as high as fifty cents for the immediate use of a toilet." Jim Kinnear remembers the bidding up to two dollars for a place in line. "The boys'd sell their place, go back to the end of the line and come up again. By the end of the day they'd make forty or fifty dollars."

Daniel Davis concurs with the dangers of drinking the water.

Our water was cistern water. Everybody had a cistern and we had to put a strainer on *to strain the wiggle-tails off,* and we couldn't always do that. We had a great deal of dysentery, typhoid fever, as well as other diseases. Malaria was very prominent. We were losing a great deal of children with what we called "cholera infantum." I worked day and night with children who came in looking like living skeletons, and I learned how to save them, simply castor oil, one big dose. And then after that I gave them ten drops of castor oil every two hours and worked their bowels out and gave them osteopathic treatment. Water was worth more than oil. You could buy water but the containers would get contaminated. Hard to keep them sterile, clean. The only fine water was at the Steadman farm, and the Fletcher farm. They had artesian wells and wonderful water, but they had trouble keeping their tanks sterile. Most people boiled their water, but they didn't like it.[32]

Of course, out in the oil fields water could often prove to be dangerous for other reasons. Will Armstrong, the police officer, recalls patrolling at the edge of Big Hill one night "and the road went right off into a ditch that had been dug about eight foot deep, and it was full of water. There was four boys coming out of one of them houses, had tuxedos on, plug hats, silk hats. And they were walking right behind one another, just two feet behind each other, and they just went right plum out of sight, one after the other, like a bunch of ducks jumping off into a pond. If that wasn't a mess to look at. You'd think one of them boys would fall in the others would stop, but they all went right in."

And the cold of winter stretched to the very bones of every man, woman, and child. Says Frank Redman, "Let me tell you when winter come it was cold up there about eighty feet in the air [on a derrick]. Holding that swivel, you know, and putting the elevators on to let the pipe back in the well. That's cold, cold, cold. No fire or nothing. But we was fat and healthy and stout."[33]

Dr. Davis remembers the mud that first winter after he and Grace arrived,

so deep that I saw one time a team of mules suffocated at the corner of Calder Avenue and Magnolia. They got all tangled up in their harnesses and the mud was so deep they got their heads down there and before they could get them loose and get them out, the mules were literally suffocated.

Wagons sat there all winter with mud clear up to the bed. We had no drainage and we had rain, I mean rain. Pearl Street had become flooded, and I saw a boat, a skiff, come up Pearl Street and they run it right into the front door of the Federal Bank on Pearl and Liberty. And one time out on Carter Avenue at Eleventh, they were driving their horse in the small ditch on the side of the road and the horse was just swimming across the street there.

One of the stories has the boys sitting on a roof downtown, taking bets how long before a wagon would completely disappear under the street's river of mud. And Davis's recollection of the skiff on Carter is not too far removed from another tale, of Jim Hogg taking off from the Oaks in a skiff, dressed flamboyantly in a bright green slicker and yellow umbrella, heading up Calder Avenue toward the Crosby House like he was in a gondola on parade![34]

With the incessant spring rains and the mud came, of course, the mosquitoes of legendary Texas size. "If you could stand the mosquitoes, you were all right," declares Sam Webb, who was twenty when he came to work for Walter Sharp. "I seen horses and cattle gather around the smoke fires, run the fellas off, just to keep them mosquitoes away. Pretty tough on the families that came out there to live near the fields. They mostly lived in tents, mosquitoes and flies, no window screens."

"They'd eat you up if you got outside," says Bud Coyle. "Had to put two mosquito bars over your bed to keep them out, and even that wouldn't be enough for some. Didn't bother you at the rig much, with all the steam and the oil and such in the air. There was an old mule out in the field, he'd come right over and stand right there in the steam. You couldn't get him out, it kept the mosquitoes off. Bright mule."[35]

T. C. Stribling was an oil promoter who believed that the pressure beneath the salt dome at Beaumont was connected subterraneously to the volcanoes of Mexico! After forewarning in a Houston newspaper that "there will be the greatest volcanic eruption at Spindletop that the world ever saw," Stribling began work on drilling a well away from Big Hill and on the banks of the Neches to the east. He finally called off his crew and quit the operation because the mosquitoes were so bad as to defy the oily air and any attempts to fend them off.[36]

An indelicate tale of the blight of the mosquitoes comes from Bud Coyle, who remembers that the insects were particularly awful over in the nearby marshes, and that a group of "high-brow Negro ladies came to Spindletop from across the marshes to see if they could make some money." Some roughnecks and pipeline workers "jumped them out there and stripped them naked. Set their clothes on fire and chased them into that marsh. I don't know how those wenches ever got out of there alive, as bad as it was."[37]

"THE GREATEST BANQUET EVER GIVEN IN TEXAS!"

November 12, 1901, Main Ballroom, Rice Hotel, Houston—In honor of John Henry Kirby, president of Kirby Lumber Company, Beaumont, and oilman, a dinner was served featuring promoters, politicians—including Texas Governor Joseph D. Sayers—and oil corporation executives from all over Texas. Miniature oil derricks served as table centerpieces; pine logs and cones, rice sheaves, roses, and chrysanthemums adorned the ballroom. The gourmet menu announced the following repast by courses:

Absinthe   Astrakhan Caviar   Celery   Oysters   Canape Lorenzo
Stuffed Olives   Green Turtle Soup   Amontillado Sherry
* * * * *

Soft Shell Crabs   Salted Almonds   Sauce Tartar   Cheese Straws
Dressed Cucumbers   Haute Sauterne
* * * * *

Small Pates a la Financiere
* * * * *

Filets of Breast of Spring Chicken (Peregord Style)
   Chateau La Rose
Diamond Back Terrapin (Sam Ward's Manner)
* * * * *

Champagne Punch   Roast English Snipe with Cresses Chamberlin
   Artichokes
Lubec Asparagus
* * * * *

Charlotte Russe   Assorted Cakes and Cheeses   Metropolitan Ice
   Cream
Cigars[38]

For all of the prosperity that spilled across the ground and through the city streets in those first months of 1901, the city and citizens of Beaumont were stretched to the limit in dealing with the darker side of the boom: overcrowding, rowdiness, promiscuity, and violence. Saloons and brothels popped up like dandelion weeds in the springtime, the fluffy white seeds floating through the air and spreading the infestation. Authorities from a tiny police department and a thin sheriff's office called in help from the outside, often too little too late. Infiltrated in the mob of speculators and entrepreneurs were thieves and brigands from all walks of life. Their "contributions" to the Spindletop experience are part of the story as well.

5

Dark Side of the Moon

E. W. Mayo pressed his way through the crowds at the station, scribbling furiously as he elbowed through the churning masses. "Maelstrom," he wrote down for future reference. Just in from New Orleans, the reporter for *Harper's Weekly* had already written copious notes while staring out the train window as it crossed the flat Gulf plains into Beaumont. The confusion on and around the platform extended out into the muddy June streets and over to a two-story building with the word "Crosby" painted over its balcony. The people—thirty men for every woman or child—milled about in groups of three or four, but the whole mass curled like a serpent for a block, always changing its position, writhing in anticipation of something to strike out against. Keep that sentence, Mayo thought to himself with a smile.

HARPER'S WEEKLY

"The dirtiest, noisiest, busiest, and most interesting town on the continent today," Mayo had his opening sentence in block letters across one page of the notebook. The editors had rushed their crack reporter to southeast Texas after the telegrams announcing Scott Heywood's fabulous gusher at the end of May. Mayo had missed the sight because it had been capped when he arrived, but people were still more than willing to describe it for every stranger who inquired.

As he headed for the Crosby House and, hopefully, a room, Mayo noticed three women standing at the edge of the balcony above him.

Dressed alike in white sleeveless blouses and long black skirts, their long raven hair up in a tangled bun, the three waved into the crowd at no one in particular, bright smiles on their faces. A few men waved back, and an occasional holler went up in their direction. Mayo didn't have to guess their occupation: New Orleans' balconies were usually filled with the same types. As he stepped onto the hotel porch, two men in soiled overalls burst out the front door from the lobby, their arms and legs intertwined in a mad scramble of fists, sweat, and curses. Mayo stepped gingerly aside as they rolled past him and disappeared into the teeming crowd. No one seemed to notice the fray.

In the article he would publish June 22, E. W. Mayo recalled two men who had accompanied him on the train trip busily planning their "oil company" operations. "A few moments after the train arrived I saw them talking with one of the grizzled farmers who are to be seen standing about the streets with cards in their hats announcing that they own four acres of land only eleven miles from the gushers, which they will sell for $400 the acre." Mayo noted also that some twenty-five companies appeared to have been organized just that one day alone! He learned later that the two travelers had become president and treasurer of their What Not Oil Company—Mayo's personal favorite title—capitalized at half a million dollars and already selling stock from the street corner cafes.

Using his jotted word, Mayo wrote: "The maelstrom of the speculative movement is the Crosby Hotel, which is only a few hundred yards from the Southern Pacific Railway station. Here pandemonium reigns day and night." The most sensational sight, though, was the money: "Men carry about great wads of thousand dollar bills with them." Although, the reporter noted wryly, for all of the money that was available and unlike in New Orleans, "it was impossible to obtain a decent meal in this town. Food cannot be brought in and cooked rapidly enough to supply the boomers." Yet despite the poor fare, "guards are placed at the restaurant doors to keep them from being swamped by the hungry speculators."

Later that same day, Mayo headed for the Spindletop oil fields to get his first look at the reason for all the chaos—the derricks that spewed heavy green oil from a thousand feet below the otherwise nondescript Texas surface. "The old darky who drove me from the station to the oil fields in a wagon dangerously near collapse," the reporter later included in his article, "hitched behind a pair of skeleton horses owns a tumble-down shanty, and a lot just large enough to hold it, on the outskirts of town. He had been offered $2,500 for this unpromising bit of real estate, but he 'guessed he'd hold on a little longer, suh, before selling it.' He is making twenty-five dollars a day driving visitors to the oil wells," Mayo continued, "and his ideas of money have been considerably readjusted within the past few weeks."

Standing on Big Hill watching the feverish pace of the workers and the endless procession of wagons and carts and hacks that ambled in every direction between buildings and derricks, Mayo could not help the hyperbole that filled his text. "If the Texas oil field does not prove to be the greatest oil-producing region in the universe there will be tens of thousands of bitterly disappointed persons in different parts of the United States.... Not since the days of the Pithole and Oil City booms has there been such excitement over the discovery of petroleum as rages now all over eastern Texas. And not in the history of the world have there been such wells as have been tapped beneath the sandy soil of this region."

As for the crowds and confusion, Mayo observed that "this section has undergone a transformation such as no region ever experienced excepting possibly Cripple Creek or some of the other bonanza gold camps of the West. The quiet streets of the sleepy little town have become surging avenues of seething, sweating humanity." It was the dark side of the bonanza that Mayo witnessed swirling around him, and it would not be an altogether optimistic or friendly article that would appear in the magazine with his name over it. "There are dealers in oil lands, promoters, sellers of maps, pickpockets, tipsters ready to put the newcomer on to a good thing, and all the human flotsam and jetsam that ride on the crest of a boom."[1]

"RIFF RAFF FROM ALL OVER"

There came a clamor of voices, rising above the pounding of hammers and the sounds of labor in the neighborhood. The yells grew louder, and yet louder, and the boys dashed to the open window of the house.

Everybody in the room was on his or her feet, and all seemed to be shouting at once. It was impossible to see many in the crowd, but two men close by the window made a little drama all by themselves. They were Mr. Sahm, the plasterer, owner of one of the "little little lots," and Mr. Hank, the ex–gold miner, owner of one of the "big little lots;" they were shaking their fists at each other, and Mr. Sahm, the party of the first part, was shouting at Mr. Hank, the party of the second part, "You're a dirty, lying, yellow skunk!" To which the party of the second part answered, "Take that, you white-livered puppy!" and hit the party of the first part, Biff! a crack on the nose. The party of the first part countered with a nasty upper-cut to the jaw of the party of the second part, Bang! And so they went to it, Biff, bang! Bang, biff!—and the two boys gazed through the open window, horrified, enraptured. Whoopee! A scrap![2]

Two constants defined Beaumont in those early days after the Lucas well came in: oil and violence. As Mayo indicated in his magazine article, Big Hill witnessed much of the same kind of untethered excitement and brawling that went with nearly every "bonanza town" across the American West in the nineteenth century. The unceasing crowds that pushed and shoved up and down the streets of the city couldn't help but turn the jostling into fisticuffs. Knives and chains and oil field tools became the weapons of choice when the good-natured wrestling matches took a serious turn. The causes were manifest: oil deals gone bad, soured partnerships, jealousy, drunkenness, and cheating seemed to top the list over at the jail. Scam artists and card sharks made the rounds of the saloons, and a fair share of them met their end in the Neches River nearby. Judge Edgar Townes also noted that "probably there was less organized crime than has existed in any other place with that number of people. This was due to the fact that people did not know each other. There was not the quick opportunity for organization and cooperation between the illegal element." More often two men or a man and woman would team up to rob their unsuspecting victims.[3]

The huge sums of money—cash money—that lay about in the hotels and saloons of Beaumont and Gladys City heightened the desire of the unsavory character to make his or her way to this boom town: barroom brawls were one thing, robbery and murder quite another. Frank Redman recalled that when the derrick crews "wanted to come to town we'd catch that oil train out of Spindletop, but never go out unless there was a gang of us, cause they'd knock you in the head for $5. Hijackers everywhere. . . . Nothing at Spindletop but houses and saloons and gambling houses all over the hill, and eight or ten thousand men on that hill at a time. Lots of them just bums all they were. Riff raff from all over."

And as the violence intensified, the corresponding law enforcement, as a rule, did not keep up with the demand for order. Officers such as Will Armstrong and Ras Landry did the best they could, which in most towns would have served them well. But Beaumont became a different kind of jungle, where predators and prey stacked atop one another in unnatural density. "I suppose there were few nights that there were not murders committed," continues Judge Townes, "and bodies thrown in the river. The officers did the best they could but their position and the circumstances made their duties very difficult."[4]

Ray Sittig tells a story that was oft-repeated over the years in one form or another.

> In the old saloon days at Spindletop, there seemed to be killing every night. There was a fellow there who ran a hamburger counter and they called him Hamburger Bill. And there was a barfly called Spindletop, and he was a great big man, looked like a rig he was so big. And Spindletop was always mooching money for drinks and such. Someone gave him 15 cents and he went over to Bill's place and bought a hamburger for ten cents. And he said, "I'll use the five cents later." A few hours later old Spindletop come back and said, "I want another hamburger now." Bill said, "Not until you give me another five cents."
>
> Now Spindletop was much bigger than Bill so he grabbed up a bunch of ketchup and sauce bottles and started around the counter after him. And he started hitting Bill over the head with a ketchup bottle. And Hamburger Bill had had enough of this, so he came around from behind the counter and grabbed a big old knife and he cut Spindletop right through. And Spindletop went down, cussing right 'til his last breath.[5]

Spindletop the barfly may have gone down, but as long as the oil flowed from under Pattillo Higgins's salt dome, the blood and the sweat poured out across the fields and streets and saloon floors.

H. P. Nichols considered Beaumont

> the most congested place I had ever seen, a little town of nine thousand trying to absorb fifty thousand uninvited guests. Lawlessness and hijacking became rampant. Mayor Flincher hired an able officer [Ras Landry] from New Orleans, and he soon had matters under control. If my memory serves, for nine consecutive mornings a floater—a dead man—was found in the muddy waters of the Neches River. Later a bartender and a Black porter were charged with the murders.
>
> There were men in those unmarked graves the same as I was, maybe workmen, but generally the men who were killed were fellows who had flashed some rolls of money. A man would come into this bar and flash

that money. The bartender would put a knockout powder in his drink; the porter would drag him out the back, and during the early morning hours they would take him and throw him over into the river.[6]

Although most of the violence was concentrated at the southern and western edges of Beaumont and out toward Big Hill, many recall the most dangerous place to be Red Town. North and west of Beaumont some two miles, out Concord Road, stood a stretch of a dozen buildings all painted red for some unknown reason. The Friday and Saturday night life there became so unruly that the neighborhood gained a reputation for being the bloodiest street in the county during the boom days. This was also an area where drugs were more prevalent than most anywhere else. By 1902 it became necessary to station no fewer than four police officers on that beat alone.[7]

Police officer Will Armstrong had a lifetime of memories from those days when he and a handful of others tried to keep order in the boom town.

You could get in a fight in Beaumont most anytime you wanted. I had a black eye myself most of the time, and I was pretty husky. Never did have to use my six shooter or my billy club or nothing, though. Well, except one time. Only man I ever beat up real bad I had to get after him. He kind of cussed me a little bit and I hit him with my fist. He didn't even bat an eye! So I took my six shooter and worked him over. He'd brought two women into a saloon and I told him to take them home. I didn't want them running around town like that. And he said, "Well if you'll stop hitting me I will." And I said, "If I don't stop hitting you?! Why, I'm gonna shoot you the next time!" He took the women and left town.

They fought in and out of the saloons, and they were everywhere. There was the Coney Island, the Klondike, Two Brothers, and Charlie Houston's, and the Little Casino. And the Blue Goose. Joe Broussard ran one called Joe's Place. Nothing fancy about the saloons. Just common old oak, glass bottom mirrors behind the bars. No fancy stuff. Didn't need it.

A fellow one night had a gun with him, a .32 six shooter on a .45 frame, and he was coming down Crockett Street looking for trouble. Well, he went down in a mud hole and that gun stuck in that mud right up at his shoulder. And it went off and blew a hole out of that mud you could have put two men in. Next morning he gave me that gun and says, "Will, you keep it. I nearly killed my best friend with it last night." And there was another fellow named Johnny, Old Popcorn Johnny they called him, and he came down into town one night and he got foxy and was going to shoot old man Sam McGrury. But I talked to him and he gave me his gun and I kept it for two years before I sold it to someone else.

One night I had a fellow down there, he'd done something or thought he had. He saw me and took off running. Well, just for curiosity's sake I ran a few steps after him. He took off down a side alley. Now I knew there was a guy wire down that alley and I didn't want him cut too bad. But he hung on that guy wire right under his neck, by golly. Took two hours to bring him to.[8]

Bud Coyle joins in. "I'll never forget one fellow on horseback, riding a gray horse and he had a rope, and he was chasing another man right down the street. I was in Beaumont calling on my girl when they run right by me. The man running had a big suitcase he was toting, but I swear to goodness he outran that fella on the horse for a good 300 yards, right down the road. Jumped over a fence and got away. Don't know why he was running. Never did drop that suitcase, though."[9]

Will Armstrong recalled two robberies among the many that occurred those days in Beaumont. Both had to do with the theft of diamonds.

I had a diamond crook come into my beat one night. There was a little Indian woman told me he was there and to watch him. He went up to a room with the landlady, got her drunk. In about thirty minutes she was snoring so loud you could hear her all the way to the depot. He raised up from the bed and looked at her, listened to her. Eased out of bed, he had a pair of rubber shoes on. Got the keys from the pillow under her head, opened the box where she kept her diamonds. She had about $50,000 worth. Put them in a little sack. *I stepped out from behind the curtains* about that time and I said, "Buddy just hold your hand still now. Don't move cause I don't want to kill you." He offered me everything in that sack if I'd let him go. Offered to get a running start and for me to shoot at him but not kill him, and he'd give it all to me. I said no. Took him in.

The other situation didn't turn out as humorously.

One night I was making my rounds, and there was a boy there, they called him Doc Bush. And he said to me, "Bill, I'm leaving here tonight and I'm going up to Kansas City to get work there. And I want you to wake me up a little later." And I said okay I would. In about two hours I was making my rounds and I looked up and there was a curtain on fire in a room over the saloon. And I went in and said to the bartender, "Go upstairs and wake Doc up right quick." I turned on the fire alarm there at Neches and Crockett. And the fire wagon got there, and another man and I started up the stairs. The other man got up to the roof and fainted right there and fell down.

They got Doc out of that room. Now he always wore a diamond right on the front of his shirt. And they never did find that diamond. His face was burned off 'til his teeth had cracked. His leg was burned off from his foot to his hip. And his arms were burned clean off. And I always believed somebody robbed Doc and took his stuff and set him afire.

The tragedy broadened when Doc Bush's girlfriend Mae arrived on the scene. Horrified by the sight, she returned to her room in another hotel, emptied a bottle of whiskey downing a handful of pills, and was found dead the next morning.[10]

Ralph "Ras" Landry was sheriff in Beaumont those early days, and many of the old-timers remember him with respect. Louisiana-born, he is described as tall with angular features and a handlebar moustache under his ever-present wide-brimmed white hat. His smile could disarm a crook as well as his intimidating stare. Landry sported two pearl-handled pistols, both of which he could draw with lightning speed and shoot with accuracy, and fancy cowboy boots. Dr. Davis recalls that the shootings

were quite frequent and pretty rough the two or three years after I got there. Ralph was a good sheriff. He kept order pretty well, exceptionally well, I think, under the circumstances. He had good men with him. . . . One time Ralph started out to arrest a Black fellow and they were out on the edge of town. The man laid his gun down on them and made them all get on their horses and ride into town in front of him. They came to a bread truck on the street and the man got over on the seat and made the fellow drive while he held his Winchester on him. They stopped at a saloon after a bit and the man went inside, with his gun still on the driver. The officers tried to get the drop on him but they couldn't.

When they got over to Pearl Street and started into a saloon there Ralph decided he was going to get the man. So he pulled his gun and fired. But the man threw his Winchester at Ralph at the same instant and that bullet went right into the rifle barrel and plugged it! The man took off running and went around the corner. Somebody grabbed the Winchester and chased after him. When he got close he tossed the rifle toward the man, who stopped and lunged for it. Ralph shot him dead. Quite an excitement.[11]

George Walker Weller, son of a Beaumont merchant during those boom days, remembers the time he was riding through town on his bicycle when some excitement began right in front of him.

Sheriff Landry and a posse went out of town to get a fella who had killed a man on Pine Street. But the fella got the drop on him [that seemed to happen a little too often for comfort]. They convinced him if he'd come into town they'd take him to the First National Bank and give him $350 if he'd leave town.

So they all rode into town and got to the bank. I had just come out of Nathan's store and was riding my bicycle, and I started following them and watching them. Ras Landry got down off his horse and the fella got down, too, and all of a sudden he started shooting at the sheriff. Ras pulled his gun and shot the fella in the arm. The man started running down the street and he was shooting everywhere. I rode over to the Lewis Brothers store and run and got under the counter. They chased the fella behind the post office building and killed him. He nearly got Ras that time, but Ras made that real quick shot.[12]

Not every incident ended in tragedy. The young teamster Hiram Sloop was delivering groceries to the Pickwick Saloon one day. "The Pickwick was run by a woman. She dressed like a cowgirl all the time, and she was always in the saloon. And she always walked up and down that saloon, never sat down, advising men and women there about drinking and everything, always giving instructions and orders. Some man rode his horse through her saloon one day and right out the back door. And she said, 'I sure wished he'd ride through here again,' real loud. And she always kept a couple of guns around, hung a small one and a big one on her, and had some others hidden around. Well, he started back into her saloon on his horse and she shot the reins right off that horse! He never did ride through that saloon anymore."[13]

"There was always somebody getting in an argument," recalls Harry Paramore.

One couple got in a fight one night and they stepped outside onto the street. I was walking right by them in the doorway as they came out, and a bullet came right down through the floor where I was standing. . . . They used to have knock down drag outs in Beaumont. One time there was a general fight going on upstairs over the post office after a dance, and this one fellow got knocked down. His wife said, "Get up, Honey." And he says, "Hmmph. What's the use? They'll just knock me down again."

Some boys got into an argument over at the Alamo Saloon, and one of the boys just couldn't take it anymore. He came running over to the pump where I was working and said, "Anybody here got a six shooter?" I said I had one and he asked if it would shoot and I said Yeah it'd shoot. I took it out and fired two shots into the ground. It was a Harrington-Richardson, black. "Will you take $3.50 for it?" he said pulling some money out of his pocket. I took the money and gave him the gun. He emptied it out on the ground, walked back into the saloon and broke it right over one of the boy's head.[14]

The fighting went on in town and out, and plenty of time the fighting would begin where the oil field workers came into town. "The toughest outfit that followed the oil fields them days were the tank builders," says Bud Coyle. "Oh man, they'd heat them rivets and beat them with hammers and stand there in all that. And they'd fight all the time. I come there one day with a man named Peak from Dallas, and old Wallace was there and there was ten of them fighting, five pairs of them fighting each other at the same time. And I says, 'What the dickens are they fighting about?' And Wallace says, 'Believe it or not, there's not a one of them fighting about the same thing.'"[15]

Wilson Hudson worked the derricks in Spindletop and recalls a peculiar fight between Tom Lane and Old Dan.

They were arguing in the bed of wagon and Old Dan picked up a two-foot long piece of steel and swung it at Tom. Tom fell out of the wagon and Old Dan he jumped out on top of him and they both grabbed this steel bar. And they got caught up in the wheels of this wagon and spooked the horse and he started ambling along, pulling these guys down the road while they were still fighting each other. By the time I got there and stopped the wagon, they were both all tangled up underneath, arms and legs and wheels. But by God they hadn't either one of them let go that steel bar. I finally pried it away from them. One of Tom's buck teeth was about a half inch longer than it had been. He pulled the other man onto his feet, said, "Well, Old Dan, that was a pretty good trick, wasn't it?" and they walked off together.[16]

Jack Hunter ran the bar at the Log Cabin Saloon out on the hill. He remembered nights when a fight would break out every hour. It didn't take much more than a raised voice or eyebrow, or an argument brought in from the field. Sometimes the fights were over "bragging rights" between the derrick crews. It gave the roughnecks an excuse to let off some steam of their own; generally everyone left arm in arm when the brawl was halted—usually by Jack Hunter's shotgun fired out an open window.[17]

Sometimes the fight just finished what had begun earlier in the day, out in the oil patch. Frank Redman recalls some Irishmen who got into it. "There was an old Irishman named John Dollinger, about sixty years old, and he was working one of the locomotive tanks, pretty heavy, and they'd put them on floats, two horses on each one, to move it. And the old man was standing there watching the men moving the tank, and Dollinger hollered, 'Pat, you ain't lifting a damn pound!' And Pat turned and said,' Well, Uncle John, I'm lifting a damn sight more than you are.'"

The Irish often ended up the butt of oil field jokes, like this old saw that always made the rounds: a big Irishman was sleeping at a boarding-house one night when the building caught fire. This roughneck's feet were so big he had to put his pants on over his head, so while he was rushing to get out alive, he pulled his pants up backward and jumped out the window to safety. A fireman asked him if he was hurt. "No," he replied as he surveyed his pants legs sticking in the air, "but I gave myself a helluva twist coming out of that window."

It was no joke, but a great free-for-all on St. Patrick's Day, 1902, when the Orangemen and the Sons of Southern Ireland took each other on out on Big Hill. Some who witnessed the all-day brawl said it was the biggest fight in the history of the West; others recalled that the night's drinking afterward may have set a record as well.[18]

Women more often than not seemed to be in the middle of the disputes. Hiram Sloop tells of "a big brawl outside a saloon once, when a wagon load of women showed up on the street outside. And the men were inside the saloon, so the women were hollering for the men to come out or they'd come in there, and there was some confusion, and then the men started fighting. One or two men killed in that brawl."

Many of the men who came to Spindletop brought wives and children with them, and of course the city of Beaumont boasted some of the most beautiful, dignified, and distinguished women in Texas. One article in the *Journal* gave detailed instructions for women who walked through the muddy, crowded streets, how to grasp their long skirts in a feminine yet confident manner "so that in this way naturally the foot is exposed and a very dainty shod toe should peep out." But beyond the refined and the responsible were the women who came to make their own living off the Beaumont bonanza, and their stories were decidedly different.[19]

THE RESERVATION AND DEEP CROCKETT

Crockett Street moved west and got rough. It became Deep Crockett, the haven of the demi-monde, and the most notorious red-light district in the western hemisphere, if not the world. It was a street of assignation, with brothels over every saloon, dance hall and gambling house.[20]

They called it "the reservation," the block of brothels, saloons, gambling houses, and alleys filled with "cribs," melting together at the edge of the city with the gritty, oily buildings of Spindletop, west and south of the first houses of ill-repute that lined Forsyth Street near Park. No upstanding Beaumont citizen would be caught dead there, although the shadows of night hid many a husband, merchant, and local politician. Children were kept away from the area, except for those whose mothers worked the streets. Although the young men of the city often fell prey to their own desires and wandered down "Deep Crockett," it was the boomers who were the targets of these many institutions of iniquity.

The women came from New Orleans, Galveston, and Shreveport, and a number of the madams who ran the places traveled by train from all over the Midwest and even back East. Some were transient, get-rich-quick women who stayed only long enough to fill a suitcase with money and then pushed on. Some remained in the area, investing businesswomen who made as much money as the oil promoters. Many of the young prostitutes were brought in as runaways under the spell of the madams, often cast aside when no longer "marketable." They witnessed their share of violence in the Reservation, and were as often the victim as the perpetrator.

Their stories are poignant, dangerous, sad, hilarious, and bitter. As a police officer, Will Armstrong worked the beat known as the Reservation; as a physician, Daniel Davis treated their injuries and diseases, as well as the deeply emotional pain.

"There was just a long row of houses there," Armstrong remembers,

with not much behind each door—we called them cribs. There were about thirty-five or forty there. And the madams would come walking down the streets, their diamonds shining like headlights on an engine. They were the walker bosses, most of them from New Orleans. There was Ruby Belle Pearson and Myrtle Reed, Hazel and Essie Hoke, and Myrtle Bellevue. And there was Jessie George, and one named Alice and another Effie. Hazel and Essie Hoke were the best known down there. Hazel would never get drunk, but Essie would. Hazel had about $75,000 worth of money and diamonds, and owned a lot of property out on Calder Avenue. They were from Navasota.

Most of the others wouldn't come down the main streets too much, not during midday anyway. And none of them rode into town, just walked sometimes. There was a city ordinance said a woman couldn't ride down Pearl Street on horseback. The reason is because there was a gal by the name of Jessie Woods went riding out to Spindletop and back, and coming back by the court house she fell backward off her horse and got hung with her foot in the stirrup. Horse pulled her plum clear up Pearl Street to the livery stable. That settled it.

And there was a colored house there called Gold Toothed Sadie's. And old Big Annie was down there. She had eight or nine Black girls. And they wouldn't let them cross the street or go on over after eight o'clock. But they'd pay me to walk them across the street sometimes.

Jim Kinnear remembers a black cop "named Dollar Bill. He'd arrest the Blacks down there and they'd give him a dollar and he'd just walk on down the road."

Armstrong continues,

The girls charged $2.50 to take a man up to their room. They kept that, and the madams got their money off the rent and the beer the girls sold. The Black girls were a dollar. And the French women were a dollar.

There was honky-tonking down there, they had about fifteen or twenty girls. They had a little show and the girls were what we called beer jerkers. They'd get a fella in the booth they had there and bleed him dry of all the money he had with him. Sell him keys to their room, you know, and take 'em for everything. They'd shake them down, sell their keys for $5, $2, whatever they could get. Sell maybe fifty keys a night, then just take off.

There was a fella there one night and I says to him, "Why don't you go on home? You're just throwing your money away here." And he says, "Oh, I'm gonna spend the night with my girl." So I passed him again about four o'clock in the morning and he was sitting on the steps at the foot of the stairs. I says, "Why haven't you gone home yet?" And he says, "Oh, she'll be down directly." And I says, "Well, I saw her and another man beating a retreat out of here about an hour ago." That's the way it was down there.

Arthur Godkins and Miss Lou ran a honky tonk. Had a beautiful band there. They'd march right down the street with it playing, come right up Crockett Street, up in front of Old John Mark's place. He was an old Confederate soldier and he'd get riled with the band playing and come outside, and he'd holler at me, "Bill, I'm gonna give 'em a Rebel yell." And he'd let out an old Rebel yell.

They had floor shows in the honky tonk. About twenty girls doing the hoochy koochy, that was kind of a new thing back then. The men, they all liked to watch that. Girls'd charge a dollar for a quart of beer and they each got 25% of that for themselves. One night I saw Hazel Hoke sell $1300 worth of champagne to one man. They brought in a case of champagne for him, like they was going to open it all for him. He got drunk, said he was gonna marry Hazel's sister Essie. Next morning his $1300 was gone, Hazel and Essie were gone, and the store was closed up. He never did raise Cain about it. Moved back to Oklahoma.

There was some trouble started up in the Reservation, so I went down there and worked about eleven months. There were eighteen saloons on my beat, and it was three-quarters of a mile around it. We had all kinds of ups and downs, all kinds of troubles and trials. There was eleven men killed on my beat in the first nine months, in various ways. I found one one night with his head crushed where a big heavy wagon had run over it, just mashed his head flat. Another one got burned up in a saloon, over at the Stallion Saloon. And another one was looking through a window watching the bartender count his money, and the bartender looked up and saw him and picked up a gun and shot him, went right on counting his money. I came in the next evening and saw this fella lying there under the bar. Bartender didn't even know he'd killed him.

I was going around one night and there was a big woman, half Indian and half Italian. And she had a knife, sharpened like a razor, and I says, "Emma, what are you gonna do with that?" And she says, "I'm gonna kill every whore in that house. I'm gonna catch them as they come by and cut their heads off." And the women were all hiding inside. So I asked Emma if she wanted a drink, and she said she believed she would. Now I always carried a bottle of knockout with me. She drank some and in five minutes she was dead to the world. I dragged her out of the doorway and hollered at the girls and they all lit out of the house. About seven the next morning Emma came to and asked me what happened. I told her she got drunk and she was gonna cut the heads off all those girls in that house, and I asked her what she was so mad about. She said she couldn't remember, she was just mad.

We had about four hundred of those women on my beat, besides the saloon men. And of course when they got drunk they were troublesome. I went down there one night because old Mayor Langham didn't want the girls working after Saturday midnight until Monday morning on account of the Sabbath. So I told one of the madams and she said they weren't going to pay attention to old so and so, and what was I gonna do about it anyway? I said, "Well, I'll just get the wagon and round you girls up and put you in jail, I guess." And she said, "You'd better wait and see who's in here first." And I said, "I don't care who's in here. I'm the policeman, and I'm in here."

So she hollered down the hall and pretty soon the chief of police came out of a room. And then she hollered again and after a while Mr. Flincher the mayor pro tem came out of a room. And she said, "Now you boys gonna let this policeman close me down?" And they said, "Will, have we done anything wrong?" I said, "No sir you haven't." So they said, "Well, he's the policeman and it's his beat." So I closed the place down and took the girls in and put them in jail. Next morning the judge fined them $200 each.

Later I told the judge I'd close the places down on Sundays if he wanted me to, but that there was no one down there to bother about it much. The girls had a hard row to weed anyhow. The judge says, "All right. Do as you please about it then."

Not too long after I was in court again and this lawyer asked me if I ever saw anybody in the Reservation that didn't have no business being there. And I said yes, I'd seen quite a number of them. And the lawyer asked me to name some of them, and I said I didn't think that was right for me to have to tell because some of them were from good families in Beaumont. Well, the lawyer insisted so I asked the judge about answering that question. And he said, "Well, tell him one or two names." I asked if I could just tell one and he nodded. "Well, Judge," I said, "I see you down there about as many times as anybody else from Beaumont that has no business there." He got out of court later and says to me, "You son of a bitch, I should have shot you right there. I knew what you were going to say the minute you asked me, but it was too late to stop you." We had a pretty good laugh about it.

Wasn't so funny sometimes. I had a fellow one night was whipping this gal real bad, and I took him to court the next morning and he got up and swore that they were just playing. So I reached down and I pulled her dress up over her hips and said, "Judge, this look like playing to you?" And he said, "No, Bill, it sure doesn't." Fined the man ten dollars, told him not to play so rough next time.

One night I was walking my beat and I saw a Beaumont lady and I reminded her that she shouldn't be out after eight o'clock. She said she was looking for her husband. I knew where he was, and I made her promise she wouldn't cause a disturbance if I went and got him for her. So we went into the saloon and I called upstairs for Myrtle and told her to bring the lady's husband down stairs. He came down and his wife says, "I thought you were gonna come home tonight." And he started lying to her, so she pulled out a six shooter and laid it on the table, and said, "I promised this policeman I wouldn't cause a disturbance; otherwise, I'd kill you and go upstairs and kill that woman, too." And he told her they should go on home, but she said, "No, we're gonna stay right here tonight and talk." And they did.

Occasionally the scene was too much even for the toughest policeman.

Some of them French women did sick things down there, perversions. That's what their hobby was, I guess. I asked them what the hell they got out of doing that stuff, and they said it was just for the money and for Mac— that's what they called their men. I watched a fella in a crib with one of them one night, and I gotta tell you, I threw up everything I'd eaten for a week.

'Course there was every kind of venereal disease you can mention. When the girls first came there they were called tidbits, and the first thing they'd do is catch some kind of disease. I saw them in all stages. Gonorrhea didn't amount to much, but the syphilis would take 'em away if they didn't watch out. No precautions. No examinations whatever. You just took your chances.

The devil's the thing, though: the church people never did come down and try to clean it up. Too tough, I guess. The Salvation Army come down every now and then, stood on the corner and preached some. Never did go into the houses.[21]

Dr. Daniel Davis, the osteopathic physician in Beaumont, dealt with the diseases that came out of the Reservation. He agreed with Armstrong's assessment of both the dangers of that red-light world and the reluctance of the citizens to address it.

> The people of Beaumont were bitter about all of that going on but they tolerated it, and it was practically legalized as long as they stayed in their district. The ministers and the church people had tried some to close it down, but all they did was scatter them around Beaumont.
>
> Venereal disease was really terrible then. Men and women. I used to treat a lot of the prostitutes. Didn't have much treatment at that time. We used common potassium permanganate, different forms of different solutions, and we had preparatory remedies of all kinds. Advertised it all over the country and the downtown restrooms and toilets and had big signs printed up, medicines for different diseases. Some of them were no good, of course. Just out to get their money. The main thing was irrigation with potassium permanganate, and certain drugs. They helped out but they had no antibodies at that time. It practically ruined the females once they contracted the disease.
>
> The young men thought it was smart to contract venereal disease. They'd brag about it. They didn't know what it meant for the future. They didn't know what was coming later, and consequently they'd die young. After awhile they got out what they called 606 which was an arsenic preparation, and it was very severe but they begin to try it thinking it might control or do something for syphilis. It was pitiful the way some of them never knew how or why they contracted "the looies." Young men, some of them paralyzed before they ever knew they had it, before they knew they'd been exposed to it.
>
> And much worse in the colored population, I think because they didn't take their treatments. Their sanitary conditions were worse and they didn't take any precautions, didn't go to the doctors for treatment. They'd just carry it along.[22]

Armstrong recalled one of the more poignant moments in his Beaumont career.

> I came down there one night and there was a little French girl in trouble. She was in one of the cribs and she was crying. And I stopped and asked her what was the matter but all she could say was Mr. Policeman. I went

around to the bartender and I says, "Charlie, come around here with me and help me find out what's wrong with the French girl. I can't talk her language and she can't talk mine." So Charlie went around and found out some fellow had taken her from New Orleans and told her he had a job for her paid $300 a month, brought her here and left her.

So I picked up her stuff and took her over to the hotel, and we got in touch with her father who was in New Orleans. Few days later a train came in from New Orleans and he was on it. And I took him to the hotel and he got his daughter and he says to me, "Young man, if I can ever do anything for you just let me know. And if you ever come to New Orleans you come stay with me and you'll be at home just like you were one of my boys." I thanked him kindly and they left. I got a letter from him sometime later and he asked if I was going to come see him. I never answered the letter, though, because I knew I wasn't ever coming. I just done what was right on behalf of the girl, that's all.

Sometimes the two worlds of Beaumont and the Reservation merged in strange and remarkable ways. Armstrong tells the story:

There were two women that I know of who left the Reservation, got married and became two of the best people in Beaumont. I was on my beat one night and there was a woman crying and I helped her out of there. And I brought a fellow I knew in town to take care of her, and they got together and she made him the finest home you ever saw. Married her right out of the houses down there. And she led a respectable life after that and everybody in town respected her. They had a little girl and that girl had a church wedding as big as there ever was in Beaumont. And she was well educated and never said a smutty word or drank again.

One day a fellow was telling me about this woman and I said I knew her. And he laughed and said, "Why she wouldn't even speak to you on the street." And I wished I had a thousand dollars to bet him on that. And we were coming down the street and there she was, coming our way. And she stopped and looked me right in the eye and laughed, put her arm around my shoulder and said, "Will, where have you been so long? You come down to the office and we'll talk all day long sometime. We can talk about the *old Navajo days*. I'll never forget you for what you did." And she turned to the fellow with me and said, "Hello, Mr. Holmes." And she walked away. And I said, "Don't know her, do I, Tom?"

And the other woman, she was real big, but a fellow made up to her and asked her to marry him and she made him a fine wife. And one day I said to him, "She sure is a big woman." And he says, "Oh, she fits like a sock on a foot, Bill."[23]

THE BAPTIST DEACON

My friends and I hated to walk past a saloon, especially after the boom where there were so many of them, because our skirts drug the wooden walks where the men had spit out the door of the saloon.[24]

Not everyone in Beaumont looked the other way. George Washington Carroll, one of the most upstanding citizens of the city, a deacon in the First Baptist Church and an ardent prohibitionist, continually railed against the sordid activities that had assaulted his fair city. Because of his immense influence, the people listened, including mayors and judges and constables. The three pool halls that opened in the spring of 1901 were all closed by December because of Carroll's demands. Edgar Watkins of the Houston chapter of the Anti-Saloon League made frequent visits to Beaumont to coordinate moral strategy with the deacon.

But there seemed to be only minimal effort to actually do anything about the Reservation. To attack this problem meant going down into the den of iniquity, a proposition most preferred to avoid at all costs. Better to let men like Bill Armstrong handle the situation in their own way seemed to be the consensus at most forums. As long as curfews and other restrictions kept the riffraff off the principal streets of Beaumont, so much the better to look the other way. Out of sight, out of mind.

But not for George W. Carroll. He was determined to "get the goods" on these undesirables, and send them packing. Finally he hit upon an idea that might address the awful problem infesting his city. The deacon had sported a long, white, flowing beard for a number of years, and could be recognized blocks away as he strode the main streets of town dressed in his finest black suit, with top hat and cane, a silver watch fob glittering in the Texas sunlight. One afternoon in the privacy of his barber's chair, Carroll had his beard shaved clean off his chin and his white hair trimmed close. He borrowed some plain clothes from a local contractor, pulled a nondescript wide-brimmed hat down over his forehead, and set out for Deep Crockett after dusk.

The disguised Carroll walked deep into the red-light district, passing saloons, cribs, and brothels. The crowds of mostly drunken oil field workers bumped and shoved him as he made his way to the center of the Reservation. He stopped there, picked out one of the several gambling houses in front of him—the Ogden—and walked inside. What he witnessed in that saloon was similar to that vividly described by George Stoker:

> It was ablaze with light. Pimps, professional gamblers, drillers, gunmen, and business men stood at the bar, drinking, arguing, swearing, and telling filthy stories. Games were being played by tense, excited men. Cold-eyed, expressionless attendants of the games sat behind the tables pushing forward money or chips, or putting into the drawers the losings of the players. Earnings of a week were tossed on a number or a roll of the dice and lost. The betting ran high. Stacks of currency, piles of gold and silver stood in front of the eager-eyed players. Numbers were droned. The click of dice, the whirl of the wheel, wild laughter, and oaths filled the air.
>
> Half-dressed prostitutes stood with their arms around drunken men, sat in their laps, or danced with them in vulgar postures. Men cursed them or pushed them away if their overtures interrupted what they were doing. Old, haggard creatures with dyed hair, sensuous lips, and painted, wrinkled faces mingled with pretty young girls whose freshness had not yet hardened into a look of lust and greed.[25]

Carroll eased his way into the midst of the sinful throng. He recognized a dozen faces in that crowd, to his consternation: a store owner, a councilman, and several others who sat around him in their pews on Sunday mornings! Some of the faces he did not know, but they were so young and already had lost their innocence. The deacon sidled up to the bar and stood there for a few minutes, squirming his way into the long line of drinking men while he said a silent prayer for all of their souls. Then, with the self-assurance borne of faith and high moral purpose, he walked to the middle of the saloon, climbed up on an empty wooden chair, and gazed across the crowd.

"Fellow citizens," he shouted, his voice audible above the din. "May I have your attention, please?" For whatever reason—perhaps the tone of his voice—the crowd noise ceased except for murmurs of who this stranger might be. "I have come here to pray God's forgiveness for your sinful ways, and to ask you to depart from this place immediately! Otherwise, you are all under arrest!" With that stunning announcement, Carroll dramatically raised his hat into the air, revealing his hard eyes as he looked into theirs.

Someone in the crowd gasped. It was Mr. Carroll himself standing on that chair! The word quickly spread through the room. A few, new to Beaumont, shrugged their shoulders and turned away. Most, however, knew the man if not personally then certainly by reputation. The merchant and the councilman and a dozen others tried to disappear in the crowd, pulling hats over their eyes, looking for an escape route from the humiliation of discovery. But Carroll was calling out names and pointing in every direction, shaming his neighbors for their conduct.

The saloon began to empty, the women moved upstairs and shut their doors, the tables laid bare except for cards and drinks strewn about absently. Carroll stood on the chair for several more minutes, relishing this moment for all it was worth. Then he too walked out on to Crockett Street, a silent and nearly abandoned avenue now. It was dark. The Reservation was eerily quiet. George Washington Carroll, Baptist deacon and Beaumont citizen extraordinaire, put the disheveled old hat under one arm, and walked home.[26]

A remarkable article appeared in the October, 1901, edition of the *National Oil Reporter.* Entitled "Law and Order," reporter Frank Andrews clearly intimated that the stories of violence and killings were naught but rumors; that in fact Beaumont was a modicum of composure in the throes of the oil boom.

> Wild stories of Beaumont have been afloat since the late discovery of its oil, and, in fact, some of them have been accepted and published in papers of the Eastern cities. That these stories have worked an injury to Beaumont and Texas there is no doubt.
>
> Had this been a law-despising, disorder-loving community, as it has been painted by some space-writers, these characteristics would have cropped out in an exaggerated form during the great excitement that followed Captain Lucas's discovery, when opportunity for law-breaking without detection was greater than ever before. . . . During the three months [of the boom] but two homicides have occurred in the town since the discovery of oil. Perhaps not another town of 20,000 population could go through a similar period of excitement with the loss of only two lives.[27]

The incredibly naïve story—or perhaps it was published in order to allay the fears of those who might bring investments there!—was magnified with a quote from the estimable General James A. Huston, U.S. treasurer during the Harrison administration (1889–93): "Nowhere have I met a more hospitable or generous people. Even during the great rush there was an absence of rowdyism and an observance of law, order and decency, the counterpart of which I have never seen. During the weeks in which men went almost wild over speculation I did not witness even a fistfight. Neither did I see an intoxicated man on the streets." Andrews summarizes his staggering report of peace in the streets of boom town Beaumont with this assurance: "Not only have the more shocking crimes been conspicuous by the smallness of their number, but the crimes of robbery and theft have been almost unknown. Not a single case of highway robbery has been reported to the officers since Jan. 10th, and in no case reported to officers has a thief made way with property to the value of [more than] $50."[28]

One wonders aloud where Mr. Andrews positioned himself during those days!

"MY GOD, I'M GONNA BREAK MY LEGS!"

I went over to oil the steam head that was on top of the well that pumped the oil out of the ground, and the derricks were so thick together that you had another fellow always with you to watch you all the time. Well, I climbed up there and put some oil on it and was starting back out when the gas got me. It blew, knocked me out and I just fell. I knocked against the boards and everything, and the fella grabbed me as I fell and dragged me out of there, and all the time I was dreaming I was floating in the air and thinking, my God, I'm gonna break my legs.[29]

Accidents happened. All the time. With dozens of wells going in at the same time all over Big Hill, and literally thousands of workers at risk every moment of every day and night, the odds were ever against any accident-free work site. Wooden derricks toppled or crumpled, gas blowouts threw bodies a hundred feet through the air, and fistfights broke bones. Wagons careened into ditches; horses tossed riders. Gunshots sounded from saloons and alleyways. Knife wounds were as routine as mosquito bites.

Through these helter-skelter boom days of Spindletop, very few doctors made their way to the rescue. Old Doc R. L. Cox was one, and the equally aged Doc Cunningham another. Daniel Davis and his wife moved to Beaumont in 1902, and young George Stoker came there from a successful Virginia practice. Hiram Sloop "interned" on Big Hill, but hardly could be considered a physician. Others came and went, often to gamble away a fortune rather than attend to their Hippocratic oath. In 1904 the Beaumont directory listed a second hospital and forty-one physicians, double the number from pre-boom days.[30]

Mostly, roughnecks took care of each other: bandaging wounds, washing out poisoned eyes, setting a broken limb with a one-by-six, or applying a tourniquet with an oily rag. Sometimes it was just too late to do anything except contact the undertaker. Bill Philps remembers Bert Rambeau. "He was a good driller and a good man, but he was a little wild in pulling casing and tubing. Well, one day he was working on a derrick and everybody was hollering at him to be careful, and he yelled back at them, 'If the crown starts in, I'll get out of the way.' He turned the engine on wide open and sure enough that crown block came down. Bert made a run for it and nearly got out of there, but that timber hit him on the head and killed him dead. He never knew what hit him."[31]

In the tough parts of town, you likely cared for yourself or bled to death while the crowds stepped around you. It was rudimentary medicine, simple doctoring. Probably a miraculous number of people survived grievous injuries and wounds; a fair share certainly did not. Young Hiram Sloop retells stories of old Doc Cox; Daniel Davis recalls the primitive doctoring in boom town Beaumont; and George Stoker reminisces on the oil field doctoring.

Somebody'd come in Doc Cox's office with a leg broken or an arm broken or a leg cut off or something of the kind. And we'd all gather over there and go into his little office to watch. And I learned after a time that the way not to get pushed out was to get behind the door. And I also learned to accommodate Doc by reaching down and getting the old wash pans he had there, set them on the gasoline stove and start heating water for him as soon as someone was brought in. And after awhile he'd throw everybody else out but he'd let me stay. And he'd say, "Get kit number four, number seven, number six and put it in the water."

Well, that was big business to me and I had the opportunity to stay and see what was the matter with the man that he was going to cut, cut his foot off, or a hand, or a finger that had been smashed. Doc had no nurses, and the druggist was busy a lot over at the store. And most of the time I was the only one in there. And he'd say, "Git holt, kid." And I'd grab the man's arm or leg and hold on to it; the doc was working with all those little vessels and the blood was spurting here and there.

He'd be using his saw to take an arm or a leg off, and his old saw wouldn't work. And he'd say, "Kid, go across the street there to the butcher shop and get me a saw." And I knew which one he wanted and I'd come running back with that thing and he'd say, "Saw it off." He'd have the man's leg up between his legs holding him real tight or he'd lay it up against the bedstead and finish the job off. Then he'd trim it up. Sometimes he had an anaesthetic, sometimes not. Sometimes he didn't have time to administer it. These men were, you know, hard workers and tough. He'd give 'em a shot and then go at it. Then they'd lay around the office for a day or two until someone would come get them. Or we'd put some cots in the wagon and take them into town.[32]

Gas explosions were perhaps the most dangerous moments in the life of an oil field worker. Bob Waite of the *Journal* did a story in May, 1901, related to the problem of oil and gas and sulphur in the air, and included a profane quote from a roughneck that most shared: "The stench that greets the nostrils in that locality would give a South African mule[33] spinal meningitis!" If the force of the blowout didn't kill a man, the poisonous gas might very well blind him, even permanently. Dr. Davis dealt with the gassed eyes hundreds of times.[34]

At Spindletop they'd get gas in their eyes and have the awfullest inflamed eyes from that. There was a doctor there for awhile who fixed up a solution that would clear up their eyes and give them relief right away. In those days, of course, you didn't have any prescriptions for narcotics or such as that, and there was no telling what he was putting in that solution. He told me it wasn't anything serious, not like cocaine or morphine or anything like that. Because there had been some talk about the use of cocaine as a medicine for curing lots of ills. He left me some of that solution before he moved on, and I took it up to Big Hill one day after a gas explosion and I was treating the boys when all of a sudden I heard one of them say, "If a man were to put cocaine in my eyes I believe I'd kill him." I got to thinking I ought to find out what was in that solution.[35]

Another gas problem was *inside* the homes, where Miss Jessie Pierce remembers that "the portable stoves were so impure and full of sulphur, that my eyes and my mother's would swell shut. After the meals were served we would lay down and apply tea leaves to relieve the swelling."[36]

"Quite a lot of narcotics used in Beaumont those days," the Davises remember. "Cocaine. Morphine, too. But not by the oil field workers. For patients in the oil fields, the only thing we could do was just boil water and do the best we could with whatever injuries they had. Sterilize our hands, boiled water with a teaspoonful of salt to a quart of water, and I would just irrigate any wound they had. I'd hang the [saline] bag just as high as I could and I'd use as much force as I could shoot into it, and I'd run it through until it was perfectly cleaned, sterile. The one thing I depended on the most was that salt water. I'd run a gallon through a good-sized wound."[37]

R. R. Hobson arrived at Spindletop in 1902 and turned seventeen on May 31. "They gave me what they called a 'death warrant' to sign. It read that I was a white man, 21 years of age, and that I realized the work was dangerous and I assumed all risks, not the company. In September my brother came down. He was twenty and they wouldn't let him go to work, said he was too young. Wasn't because the rules had changed. They said he asked too many questions about the 'death warrant.'"[38]

"Another problem," says Dr. Davis, "was the food. Sanitary conditions of the food was pretty wide open. Food would be just sitting out on the curb. They didn't have any screens. The food market was put in a board shack and the food was just placed out on boards. Meat was kept in the ice box, but they'd lay it out on top so people could see it better. The rats and the mice were awful bad in all the stores. Terrible. The young boys would sit up at night with their BB guns and their .22 rifles, and shoot rats all night long in the stores."

Rats weren't the only problem in "the wilds" of the southeast Texas Gulf plains. Davis recalls,

> There was a fellow out in his backyard, and he had his hand in a bucket of coal oil and he was unloading a load of wood and a ground rattler was in the wood on the wagon bed and it bit him on the knuckle. I cut that bite open wide and filled it with permanganate crystals. The man liked to lose his arm, it swelled up until he couldn't wear a sleeve on his shirts. But he got all right, didn't die. Told me later he'd been bit by a rattler when he was a boy.
>
> One Saturday night a boy was bit by a rattler down on Village Creek and they kept hollering for me and I finally got there and they said a boy's

snakebit. And I said I didn't think it was a snakebite, it looked like he got stuck on some burnt fobs that were there. But he told me it was a snake and it was at least a foot long. Then his foot began to turn black.

Well, I didn't have a thing on me except a pocket knife, but I found a syringe and some morphine and some strychnine. Took him over to the clubhouse, and I took my pocket knife and I got a bunch of salt and I scrubbed the knife through until it was bright as a dollar. I cut the boy's foot open and mashed it out good and took a handful of salt, wet it, put it right on there and tied it up. Put him in a cot and waited. I was watching his heart all the time. When I picked him up he fainted on me. I gave him a shot of strychnine and let him rest a while longer before I brought him into town. When I left him he was sleeping like a baby.[39]

Young Dr. George Stoker inherited the practice of one of the aging physicians in Beaumont, remembering that the old doc then proceeded on to a long-anticipated drunk! When some oil field workers arrived soon after with an injured roustabout, Stoker first had to accept the response that he was "nothing but a damn kid." When he stood his ground, the supervisor said, "Well, hell, John's gotta have help. Kid, take a look at this son of a bitch's leg. He just got the damn thing tore open out in the field. Can you fix it?" Stoker did, and received what he considered a large compliment when the spokesman of the group muttered, "You'll do."

George Stoker never got over the sight of the squalid conditions of many of the oil field families. On a call to see a sick child, he

found the family living in a tent which was surrounded by mud, water, and a few rocks. Pieces of half-submerged boards kept one from sinking into the mire up to his knees. The tent had a dirt floor. Three half-ragged, tow-headed children, with sores on their faces, played listlessly in a corner. The baby lay in a large box which had contained dry goods before it had graduated to the status of a baby's crib. I found the baby a thin little yellow-faced thing with a well-developed case of rickets. I prescribed something for it, and I saw the mother's dull blue eyes and knew that she barely grasped the instructions I left with her. As I returned to my office, I thought that since I had come to Spindletop I had seen only dirt, sickness, squalor, and the lowest form of sin.

Back out in the oil field Stoker often had to make do with whatever he could find literally lying around to supplement the very basic medicine he could offer. One day, he tells the story, "I found a man on a derrick floor almost torn to pieces, bleeding from the head, arm, and leg. I couldn't move him, and had to patch him up right there. When I offered to give him an anaesthetic he refused and emptied a bottle of whiskey instead. 'Let's go, Doc," he told me. Blood was spurting from a severed artery and his arm was broken in several places. I stopped the blood and used boards lying on the derrick floor to set his arm." The crew built a makeshift stretcher and carried him home.

Stoker responded to calls in the Reservation, but the sight of the young women made him sick, "often finding them dying from having drunk carbolic acid or some other kind of poison. Many of these unfortunate women were young and beautiful, but it did not take long to destroy all semblance of beauty in that place of degradation. Once they entered that life, it seemed all hope left them, all power to exert themselves to leave departed. The only door that seemed open for escape was that of suicide."

Stoker delivered quite a large number of babies in those undesirable conditions, in tents and cribs and alleyways and brothels. He lamented that "many of the men drank and gambled, that their wives and babies were often without enough to eat and wear, to say nothing of having anything ready or sanitary for the newborn. I tried to instruct the women on sanitation, the care of themselves, the dangers of mosquitoes and flies. But the rush of riches into eager hands, the lawlessness, the lust, and the intoxication of the wild excitement caused most of my advice and teaching to fall on careless and deaf ears."

A favorite story for the young physician, because everything eventually turned out all right, began with a midnight rap on his door.

There stood a half drunk, dirty looking man, rain dripping from his hat and the tatters of his coat. He said that he wanted me to go at once to the oil field and take care of his wife. The rain was coming down in torrents. You could feel the darkness, it was so black. We stumbled and floundered through the mud until we reached his tent.

When he pulled back the flap of his tent, I gasped. In one corner was an old broken cook stove, standing on pieces of brick, its rusty stove pipe almost falling apart. The rickety table was piled with dirty dishes and a dingy pan held dingier water. A single oil lamp lit the hovel. Over in another corner on an old unpainted iron bed lay a large woman. A mop of uncombed, drab, yellow hair hung around a face tougher looking than some of the faces of the women I had seen plying their trade in the gambling houses.

She was in labor, and I beat the stork by one jump. The look she gave us from those little green eyes of hers, and the choice curses with which she greeted her husband, made me realize that at least I had an interesting patient, if not a gentle or cultured one. She cursed her husband for getting her into her present condition, and cursed me for not getting her out of it.

The woman and I worked for hours trying to have that baby. The husband finally sat down in the broken chair, tilted it back against an old box, and went to sleep. When the cursing and groaning woman was finally delivered, I picked up the baby, shoved her into the father's hands before he could protest, and said, "Here, take your baby." His face was a study of emotions, for the baby was not a very pleasant looking object. He looked down at her and began a stream of oaths. I picked up my bag and started out into the rain. The panic-stricken new father yelled, "Hey! You can't leave. What am I going to do with it?" I ignored his whining and begging and reached for the flap of the tent.

"Wait, Doc, don't go," he said. "I gotta proposition to make you. I'll shoot you the best two of three and the guy what loses, cleans and dresses the baby." I was afraid he would arouse his wife and I did not know what would be the result if she decided to sit in on the conference about who should wash the baby. I agreed to one throw of the dice just to keep him quiet. He laid the baby down quietly on the bed, tiptoed over to me and rubbed his hands on his trousers.

Fishing into his pocket, he brought out two well worn dice, and we got down on our knees in the dirt where the floor should have been. Caressing the dice in his hands, he talked and begged them to win for him in the most pleading and pitiful voice I had ever heard. With a soft groan he shot first; but his pleading was in vain, for they rolled him low and I threw high. I looked up at him just in time to see a fixed look of horror come into his face. I turned and met his wife's eyes. She was looking in wild-eyed fury at both of us, then burst into a volley of the most torrid curses I had ever heard. The names she called us were beyond my comprehension as she told us where to go and what to do when we got there.

I reached for my bag, took hold of the tent flap, turned and said quietly, "I win. Good night."[40]

One of the trademarks of the Spindletop boom—and the spread of that unique character to the other towns that would soon experience their own—was the personalities that emerged from those crowds. For all of the literally tens of thousands of people who came to and through Beaumont in those few short years, there were a handful that no one could, or did, forget. Their antics or foibles or peculiarities, whichever, set them apart from the milling masses. Some were good-natured or good-hearted; some were angry or volatile. However their stories added to the character of that world, they stood the test of time: they were remembered.

6

The Black Golconda

There was a time when Spindletop, near Beaumont in Texas, held the heart and hope of an oil-mad world. It was the Klondike of petroleum and witnessed the greatest rush since that eventful day when Drake drilled the first well on Oil Creek. It was the wonder of its day.
—*Isaac Marcosson,* Black Golconda

It almost goes without saying that scattered among the tens of thousands of boomers and Beaumont natives would be the kind of characters who make for the most entertaining stories. Already in the city were remarkable personalities like Carroll and O'Brien, and Pattillo Higgins himself. To the oil fields came Walter and Jim Sharp, the three Hamill brothers, Scott Heywood and his vaudeville siblings, and Easterners such as John Galey. Making appearances along the way were larger-than-life folks such as "Bet A Million" Gates; Colonel James Guffey; railroad magnate Colonel George A. Burt, who had worked with the French on the Central American canal project; Jack Ennis, a reformed gambler who made and lost two fortunes at Spindletop; and the debonair Brit Jim Roche. Equally strong personalities like Anthony Lucas, William Mellon, and J. Edgar Pew made their mark on Big Hill as well.

But others left their names at Spindletop, perhaps not on monuments or markers, and certainly not with bank deposits in the millions. Some of the real characters rose above the milling crowds perhaps for just a single moment, but long enough to enrich the storytelling that continued long after the gushing oil and the crushing hordes had gone. Their stories deserve at least one more telling here.

THE BOY WITH THE X-RAY EYES

The list cannot begin without remembering "the boy with the X-ray eyes," a young man named Guy Finley. The oil patch always attracted those who claimed special powers to find the stuff. There was a preacher out of Dallas who wandered the Texas oil fields with his hands raised high in the air, his eyes rolled back in his head, claiming to be able to "see" through the ground. "Oil smellers" were a dime a dozen. A Dr. Griffith—and hundreds more—poked around the fields, literally, with all kinds of exotic divining rod switches much like those who sought water below the surface. "Wiggle sticks" of every shape and size promoted outrageous claims and outrageous stories. But for a time, Guy Finley captured the imagination of the oilmen on Big Hill. He tells the story himself.

I suppose I was something like nine or ten years old when I told my father about being able to "feel" water under the ground, and he said, "Well, let's try it." I located a well and told them it was about sixty feet deep. They got down to sixty-two feet and got water. I located three wells for a fella out north of Del Rio, and another for a fella named Lee Lanford in Uvalde.

When the Lucas gusher came in, I was thirteen years old, and someone asked if I thought I could go there and find oil like I had found water. So we went there. They had buried a barrel of oil and a barrel of water and I didn't know where they were, and they took me out to the field at night. Well, I found both barrels, buried at about six feet. They said I had sharp eyes, but it wasn't ever a vision thing for me as much as it was a feeling.

I stayed with the McFaddin family while I was there, and we wrote up a contract with Mr. McFaddin for me to find oil. I went out on this one long strip of land that he owned and I located a spot at one end of the strip where I thought there was oil. But for whatever reasons, I never did know why, they ended up drilling on the other end of that strip of land—didn't find any oil there.

I was in Beaumont about two weeks, and the feeling just left me. Can't explain it. And my father took me back home. That was the end of it. People would ask me later about working for them, and how they'd pay me, but I never did take money for that. I believe that it was a gift that was given to me to give to other people—maybe it would come back if I didn't charge for doing it.[1]

Harry Paramore and Bud Coyle remember a character known only as Yorky. "Came in during the boom," says Paramore. "He was dressed up in a Prince Albert suit, carried $60,000 around in his pocket. But he liked to drink and he stayed around the hotels and the saloons and didn't do much of anything. He was highly educated and very proud, though, and he could answer any question about anything you could think of. One time we were sitting in front of Walter Berry's store and he heard someone down the street playing a piano. Said he'd like to get hold of that. He went over there and just pounded those ivories—he was quite an accomplished musician. But he just sort of hung around until he went broke."

"Fine looking fellow," agrees Bud Coyle. "Always had on a high hat and that frock coat and a cane. But one night he wandered out to Spindletop and got in with a bunch of pipeliners on a spree. They cut the crown out of his hat and put grease on his face and you just never saw anything like it. Somebody said he was a drunk lawyer from New York. I never saw him do anything. Just a pure D bum."

Wilson Hudson talks about a man he called Dr. Griffith who may very well have been the "Yorky" the others remember. "Dr. Griffith wore a long black Prince Albert coat with a stove pipe hat or a square derby. First time I ever saw him he was climbing out of a slush pit. He'd found a bunch of nice dry looking sand to walk along and stepped right into the slush pit up to his neck. His derby wasn't worth recovering."

"Yorky's folks had money, I think," says Paramore. "They were looking for him, trying to prevail on him to come home, but he always said he wouldn't go back unless he could go back with what he left with. One time he handed me some letters. They were from his sister, wanted him to come home to help settle something about the family estate, said she'd pay his way to come home. He never did answer any of them, never did go back that I know of. Just wandered off, some say he went to Batson. Just disappeared."[2]

"I remember another character," says Coyle.

There was a woman named Mrs. Shelby. She was noted all around for making good pies. She ran a little restaurant and she had a drunkard for a husband. But between the two of them they could bake the best pies—

sold those pies out of a tent for a bakery. And he'd get drunk and she'd close the bakery and put a sign out front that said "Shelby's Gassed."

Old man Lee Young opened up a boarding house and he took our cook away from us, a German. Next cook I got couldn't even boil water. But then I got a Frenchman, he was a pastry chef in a bakery for years somewhere before he came out. He made the best hot rolls, baked bread twice a week. Ed Prather and Walter Sharp came out to the camp one day and I invited them in for coffee and hot rolls that Frenchy had made. I don't know how many rolls they ate! But they wrote the date down in their books and after that they'd come by regularly to get those hot rolls."[3]

Curt Hamill, the man who drilled Lucas No. 1, recalled the penchant in the field for giving out nicknames.

We had boys out there had hobbies and some were artists and so on. Had one boy that liked to draw pictures, called him Artist. He could draw you a picture just like that that was real pretty. And I asked him one day why in the world he was out there roughnecking when he could do that kind of artist work. He said, "That may look good to you but the picture is of no account. It's just good enough that it's no good. I couldn't ever get nobody to back me in my work."

There was this boy working on a swivel board and he was always whistling and I was having trouble screwing the joint in and I says, "Music, hold this thing over this way." Well, from then on he was Music and nobody ever called him anything else for the rest of his life. There was another boy who had a sweetheart back home and he was always talking about her and calling out her name—her name was Mary. So they just called the boy Mary. And there was another boy who liked to shoot craps all the time, and everybody called him Two Bits because that was always the limit when he shot craps, two bits.[4]

Jim Kinnear remembers two fascinating women in the Beaumont crowd. Hattie Green moved faster than most people in staying a step ahead of the rent and the law. "She wouldn't stay at any one place more than two weeks, and 25 cents was all she'd pay for a meal. And then there was Virginia Shauffner. She owned some property over on the Port Arthur Road. The Texas Company come in there and was laying some pipe right through her tract. She found out on a Sunday afternoon, so she went out there and sat down at the end of that pipe until two o'clock

Monday morning, got an injunction against those fellows. Stopped them, too."[5]

Officer Bill Armstrong recalls the arrival of a national celebrity to Beaumont.

> Carrie Nation came to the Kyle Opera House once, and I was sitting up in the corner watching, and there were some packing boxes stacked outside the window where you could crawl up to watch. And some guys thought they'd pull a prank and scare her, so they got up there and were throwing those boxes in through the window, making all kinds of racket, fell down in the crowd and raised a big fuss. But Carrie Nation looked up in their direction and said, "Stand away, men. That noise sounds a lot like it did before I tore up a saloon with my hatchet." She didn't ever use her hatchet in Beaumont, though.
>
> Afterwards I was talking to her and I said, "Miss Nation, if there were more women like you things would be a pretty hard go for these boys." And she said, "I know it would! They can smoke cigarettes and chew tobacco, they can spit out yonder and wear the pants and all, but they'll never be the Father of our country!"

Ashley Weaver was just a boy when Carrie Nation came into town that night. "I was an usher in the theatre. I used to usher to get to go to see the shows free. And she was coming back down to the boardinghouse where she was staying, right in my neighborhood. And I took her grip and we were headed down the street when she just suddenly darted into a saloon. I don't know what she did in there. She didn't have her hatchet. Just gave them a tongue-lashing. I didn't stay. I put her bag down there on the sidewalk and went on home. She was quite a character."[6]

Recalls George Weller,

> One night we were coming back from Spindletop, and there was a man riding in my father's hack and he says he needed someone to lead him around Beaumont. He was a blind man. And I said I would and he told me to meet him in front of the Crosby next morning. So I did and he told me to take him to the Episcopal Church. "I want to go there to fix the organ," he says to me. And I wondered how in the dickens a blind man was going to fix an organ, but I took him down there.
>
> And he took that organ all to pieces and he'd say to me, "Now lay it in a row as I hand it to you. And when I'm ready to put it back together you

give it to me just like I tell you." So I did what he told me to do. Took him three days to fix that organ, but he did, and then he sat down and played that organ like everything.[7]

With plenty of references to the characters known as roustabouts and roughnecks, Frank Dunn gives his definition of those terms in the early days of Spindletop:

A roustabout looks after the wells, sees that they are pumping, see if they need repairs. He looks after the storage tanks, and the neatness of the field, picks up broken rods, junk pipe, connections, so there's no danger of stumbling when you're working on a well. He digs ditches to take care of the waste water, builds fires to evaporate some of the water. He washes out the boilers, swabs the tubes. Checks the mainways to see that they don't accumulate salt. Looks after the discharge lines, checks the gauges, looks after the steam engine, the amount of oil pumped from each well. He checks the band wheel and the 8" belt that takes care of the band wheel, makes sure the bearings and beams are well greased. He pulls the sucker rods out of the wells, and puts new clamps where they're needed. The "roustabout pusher" is the leader. He's the master of the engine, watches the crew take off the saddles, take the walking beam off, take care of the engine. He tells you what to do and how to do it.

A roughneck looks after the breaking out of the pipe, stacking the pipe, and so on. Doesn't have the amount of work a roustabout does.[8]

It is difficult not to include one more Jim Hogg story when one is talking about oil field characters. This one nearly got him in big trouble. One day when one of his wells had blown, and he was on hand to watch the whole process of capping it, he reached down on the ground and picked up some rocks that had come up from deep below. They were sulphur pyrite with a yellowish hue that glinted in the sunlight. Later that day Hogg went into Beaumont and let it be known he had found *gold* in his latest drilling operation. The prank turned ugly when the telegraph office went berserk with the news, and the very real threat of a mad gold rush into southeast Texas appeared imminent. Caught up momentarily in his own practical joke, legend has it that Hogg even drew up some papers to organize a gold-mining company! The gold rush quickly faded.[9]

But the boom days characters did not. They popped up again in Batson and Sour Lake, in Saratoga and Humble. A phenomenon like Spindletop brings out the frontier character in all of his—and her—glory.

GLADYS CITY

Higgins Files Suit Against Lucas for $4 million
                    —Headline, Beaumont Daily Enterprise, *May 18, 1901*

Before the Spindletop boom had run its course, the man who had first insisted that his dream—and his theory—were real had walked away from the oil fields. Ultimately Pattillo Higgins settled his various suits against those who had been brought in as the first partners. His Higgins Oil Company and other investments made it possible for the one-armed man to live a more than comfortable, though never luxurious, life. At age forty he married a young woman he had adopted some years earlier, and they lived happily until his death in 1955. In those intervening years it was Captain Lucas whom many credited with the Texas oil discovery; Higgins's name was always, however, much more than just a footnote in history.

Higgins's sense of betrayal carried him away when he wrote an embittered article entitled "Story of the Beaumont Oil Field." In a scathing attack defending his own integrity, Higgins referred to his fellow citizens as "two-by-four-headed Beaumonters . . . if we wanted to go to New York from San Francisco we would have to ride there on the bare backs of long-eared jackasses without bridles." Of certain "learned men of science," he wrote: "There are many geologists filling high positions who ought to be out on a farm making rails and following behind long-eared mules."[10]

But vindication of a sort came for Higgins near the end of 1901, when more than thirty of the men who made a fortune on Big Hill, led by J. F. Keith and State Representative Bronson Cooper, filed a document with the Jefferson County clerk's office that said in part: "We know within our personal knowledge that Mr. Higgins discovered the Beaumont Oil Field in the year 1892, and he said when the field was developed that it would be worth millions of dollars. He said that single wells would flow thousands of barrels of oil per day. He located the exact spot where all the big gushers are now found. . . . Mr. Higgins deserves the whole honor of discovering and developing the Beaumont oil field."[11]

One of Pattillo's dreams in the wake of the oil gusher in 1901 was to build a city on Big Hill. With the financial aid of men like Carroll and O'Brien, and the feverish interest of promoters and businessmen to be near the fields, the dream became a reality, of sorts. Gladys City was born in the spring of 1901 and at one time claimed more than a dozen buildings running from near the crest of Big Hill and southward along the west side. Families came to live in the higher elevation edifices; the outer edge was known to be "rough." Few people ever called it by its proper name. The post office was listed as Guffey, Texas. Most just called it Spindletop.[12]

Thomas's Drug Store stood along the one Gladys City avenue. Inside at the long counter was a soda fountain with homemade ice cream, a favorite of the women and children who lived nearby and many of the crews who may not have been so tough when it came to choosing a soda over a whiskey. In the back of the store was a small office that periodically housed a doctor. Up front, "Doc" Thomas sold medicine—which included whiskey—and in emergencies his supplies were more readily available than by wagon ride into Beaumont.

H. L. Edgerton opened a photography studio in Gladys City expressly for the purpose of capturing "scoop" pictures of the gushers when they rose to the sky. These made good money from eager newspapers all across the country, as well as marketing tools for the oil promoters in need of investors. Frank Trost and Swen Ostebee often joined Edgerton at his studio, especially when word of a possible strike went out. Ostebee, a native Norwegian, had come to the United States in 1882 and by 1900 was well known for his artistic photography of the American West. These professional photographers used the standard wooden frame "Favorite" brand cameras set on tripods.[13]

On April 18 the Beaumont Oil Exchange and Board of Trade opened its doors to the thousands of onrushing investors and stockholders. Over six hundred "oil companies" organized in those opening months of 1901, although fewer than ten percent of these ever came to more than a quick cash cow for the promoter himself. A large board was erected against one wall where stock exchange recorders kept a constant update for the watchful speculators, scribbling chalk marks of names and numbers, erasing and changing them every few minutes.

In the rear of the exchange building were two small offices. One was used as a print shop where flyers and notices could be hastily run off and distributed; the other came and went as a law office for several entrepreneurial attorney-types, including at one time or another J. S. Daugherty out of Dallas and Charles E. Anderson of Austin. Judge Edgar Townes notes that the law business at that time "and for several years after was principally taken up with receiverships and suits for debt with foreclosure of lien and attachments, and so on. The higher class of business was mostly related to oil and to land litigation. There were two justice courts [in Beaumont] and each vied with the other in an effort to get most of the suits that should be filed. Lawyers who had filed a great many suits got a little better treatment in the trials than those who had only an occasional suit."[14]

General stores dotted Big Hill and Gladys City. They sold nearly every product imaginable, from produce to canned goods, and from dry goods to oil field supplies and small equipment. A consumer could purchase fresh-ground coffee, fresh-baked bread, and homemade soaps and candles in addition to a sack filled with all the other necessities: flour, sugar, beans, corn meal, rice, and such.

Dry goods stores, although larger and better stocked in the city, still held out primarily to sell to the poorer oil field worker and his family who could not make the trip into Beaumont or afford its wares. The clothes sold here were basic and simple, whether work or dress clothes, of standard tough cotton, corduroy, or denim material. They also sold boots and shoes. The owner of both the grocery and the dry goods store generally lived upstairs above his establishment.

Inside the Guffey, Texas, U.S. post office were two windows, one marked "Money Orders" and the other "Mail." The two processes had to be kept separate by federal law, although usually there was just one postal worker working both windows!

August Nelson and George White partnered up and built the Nelson & White Surveyors Office at Gladys City. This operation was indispensable for the oilmen and the drillers. Land tracts were being bought and sold on an hourly basis sometimes, and parcels as small as 1/64 of an acre came to be standard especially in the Hogg-Swayne tract on Big Hill. Nelson and White drew up the first map of the Spindletop field and sold it locally as well as nationally to such as Standard Oil, the Pennsylvania promoters, Sun Oil, and so on. George White lived in the back room of the building.

The Walkenshaw Tank Company put up a warehouse in Gladys City, along with a small office, and a factory site where it built wooden and metal oil storage tanks. Tanks of various sizes, especially the larger ones, could be built in Corsicana, Louisiana, and Port Arthur, and shipped to

Big Hill. But for the standard needs at an oil site, and for the repairs that probably seemed endless, the Gladys City sheet metal company served its purpose well.

Alex and Joe Broussard of Beaumont owned and operated several establishments in the area, including Alex's livery stable at Gladys City, one of four in the vicinity. The huge painted sign that hung above the two stable entrances actually said: "A. Broussard, Undertaker, Livery & Boarding Stable." It's not clear which business he got into first, but he made a good living constructing and delivering coffins as well as stabling horses.

Nearby was Hyman Perlstein's blacksmith shop, the Southern Carriage Works. H. A. and his wife Mamie lived more than comfortably back in Beaumont, but the smithy knew that his business would soar on Big Hill, where tool and cable repair was always needed in a crisis mode. The carriage operation was actually secondary during the boom days; Perlstein's employees also shod horses and built various brackets and equipment to meet the needs of the derrick crews.

Homes, some of them no more than glorified tents and lean-tos, dotted the landscape around Gladys City. As one moved south along the side of the hill, the mud got deeper and the crowds got rougher. Down at this end of Gladys City stood Grinnell's infamous Log Cabin Saloon. Known for its boisterous patrons and nightly brawls that would carry out into the street, the Log Cabin served all of the usual bar drinks and was the sole distributor of Pabst Beer in the area. Grinnell served a "driller's lunch" daily, and an upright piano contributed what entertainment might risk being in the middle of the rowdies on any given Saturday night. Built next to and up against the Log Cabin Saloon was a barber shop with two chairs: one for cutting hair and the other for dental work, mainly pulling teeth! These two necessities of life had to be completed in just a few minutes so that the roustabout could grab a bite to eat and get right back to work.[15]

CULTURE IN BOOM TOWN BEAUMONT

In Texas the excitement has assumed all the phases of a craze, like the tulip mania of Holland, the Mississippi bubble of France, the South Sea bubble of England, and the oil craze of Pennsylvania in the latter sixties. Barbers and bootblacks, printers and reporters, cooks and chambermaids, salesmen, railroad hands, small tradesmen, and others mostly in the humbler stations of life, are investing their savings in so-called oil companies, with the chances at forty to one that they will never again see a dollar of the money so expended. Of course, it is useless to preach to these deluded souls. Nothing but their own experience will open their eyes or do them any good."[16]

Those *not* constrained to the humbler stations of life, however, enjoyed a lifestyle of the rich and famous, replete with the extravagances that come with money, old or new.

By the end of 1902, Beaumont claimed at least four clubs organized for the women of the city. The Neches Club was the most exclusive, something of a Junior League in its high society profile and magnanimous charity benefits. There was a Shakespeare Club whose members frequented the Kyle Opera House and theatre. The Texas Women's Relief Corps served meals to the needy on special occasions, collected money for various projects, and often worked in cooperation with the several prohibition, or temperance, groups that would pass through Beaumont. The Council of Jewish Women met in the new synagogue that was organized in 1901 under Rabbi Aaron Levy and expanded when Rabbi Friedlander replaced him. Mamie Perlstein was an active leader in the CJW. In addition, the Young Ladies Oil Company organized with a half-interest in a well. It had stockholders from Joplin, Fort Smith, and New York as well as Beaumont.

Churches in Beaumont underwent transformation during the boom days. Although most histories of those wild days assume that everyone who came to the oil fields were heathens, in fact the mainstream denominations grew in more than respectable numbers between 1900 and 1904. This included growth in the Sunday School programs and various activities that included children and families, for there were hundreds of families who came to live near Big Hill and support the husband who worked on the well. First Baptist Church of Beaumont added members throughout this period under the able ministry of the Reverends John Allen Smart and George Washington McCall. First Methodist Church grew under the Reverend M. I. Brown and added to its buildings. The congregations of the Methodist Church, South, and the AME Church also experienced the challenges of unexpected, overnight growth. Two religious newspapers, the *Texas Baptist Standard* and the *Texas Christian Advocate,* sold well in Beaumont and gained enough interest in the boom to invest in oil companies themselves![17]

The churches had mixed reactions, of course, to the increased social activities upon which they generally frowned—dancing, for instance. Harry Paramore notes that "there was some music played [in the saloons and hotels]. Different bands would come into town, five piece bands and such. They'd have a fiddle, a guitar, a violin, a bass and a viola. They played songs like 'Over the Waves' and 'Beautiful Ohio,' popular in those days," and forgettable tunes like "How'd You Like to be the Oil Man."[18]

George Weller talks about the dancing and courting that went on.

> Out at the Catholic Church there was a pavilion and we used to dance out there. They'd have a dance every other Saturday evening and we'd all go. The boys and girls would pay a dollar a couple. And we'd walk the girls there and then we'd walk them home.
>
> And then sometimes we'd go down to Port Arthur to dance or go to the pier. My brother-in-law was conductor of the train so it didn't cost me anything. We'd go to Port Arthur, and then catch a boat over to Orange, dance until morning, and then catch the train and come back to Beaumont.
>
> They'd have these string bands and every now and then we had these colored bands, five piece bands. And down in Port Arthur they had twelve piece bands. We'd two-step and waltz and such. There was a Professor Cheesman who was a teacher of dancing and he used to have a dancing school over on Crockett Street above the Congress Café. Every week he'd give a dance and all the young people would go.[19]

An athletic club was formed in 1902, and it featured baseball and football teams that played in semi-professional leagues around Texas and Louisiana. Beaumont boasted several winning teams during those days, often because the roustabouts could be persuaded to join. One of the first organizers in the area was Dr. Daniel Davis.

> I was crazy about football when I came here. I finally found a few boys who had played football in other places, but there'd never been a team, never been a game played in Beaumont. I got together a bunch of fellows under a streetlight and coached them, gave them the signals and we practiced for several weeks until we finally got up a game over in Lake Charles.
>
> They came over here first and we played at Ogden Park, and while we were playing we made so much noise that some of the ladies in that neighborhood looked to see what was going on. They thought something ter-

rible was happening, some big fight going on in the park, and they called the sheriff! He showed up to stop whoever it was that was "disturbing the peace," but by the time the game was over he was standing on the sidelines hollering "Go Beaumont!"

And we had a return game in Lake Charles, so we got over to the train depot near Sunset Park. But there was only ten of us who showed up to go to the game, we were one short. Someone spotted Mr. Reeves, who was a lawyer and the assistant superintendent at Beaumont High School, standing over on the corner. So we sort of kidnapped him and put him on the train with us and we took him to Lake Charles to play on the team.

Davis also remembers the adventures out north of the city, toward the Big Thicket. "That place was a paradise for hunting and fishing and sport. We'd go out there and come back with geese and ducks and quail, jacksnipe and dove, prairie chicken, all on one hunt. And we could go out to any stream and catch bass, perch of any kind."[20] (A local restaurateur did his own hunting in that area, and as Ed Cotton tells it, "he killed old black crows, cleaned them up and sold them in town as prairie chickens."[21])

Wilbur Gilbert, a teen in Beaumont when the boom hit, agrees with Davis's assessment.

> We were near the Big Thicket, quite a big hunting preserve and lots of fine timber, big thick undergrowth and a wonderful habitat for wild game. People who lived in there were self-reliant, made it on their own effort. There were lots of species of flowers, too, even wild orchids. We would take some of the prominent people hunting there. The place was full of deer and bear and all kinds of squirrels and fox and quail. And there were thousands of wild hogs and even some cattle that'd gone wild. Did a lot of hunting for razorback hogs. Got to have two or three fine hog dogs to do that. We'd be on horseback with a rifle, and there'd be a wagon following us. And the dogs would go trailing and get close and start barking and all the hogs would get in a bunch. We called it "rallyin' them." We'd just pick one to shoot that had plenty of fat on it.[22]

By 1904 there were two riverboats that ran up and down the Neches River as a leisure activity for families who could afford it. One was named the *Laura* and the other the *John Henry Kirby*, after the lumber and oil magnate from Beaumont who subsidized the two vessels. Wilbur Gilbert remembers when his father's steamboat got in a race one day.

It was called the *Gypsy*, it was a sixty footer, and a Mr. Blankenship had a pretty mahogany gasoline boat about forty or fifty feet long. And we were taking our boat out on the river one afternoon and Captain Garvin said to my father, "Mr. Gilbert, there's that Blankenship boat. How about a race?" My father said, "Boys, get plenty of steam up and run alongside of him and we'll give him a good race. And if you can outrun him I'll give you a Stetson hat."

Well, the race started out in good shape. We were outrunning them and we passed them right by and they looked like they were having engine trouble. Someone said we ought to slow down and help them out, but Captain Garvin says, "Oh, that's just a gag. There's nothing wrong with that boat." We were running about sixteen miles an hour racing down the river.[23]

THE BRITISH ARE COMING! THE BRITISH ARE COMING!

The mayor-elect of London frowned at each of the men who sat around the long, dark Victorian-style table. He had only one question for them, but none seemed to have any response. All the Lord Mayor wanted to know was, "Where *is Beaumont?*"[24]

Against the backdrop of the Texas oil boom swirled an intrigue that spread across two continents and an ocean, and involved the most high-powered petroleum interests in the world. While tens of thousands of get-rich-quick wannabes milled about along Park Street and down Highland Avenue, five thousand miles away deals were being struck, and deals were being struck down, that would affect the use of fuel oil for the rest of the twentieth century. Although most of the boomers in Beaumont knew all about the specter of Standard Oil that hung over the salt dome gushers, almost no one had an inkling of the mighty struggle that carried on involving two of the other world giants—Royal Dutch and Shell Trade & Transport. For these shipping titans, Spindletop was little more than a playing field for the next international, corporate confrontation.

The complex power plays involved several of the most intriguing characters in the fuel industry. One was a Dutchman named Henri W. A. Deterding. No one came away from an encounter with Sir Henri without some sense of awe. Dynamic, tough, charismatic, Deterding worked unceasingly and expected the same with every partner and every employee. He lived on a difficult regimen of exercise that included horseback riding and swimming, and his lifestyle was equally demanding. He harbored no illusions as to social responsibility or moral processing: his life's goal was raw power. Said his private secretary F. C. Gerretson: "He never aimed at something exalted and wonderful: to serve the public interest, to create a new economic order, to build up a mighty commercial concern. His purpose was that of any merchant, great or small, something extremely matter-of-fact: to make money. He was ever a merchant in heart and soul."[25]

In the late 1890s Deterding found himself in a power struggle with a fellow partner of the Royal Dutch Company, J. B. August Kessler. The two had matched wits and coordinated efforts to bring together one of the mightiest shipping conglomerates the world had ever seen. Providence intervened on behalf of Sir Henri in March, 1900, when Kessler drowned at sea. Royal Dutch now belonged to the thirty-three-year-old, and its direction into the new century would be at his disposition.[26]

One of Deterding's competitors was the equally ruthless American company of John Rockefeller, Standard Oil. It did not seem to Sir Henri that the two could "share" the world, and he set out to win at any cost. It was at this juncture that Deterding came across a businessman who brought to the table just the ingredients that, in combination with Royal Dutch, could beat Standard at its own power game. That man was Marcus Samuel.

Samuel was a completely different personality. Thirteen years older than the Dutchman, this Englishman of Bavarian Jewish ancestry had risen through the social ranks as first Viscount Bearsted to the position of alderman in London, to be appointed Lord Mayor of that city in 1902. Sir Marcus's father had been a tradesman in the seashell business, known in smaller circles for his decorative shell boxes and other merchandise. When Samuel created his own trading company he named it after his father's wares, thus the name Shell. The younger Samuel was patient, disciplined, and astute. He looked to the future with a creative imagination. As each ocean-going tanker slipped from its shipyard dock, Samuel searched for new ways to improve his international transport industry.

It was Marcus Samuel who read the small article in the London newspaper that January day in 1901; it was Sir Marcus who understood the implications of the gusher somewhere in Texas. For months the trade magnate had been toying with an idea that would switch his steamers over to the more efficient liquid fuel instead of coal. Not only was the idea itself intriguing, Samuel also believed that his country would benefit all the more if the Royal Navy were to switch as well. The growing threat of the Kaiser's naval capacity disturbed those who possessed a historical perspective.

Now, there in Beaumont, wherever in the world that was, rose into the sky the solution for which he sought. If, as the report suggested, this Texas crude was too heavy for the production of kerosene, it would surely be the perfect base for a locomotive fuel oil product. Shell Trade & Transport could corner this new market, reasoned Samuel, convince Parliament to switch the navy over to liquid fuel, and the mayor-elect of London would be the merchant whose oil would change the world.

Samuel set to work immediately. His staff had to borrow a world atlas from a neighboring office to *locate* Spindletop first. That finally accomplished, the telegraph office was kept busy finding the contact person, who turned out to be a Pennsylvanian by the name of James M. Guffey. Samuel rushed his brother-in-law Henry Neville Benjamin over to the United States to strike a deal with this Guffey. It took weeks for Benjamin to make the connection, with a comic twist in the first encounter: Benjamin admitted that he had never heard of Guffey or Beaumont, to which the "colonel" responded that he understood, for he had never heard of Shell Trade & Transport! Benjamin patiently explained that Shell was one of the largest transport companies in the world, and a worthy adversary of Standard Oil. That gained Guffey's attention, although Benjamin was also forced to purchase a world map to point out Shell's international influence, and from that point on the two men actually got along quite well.

The next problem then presented itself into the negotiations. Guffey, anxious to promote his Texas crude in Europe, had retained the services of a man named John Hay, a small-time broker who knew his way around London and Paris and Amsterdam. Samuel would have to deal with Hay, Guffey explained. When Sir Marcus received that news from his brother-in-law, he flew into a rage: he would not stand to deal with some go-between on a deal of this magnitude! Samuel suggested that Benjamin find a way around this procedure at once.

One way around, Benjamin discovered, might be to go to the real power behind Colonel Guffey: the Mellons. Andrew and William Mellon pulled the purse strings of the Guffey Oil Company and, although much less congenial to deal with than the enigmatic Guffey, all the more influential. At an earlier point, in fact, the Mellon brothers and a nephew had first negotiated with Standard Oil to get into the Texas oil field. Spokesman Henry H. Rogers had ended that talk succinctly: "After the way Mr.

Rockefeller has been treated by the State of Texas [anti-trust laws], he'll never put another dime there."

In a series of New York meetings that ironically concluded about the same time Guffey's contract with Hay ran out, a lucrative deal was struck between the Mellons and Shell to market Guffey's Spindletop oil abroad. For the next twenty-one years Guffey Oil Company would sell half its total production to Shell, an estimated 14.7 million barrels of Texas crude. By June, 1901, Shell Trade & Transport found itself in the oil business.[27]

But the negotiations and reports of the final contract did not go unnoticed. Standard Oil knew it had a major competitor on its hands now. And Henri Deterding wanted Royal Dutch in on the action as well. Royal Dutch was already involved in trying to break Shell's holdings in the East Indies, and the aggressive Dutchman saw an opportunity now to deal with the English Jew. Deterding began to court Samuel with promises of an amalgamation that would destroy Standard Oil overseas and put "Royal Dutch/Shell" at the top. He retained the services of Fred "Shady" Lane, a well-known shipping broker, to mediate and negotiate the deal.

For three months the chess game continued. Samuel seemed poised to sign the deal that would make him head of the powerful shipping and oil corporation while giving Deterding the day-to-day management of the company. But Deterding's overbearing personality, and Lane's less than savory reputation, suddenly complicated the process further. Lane called in his own backers, the European powerhouse Rothschilds, and Samuel sailed to New York to entertain a counter offer from Standard Oil! All of the world's major players in liquid fuel and petroleum were now heading for a collision on the same chessboard.

On November 4, 1901, with Samuel rebuffed by Standard Oil, Lane convinced the Englishman that the first deal was still the best way to go, and papers were drawn up to create the "Shell Transport Royal Dutch Petroleum Company." One last moment of drama awaited. On December 23, Standard telegraphed a staggering $40 million offer to purchase Shell. As Samuel wavered, Deterding instructed Lane to "make the deal" at any cost. Lane succeeded. The papers were signed on December 27. By early the next year, "British Dutch" was moving into Texas, building storage and shipping facilities at Port Arthur, constructing pipelines from Big Hill, and making plans for refineries and the conversion of its tankers from coal to oil.

Deterding's interests in North America never wavered. By 1912 he had incorporated the American Gasoline Company; one year later, it reorganized as Shell Petroleum of California, the predecessor to Shell Oil of today.[28]

The house of cards for Marcus Samuel, however, came tumbling down after June, 1902, in a dazzling array of misfortune and mismanagement. Shell had been buried in the paperwork by Deterding. Although Samuel held the highest office in the new company, he was little more than a figurehead: Sir Henri ran the company and had secured a "lifetime" directorship from its board. When Lane's investors wanted in, Deterding brought the Rothschilds in to what soon became reorganized as the Asiatic Petroleum Company. What little parts of the trade and transport company still existed as subsidiaries were now in deep financial trouble. Further, lobbyists had succeeded in halting any debate on the conversion of the Royal Navy to liquid fuel. And to make matters worse, the September fires on Big Hill and continued overproduction there were rapidly sinking the Texas connection.

Later that fall, as the vanquished Sir Marcus duly accepted the laurels as Lord Mayor of London, his grand banquet celebration seemed empty somehow. All of his plans, all of his dreams, cut short despite every effort to wedge himself back into the picture. "I can withstand ten Lord Mayors," Deterding claimed upon hearing that Samuel wanted to fight his way back to the top. He could and did. The first Viscount Bearsted had lost.[29]

And all Sir Marcus had done was read a tiny newspaper article about a gusher half a world away.

RULE OF CAPTURE

The white-tailed deer burst out of the woods, his impressive rack held high as he approached the stone wall. Without a moment's pause he gracefully launched himself into the air at full speed, easily topping the four-foot wall and landing soundlessly in the high grass on the other side. His zigzag pattern across the open field caused the hunter to miss his shot at the majestic buck, who disappeared into another distant patch of foliage.

The hunter cursed his misfortune as he wandered out into the edge of the field. He was startled when he heard a loud shout from off to his right. It came from across the stone wall, and in a moment a second hunter appeared there, his fist raised in the air in anger. "That was my deer," he screamed. "You shot at my deer!"

For centuries English common law dealt with these kinds of disputes by what it called "the rule of capture." The country courts had reasoned that wild game such as the deer could not be considered as belonging to anyone's estate unless illegally constrained there by protective fences or wide, deep moats. If such game wandered over onto another's property, it was, as the saying became, "fair game." In the late nineteenth century none of the states in America had any law on its books to deal with such matters specifically, although the concept was debated out in the Western states when it came to water wells and rerouting rivers for irrigation.

The concept soon gravitated to the petroleum industry in Pennsylvania through a unique set of legal relationships, when in 1889 the Pennsylvania Supreme Court decided that the "rule of capture" pertained here as well. Oil, unlike the solid minerals whose ownership could be simply determined by survey and land contract, *moved* beneath the surface, especially when it was being drilled out of the ground. Wherever a well hit an oil deposit, an area of low pressure formed, causing the oil and gas pressure from the extreme edges of that same deposit to press the oil into that void. Thus, a single well could ultimately pump the oil not only from directly below the mineral rights owner's derrick, but empty out the deposit that would surely lay under adjoining property as well. In the oil business, this would undoubtedly cause more than a fist-shaking reaction![30]

At Spindletop, the consequences would be enormous, and finally catastrophic. The Texas courts followed the Pennsylvania precedent, which declared that "a lease contract for oil contained an implied obligation on the part of the company drilling the well to protect the interests of any other company who would be affected by that well." Thus, as William Owens explains, "if one company held leases on the farms of A and B, and had completed a producing well on A's farm, it must, even though the oil could be recovered by the single well, drill immediately on B's land; otherwise A would get the oil that had been in place under B's land. If they had [instead] agreed to restrict production, they would then be subject to prosecution under the anti-trust laws for an agreement in restraint of trade!"[31]

Wells would be drilled, according to this interpretation of the law, that would be completely unnecessary; suits would be drawn out for years in the courts by companies who believed they had been "sucked dry" by a rival next door; and an unnecessarily feverish pace would accompany any new discovery, not just to get rich but to get the oil before one's neighbor.

In addition, literally trillions of cubic feet of *gas* were wasted in the early Spindletop years because of the race to equalize or beat the pressure fluctuations. With the easing of the subterranean pressure, much of the oil that might have been pumped out of the deeper reservoir sands was lost altogether. The overproduction from this too-heavy activity drove the price of crude oil so low as to make it unprofitable—three cents a barrel at its nadir—and depleted the oil deposits much more quickly than a responsible operation would have done. And finally, when a field was "drilled out," its consequences to the boom town were essentially fatal—economically, socially, and psychologically. The boomer moved on; the detritus left behind would take years to clean up.

The above scenario is precisely what occurred on Big Hill between 1901 and 1903. And although many Beaumont citizens breathed great sighs of relief when the last boomer took the last train out of town, it took years—and at least two more Big Hill booms—to regain the economic foundation that Lucas No. 1 had bequeathed it.

Perhaps if that first deer hunter had been a better shot. . . .

THE FIRE THAT TOOK IT ALL

He turned and ran for his life, everybody scattered in every direction. He looked once or twice as he ran, and saw the casing-head and a long string of casing up in the air, for all the world like a Dutchman's pipe, only it was straight. When the pipe stem got too long, it broke off and crashed over sideways, taking part of the derrick with it; and out of the hole there shot a geyser of water, and then oil, black floods of it, with that familiar roaring sound—an express train shooting out of the ground! He gave a yell or two, and he saw his dad waving his arms, and presumably calling; he started toward his father—when suddenly, most dreadful thing of all, the whole mass of oil up in the air burst into flame!

They were never to know what did it; perhaps an electric spark, or the fire in the boiler, or a spark made by falling wreckage, or rocks blown out of the hole, striking on steel; anyhow, there was a tower of flame, and the most amazing spectacle—the burning oil would hit the ground, and bounce up, and explode, and leap again and fall again, and great red masses of flame would unfold, and burst, and yield black masses of smoke, and these in turn red. Mountains of smoke rose to the sky, and mountains of flame came seething down to the earth; every jet that struck the ground turned into a volcano, and rose again, higher than before; the whole mass, boiling and bursting, became a river of fire, a lava flood that went streaming down the valley, turning everything it touched into flame, then swallowing it up and hiding the flames in a cloud of smoke. The force of the gravity took it down the valley, and the force of the wind swept it over the hillside; it touched the bunkhouse, and swallowed it in one gulp; it took the toolhouse, everything that was wood; and when there came a puff of wind, driving the stream of oil and gas to one side, you saw the skeleton of the derrick, draped with fire![32]

In a novel the excitement and drama of an oil field fire spurs the imagination, touches the soul. In the crisis of a real fire, there is another whole set of emotions: fear, devastation, discouragement, and courage. In the fall of 1902, Big Hill experienced its worst set of disasters. Not only was each damaging on its own merit, but the combination, the unceasing turn of events, the exhausting pattern of crisis after crisis, signaled for many an end to the boom itself. As other strikes less than twenty miles away enticed the speculator and the gambler, so too did the conflagrations of 1902 drive thousands away from Spindletop. Michel T. Halbouty tells the story too well to be rewritten:

> Spindletop raged with a fire for a solid week in September when the T. J. Woods well ignited from a cigar carelessly discarded by a driller. The well was gushing high above the derrick top when the flames reached it. There was no chance to close it in, as valves had not been installed. The fire was an awesome spectacle, colorful and belligerent. It marked the first use of steam and sand in fighting fire.
>
> In late October the Hogg-Swayne tract was completely wiped out by a series of fires. Twenty-six derricks and pumping units were destroyed in the first blaze, but few wells were lost, due to the fact that most of the valves were closed and the well-heads covered with sand before the flames reached them. The fire started when a small wooden tank in block 38 collapsed and the oil spilled over a boiler. Among the gushers lost were the Lucky Dime, the Live Oak and Wild Gusher wells which turned into blazing fountains of oil. The wells lost were all located on less than an acre of land.
>
> This fire was almost under control when the second started in another section of the Hogg-Swayne tract. As a worker [Forrest Bottomfield] lifted a lantern to blow out the light the gas fumes ignited and set off a tremendous blaze. A roughneck, trapped between walls of fire in the first few

minutes of the excitement, was burned to death. Wooden derricks, some seventy-five of them, were quick fodder for the inferno. J. S. Corbett's giant settling tank caught fire and added to the spectacle.

Hundreds of citizens joined the field workers in battling the flames, but by the next morning the Hogg-Swayne tract was a smoldering ruin, a shabby sight for a train of excursionists to see. There were no gushers for the promoters to show that day.[33]

It is told that Forrest Bottomfield left Texas and got out of the oil business completely after that disaster of his own doing. Legend has it he went north and got into the funeral business. Others remember him returning to Texas some years later as a snake oil salesman, selling jars of crude oil for $2 each and making a good living with his "medicinal remedies."[34]

Halbouty continues the remarkable story,

> The last burning embers of the [October] blaze were cooling when lightning hit a Guffey tank during a thunderstorm. The flames leapt to an adjoining tank and carried on to the thick patch of wells in the Keith-Ward tract. Great walls of flame, a pall of smoke and flashing lightning combined to produce one of the weirdest spectacles of Spindletop. Hundreds braved the heavy storm to climb the hill and watch the fireworks. Lightning struck a number of installations on the hill, including a Negro church in the South Africa area where a funeral was being held. A mourner killed by the lightning was the only casualty of the day. The heavy rain drenched the fire. Its waters created a blinding steam that choked off the flames. When the twelve days during which the hill was a constant hellfire finally came to an end, only the Yellowpine district stood intact.[35]

Doc Stoker was there.

> I awoke with a start from a deep sleep. Outside my window there was a great commotion. My room was filled with light. People were running in the streets, cursing, yelling, and crying. Alarmed, I reached for my clothes and somehow got them on. The crack of pistol shots rent the air. Just as I finished dressing, there was an explosion which rocked the earth. My heart almost stood still from fright, as I ran out on the street. It seemed that Judgment Day had come, and the world must be burning up.
>
> I asked a white-faced, wild-eyed man running past me what had happened. He replied that a steel oil tank had blown up and the Spindle-Top

field was on fire. Bang! Crash! Boom! Explosion after explosion followed, as large and small tanks and derricks went up like dynamite. The sky was a sea of flame. Tongues of fire shot hundreds of feet into the air. The dense, rolling smoke curled itself into fantastic shapes. Great quantities of gas formed livid balls of fire which exploded and burst into flames high in the air. Flames, twisting and writhing like hell-tossed snakes, leaped from derricks, pump houses, and shacks, leaving them flaming torches as they passed.

Hard-faced men sobbed and wept like babies as they watched their wealth vanish in a moment. Women screaming, crying, and dragging children or some piece of treasured furniture, rushed to safety. Orders and countermand orders were hurled through the air. Men, wild with fear, tried to save their tanks, wells, derricks, homes, and places of business only to be relentlessly pushed back by the mocking flames. The night was never to be forgotten. . . .

On the ground lay the burned, injured, and dead. . . . I worked feverishly over my patients and was soon staggered with fatigue. Before me stood scores of men temporarily deranged from shock and loss of fortunes. Many of these cases were worse than those of the physically injured. . . .

Spindle-Top was a "sucked orange," lifeless, dry.

Big Hill was rebuilt. Later that fall, 440 gushers spewed all over the hill. Men made money, new companies incorporated, trainloads of spectators still came. Beaumont continued its frenetic pace of social life, gambling, crime, and unprecedented wealth. But something was happening around Spindletop. In spite of the rebuilding that went on, the several new wells that would be drilled, and the thousands who worked day and night to bring in that next gusher, a change was taking place. More and more of the men and women who had come to Spindletop in 1901 were packing up, moving on. Many believed that the hill was almost "played out" now. The first flush of the Lucas gusher and its helter-skelter aftermath had flowed and now ebbed.

"Mrs. Kooney turned to Dillon and said, 'Honey, don't stay down here all night. Me and you have got some talkin' to do. I'm a-feeling it in my bones, honey. The old bubble's getting ready to bust. And when it does, we want to make a run for it. We want to hit the next boom town before all the good squatting places are took.'"[36]

And new names were on everyone's lips: Sour Lake, Saratoga, and Batson Prairie. The boomers were moving on, the excitement transferring to the north and west, the focus now concentrated on the edge of the Big Thicket. Doc Stoker was one of the throngs that pushed out. "I turned the office over to the druggist and went to Beaumont. There I bought a supply of medicines and instruments and an operating table. Without a backward glance at burned out Spindle-Top, I left for Sour Lake and Saratoga."[37]

Guffey Co. Well No. 2, Sour Lake. Photograph by H. L. Edgerton. Courtesy
Texas Energy Museum, Beaumont, Texas.

Sour Lake No. 1, 1902. Photograph by H. L. Edgerton. Courtesy Texas Energy Museum, Beaumont, Texas.

(right) Building a platform in the mud, Sour Lake. Courtesy Texas Energy Museum, Beaumont, Texas.

Sour Lake drilling crew, 1904. Courtesy Texas Energy Museum, Beaumont, Texas.

Sour Lake. Courtesy Jack Whitmeyer Collection, Sam Houston Regional Library and Research Center.

Sour Lake bath house and hotel. Courtesy Texas Energy Museum, Beaumont, Texas.

Saratoga oil field. Courtesy Jack Whitmeyer Collection, Sam Houston Regional Library and Research Center.

Saratoga Main Street. Courtesy Texas Energy Museum, Beaumont, Texas.

A muddy street in Saratoga. Courtesy Texas Energy Museum, Beaumont, Texas.

Batson drugstore, 1904. Courtesy Jack Whitmeyer Collection, Sam Houston
Regional Library and Research Center.

Main Street, Batson. Courtesy Jack Whitmeyer Collection, Sam Houston Regional Library and Research Center.

Posing for a "Round Up," Batson. Courtesy Jack Whitmeyer Collection, Sam Houston Regional Library and Research Center.

Treehouse near Batson. Courtesy Jack Whitmeyer Collection, Sam Houston Regional Library and Research Center.

The hard life in the Big Thicket. Courtesy Jack Whitmeyer Collection, Sam Houston Regional Library and Research Center.

Out in the Big Thicket, 1904. Courtesy Jack Whitmeyer Collection, Sam
Houston Regional Library and Research Center.

Hauling boilers to Batson. Courtesy Jack Whitmeyer Collection, Sam Houston Regional Library and Research Center.

(left) Striking a felonious pose. Courtesy Jack Whitmeyer Collection, Sam Houston Regional Library and Research Center.

Young women of Batson Prairie. Courtesy Jack Whitmeyer Collection, Sam Houston Regional Library and Research Center.

7

Big Thicket Oil

Joe Pivoto stood at the edge of the underbrush, a study in consternation. One of the freedmen had vanished. He and his partner C. T. Cade had freed their slaves when the war ended, and had even given them a hundred acres of land down on the bayou, theirs, free and clear. They didn't have to stay, of course, but where else would they go? In 1866, traveling around Texas or over into Louisiana would be more dangerous than liberating. And now one of them was gone.

Bazile Brown, as he called himself now, a sturdy man in his forties who carried a noticeable limp after being thrown from a bronco years before, had apparently launched out on his own into the thicket. The others weren't sure when he had left the camp, or exactly which direction he might have wandered. Now their former owner had to decide whether it was worth the trouble to go looking for him, or just let him go. The slave was an odd one, actually, given to mysterious incantations and such. He'd been a steady worker and a good cowboy for Pivoto and Cade, but as an ex-slave he had every right to head out on his own, odd or not.

All of these questions disappeared the moment that Bazile appeared from out of the deep brush. He looked terrible, covered from head to toe in caked-on goop, like he'd been wallowing with the wild hogs that wandered the thicket. Pivoto waited patiently as the other freedmen clapped Bazile on the back and led him eventually to his former owner. The stray had a big smile across his grimy face, his eyes still lit up and wide as they usually were. Pivoto knew there would be an explanation, of sorts, forthcoming. He crossed his arms and waited patiently.

"Ah foun dah cow, Suh," Bazile finally said. "Ah found her in dah swamp deah." He pointed casually over his shoulder from whence he'd come.

Several head of cattle had indeed wandered off three days earlier, Pivoto remembered, not an unusual occurrence. And those that vanished into the thicket, well, vanished. "Uh huh," was all he could manage in response.

"An de one dat wuz sick she's all well now, Suh. All well." Bazile's grin widened another inch.

"Why, that's wonderful, Bazile," responded Pivoto. "You found her, did you? And you made her well?"

"Oh no, Suh," the freedman shook his head. Chunks of black dirt flew in both directions. "It were de mud, Suh. It were de mud that healed her. I found her in de swamp, up to heah"—he pointed to his shoulders—"in dat stuff out deah. And she was all well. Stepped right out to me, Suh. Stepped right out."

Pivoto couldn't help but smile back at the eager freedman. You're a strange one, all right, he thought, a healer of cows. He gave Bazile a once over, then reached over and patted him on one shoulder.

"Dr. Mud. That's you, Bazile. Dr. Mud."[1]

SOUR LAKE

On the east side of the meandering Pine Island Bayou stand the small hamlets of Sour Lake and Saratoga, about ten miles north and south of one another as the crow flies but longer for the oil field worker who had to make that trek in and around the Big Thicket. The area around Sour Lake, just west of Beaumont, was settled by the Stephen Jackson family in 1835. Stories of the healing powers of the "sour springs" already had their circulation by then, and the Alabama Indians in that edge of the Big Thicket had long used the local mud for a variety of remedies. In 1851 three entrepreneurial Texans bought a piece of that land and established the Holland Freeman Company a.k.a. Sour Lake Watering Place. Their circular proclaimed that "[h]undreds can testify to the medicinal virtues of the waters, where indeed more wonderful cures have been effected in proportion to its number of visitors, so that the reputation which they now enjoy is no more a result of accident than of effort." Bird Holland and Ira Freeman wisely marketed their "Spa" by having Dr. Alex Sears, M.D., on board to verify the medicinal importance and to care for the patients who came there.[2]

The spa enjoyed decades of success even in spite of and through the Civil War and hard Reconstruction years. In 1896 the Sour Lake Company bought 845 acres in that area, which included the then-named Sour Lake Health and Pleasure Resort. Their circular picked up where the former had left. "This is without a doubt the most wonderful collection of mineral water, mineral mud and tars known. The mud baths have proven an infallible cure for exema [*sic*]. . . . Many persons come to Sour Lake and are cured after trying the Carlsbad mud of Europe and many others in vain to find relief." The company promised to "cure women of those diseases that are particular to their sex and nine out of ten women are thus afflicted," it reminded potential patients! The list of ails the sour springs mud would cure was exhaustive, from "sores, ulcers, skarslous or syphilitic boils, carbuncles, burns, bruises, piles, and other skin eruptions— as well as sore throats, catarrh of the stomach, and diphtheria." A new hotel was to be built, with natatorium and sanatorium and "a large, modern bath house."

For enterprising investors, the company reminded them that the "Sour Lake tar which is the salve in large quantities sells readily for \$8.00 per gallon wholesale or 25 cents per ounce bottled. It can be placed on sale at every drug store in the United States. The health mud sells for ten cents per pound and the supply is inexhaustible." The Sour Lake Company proved a successful venture, and the Hotel and Spa was operating by 1898.[3]

The community that grew up around the resort and spa claimed a sparse population of 150 in 1885, and then declined to a third that number by 1896. Two post offices opened and shut between 1866 and 1880 and then finally opened permanently in 1895. The town boasted two general stores, two hotels, and a school with an enrollment of twenty-eight. Private schools had already come and gone by the end of the century, including the Devers School founded by a Dr. Tucker, and the nearby Hatcher School in what is today the village of China. J. J. Bevil organized a one-room school in an old log cabin, then moved it to a church on Coon's Marsh. It closed down when the parents discovered that Mr. Bevil's old powder horn, which he kept at his side as he taught, was generally filled with corn liquor! The school identified at the turn of the century was situated in the Lacy home and the teacher was Frank Tebbs.[4]

Saratoga was an off-shoot of the engaging operations in and around the sour springs to the south. In fact at one time the small village there was named New Sour Lake. However, the enterprising P. S. Watts bought into the area in the 1880s, built campsites, spas, and a small hotel, and renamed the area Saratoga after the world-famous spa in upstate New York. By the end of the century, Saratoga, Texas, though not rivaling its neighbor to the south in quantity, certainly had its own share of success with the "healing mud." Doc Stoker did not share the vaulted view of Saratoga when he moved there in 1902. "There was a run-down two story building with a rambling gallery running the whole length of the house both back and front, completing the dilapidated place. About ten yards behind this place stood an equally shabby, old, one story house, which was used for the dining room and kitchen. . . . This unsightly place had the pretentious name of 'The Hotel Saratoga.' Two other houses, an old log cabin and an old general store, completed Saratoga."[5]

But the transition that took place in these two communities was the discovery of oil, gushers of oil. J. Fletcher Cotton surveyed the Saratoga area even before the Civil War, and followed up on an old legend that wild hogs—rooters—would appear from the thicket covered in oil. It turned out to be true, and Cotton drilled test water and oil wells in 1865. These proved largely unsuccessful, but in 1887 a small, shallow well puddled oil onto the surface. Ed Cotton remembers "Old Uncle Bill" Jordan who, like Pattillo Higgins twelve miles away, enjoyed treating neighborhood children to the sight of burning gasses out in the fields. Jordan would punch an open can into the ground, then light a match inside. The seeping gas would explode in a delightful moment of entertaining fireworks: a more ominous danger awaited.[6]

Similar experiments in shallow wells had been launched in the Sour Lake area before the turn of the century. In 1878 Dr. B. T. Kavanaugh issued his now famous report: "I visited Sour Lake, where I found oil upon the surface in greater quantity than at any other point." Twenty years later Nathaniel Jordan and John Savage formed a partnership to refine oil from asphalt, but the resulting product was so flammable as to make it dangerous to store or ship! They hired teenage boys from the area to help them chop huge chunks out of the earth, extracted the giant clods with pitchforks, then fired them in pots, most of which were consumed by the flames. When they finally managed thirty barrels of the product and sent it by mule wagon to Galveston, the entire load, pots, barrels, and wagons, burned up on the road before reaching its destination.[7]

The combination of devastating fires at Spindletop and a waning productivity in 1902, the considerable advance in drilling technology, and the arrival of experienced oil men such as Walter Sharp, Bud Coyle, and James Guffey's operations, brought these two communities into the boom town oil business. The famous Savage brothers wandered up to the Sour Lake area after drilling all over Big Hill, and in 1901 brought in a shallow producer, not enough to spur the rush but enough to convince others that there might be a future in the Big Thicket for oil companies.

Wells were being drilled in the Saratoga area in 1901, but the first true moneymakers came in 1903 under the watchful eye of the Great Western Oil Company and the Hamman Oil enterprise. The Saratoga Townsite Company capitalized on the growth that same year, and the next year a side track of the Gulf, Colorado, and Santa Fe Railway linked Bragg to Saratoga. (The legend of the brakeman's ghost who still walks that old rail link emerged soon after.) The operations of the Townsite Company may have helped keep Saratoga from the overwhelming violence and law-lessness that would sting Sour Lake, and later Batson, although the boom town on Pine Island Bayou certainly had its share of stories.

Sour Lake came of age in the spring of 1902 when the Atlantic & Pacific Oil Company's Well No. 1 came in at 682 feet, and partly because the field was considered at the time the "shallowest oil field in the world," with an average tested depth of only 90 feet. Then in January, 1903, Bud Coyle brought in the Fee Well No. 3 for the Old Producers Company, the forerunner of the Texas Company. At 1,088 feet, the first true gusher flowed at 5,000 barrels a day: the boom was on! By the end of the year seventy-five wells operated around Sour Lake, and another seventy-five had already been shut down due to low pressure from the overproduction.[8]

Famous oil men made their presence known at Sour Lake as they had on Big Hill: J. N. Pew, Jim Roche, John Warne Gates, and J. S. Cullinan invested financially and personally, and Scott Heywood's company drilled successfully there at the edge of the Big Thicket. A Sour Lake employee named Charlie Meider is credited with the contribution of a five-pointed star as the eventual emblem of the Texas Company whose descendant corporation still carries it today.

In 1903 booming Sour Lake boasted a handful of log cabin residences, an array of oil company camps, a dry goods store, several grocers, the hotel and spa, a Methodist church, and *52 saloons*. There they were known as "blind tigers"—saloons in a legally dry town where the constabulary "closed its eyes." One enterprising would-be saloonkeeper rushed into town, recalls Alice Cashen, "with six bottles of whiskey, swiped a rived board from a corn crib, nailed it between two trees, and Sour Lake's Big Buck Saloon was in business." Mrs. V. B. Daniels shudders when she thinks of that oil patch: "My husband and brother were already working there when I came down from Bastrop. It was a real jumping-off place. Oh my goodness, it was bad. My brother told me I couldn't go out in the streets alone. The ladies just didn't dare. I think the town had about 10,000 inhabitants. It had a daily paper *and 105 saloons.*"[9]

Three banks opened in Sour Lake in a period of less than thirty days. The Miller Hotel and the Rodgers Hotel competed with the spa resort and all were overfilled for months at a time. In November of 1903 there were 758 houses and 1,297 tents at Sour Lake, an estimated population of 7,000, and a business district four blocks long on a widened Fannin Street. The Beaumont Sour Lake and Western Railway made its first run in June, 1904, one year after the T&NO established its depot. A conductor by the adventurous name of Kit Carson ran the "High, Dry, and Windy" along its route.[10]

Residents such as Preston Mowbray shot wild game to put on the Sour Lake Hotel plates—"enough ducks and geese one time to fill five feather mattresses." The hotel fare included four different venison favorites, squirrel stew and squirrel and dumplings, and a recipe for a bear meat marinade that included soaking a six-pound roast for twenty-four hours before cooking.[11]

The Sour Lake field faced the same danger—fire—that the others had experienced before it. Fires decimated wooden derricks on August 24, 1903, and again on September 23 and October 14. A fire of suspicious origin began on the second floor of the First National Bank and burned nearly the entire town on January 24, 1904; rebuilt, Sour Lake continued its rowdy ways without more than a pause. W. T. Block dramatically describes the scene: "Screams of women and children, the raucous yells of frightened men, the falling timbers and sidewalls, the billowing flames, the mad dashes of runaway teams and wagons and riderless horses, people tumbling into tanks or pools of water, others dashing with hands and arms full of personal possessions and savings were sights and sounds etched indelibly into the minds of everyone who witnessed them. Reckless men even dashed into burning saloons just to rescue a bottle."[12]

The *Houston Post* recorded the horrors of the city conflagration: "Any loss of life will probably never be known. Hundreds of men and women, half of whose names were practically unknown, roomed in the second stories of these buildings that were destroyed and the majority could as easily have been burned to death and never be missed. Screams were heard at different times, but the destruction was so complete that no charred remains can be found, or if they were, they could not be identified, despite those who fought manfully, heroically, desperately until the red-tongued demon was ultimately vanquished." No less than forty-nine businesses were consumed at a loss of over $200,000. Governor Hogg's Fort Worth oil partner Jim Swayne was badly injured when falling timber collapsed on him as he tried in vain to save the lives of those who perished in the fire.[13]

On the other hand was the disorder. In December, 1903, and January, 1904, alone, more than 240 men, and at least 1 woman, died in the violent streets of this Big Thicket boom town. As Loither Adams says, "Of course, the killings were above and beyond the minor detail of stealing, double-dealing, and the outright beating of property owners out of their land, their royalties, and the use of their own property. Law and order simply did not exist."[14]

RASCALITY

Charlie Jeffries came to Sour Lake in October, 1903.

> Boll weevils had ruined the cotton in my part of the country, and, like thousands of others, I went to the oil field to tide over a hard time. By pawning my fiddle and six-shooter and borrowing fifty cents from a friend, I scraped up enough money to buy a ticket; I got there without a cent.
>
> Hardly had I arrived before I was introduced to one of the town's most prominent characteristics—rascality. Two young fellows at the depot came up to me and gave me a drink of beer. Then they began a game of matching nickels on the counter. After playing a short time, they invited me to join in on the game. For more reasons than one, I declined. They continued the game between themselves, but every now and then they would invite me to take a turn. When one who had lost left the room in a huff, the other boy proposed that I come in with him and we would fleece the other fellow when he returned. I knew how the trick went, and in mild tones I declined.
>
> The boy came back and the two of them started at it again, even asked me if I'd come in with them. Finally, I told them I was broke. Well, they ceased their importunities, and the game stopped. When I asked them the way to the oil field, they good-naturedly showed me the road. I grinned as I went on my way: I had got them for a glass of beer.

Things were pretty tough for a young fellow on his own, even in a boom town. Jeffries recalls meeting up with a couple of pals, but spending most of his time alone, and hungry. Poignantly he says, "I took up a seat on a syrup barrel out in front of a store. There I watched the people go by, streams of them, hundreds and hundreds of them. I'll never forget spending that Saturday evening and watching for someone that I knew." Another day, with a fresh pair of overalls and a nickel discovered in the pocket, the hungry young man headed for a bakery in town. "When I came in smelling distance of the shop, the odor of the bread drove me a bit wild. And all the way back to my tent, without water, I continued to tear off pieces of a loaf of that bread, a highly relished meal."

The saloons tended to be the hub of the wheels of outlaw activity, brawls, gambling, and just general trouble. The House of Lords had such a reputation in Sour Lake; so too the Derrick Saloon and the Big Thicket Saloon, and Dad's Saloon. Doc Stoker remembers that before the building began at the start of the boom, tarpaulins would be stretched out on the ground to serve as gambling tables. "Whiskey bottles lying in the weeds," Jeffries laments the pitiable sight. "For surging energy, unrestrained openness, and diabolical conditions otherwise, Sour Lake was head and shoulders above anything Texas had seen up until that time."[15]

Frank Hamilton arrived in the Sour Lake oil fields as an eighteen-year-old. "It was just like Spindletop," he says, "worse than Beaumont. Didn't have no laws. A few grocery stores and no rooming houses. The rooms that were there filled four or five men each. Worked twelve and fourteen hour shifts; some would sleep while others worked. The beds were always occupied. The old lady got about $3 a bed every day."[16]

Sam Webb recalls the hard work at Sour Lake. "Worked long hours cleaning up everything, putting out the fires, getting control of the fires. Billy Lyons was down there with us. My wife and I stayed with Will Young and his wife before we got hold of a house. When we'd go to bed we never did even pull off our clothes, just sleep in them and go right back to work. Never did catch up on sleep. Just got used to it. Eat breakfast and light out for work."[17]

Ed Cotton, seventeen when the boom hit, agrees. "The workers they'd just come in and set up tents and get right to work; some were portables boxed in and some were just 'flies' stretched across the ground. Came in and laid them right down, didn't matter where they were. Some had their families with them and they'd go to housekeeping soon as their tents were up. You'd go to sleep at night and next morning there'd be twenty or thirty tents set up during the night. Stores the same way."[18]

"But nobody stole anything," Hamilton continues.

Just working class people, no stealing. Gambling was wide open, though. There was roulette tables, crap games, poker, faro, anything you wanted to gamble on. . . . Easy livers, I called them. Preyed just like a lion on a lamb, anything to separate the men from their money. Sometimes they'd follow a drunk fellow around 'til he fell asleep somewhere, take his shoes off and sell them second hand in the street next day. There were disreputable women. The women had all kinds of diseases, just like you would any place where nothing was sanitary. There were some doctors, but most just said they were doctors, weren't really.

And lots of killing. Gamblers, mostly, getting murdered. Killing each other like it was Chicago. After the creek run dry they found lots of bodies, lots of skeletons, just thrown in there. The Texas Company come in there and blowed a big ditch and pumped waste oil into some tanks. Well, when they quit and moved on, they found that big ditch just full of bones. Been throwed in that oil.[19]

William H. "Billy" Bryant came to Sour Lake in August, 1902, and served six months as sheriff during the boom. His deputy was Bunk Summers. Billy had been a peace officer in Corsicana and was a colorful character all his own, given to wearing polka-dot ties with silk shirts and fancy cowboy boots. One of the first things on the new sheriff's agenda was the construction of a jail house, because Sour Lake had none. The idea apparently didn't go over well with everyone, for it was promptly burned to the ground. A more permanent structure went up soon after, and stayed up. And full.

Bryant concurs with the atmosphere of the early times there.

Didn't have time to do much but hold inquests and pick up dead bodies. You know these country boys when they get around where there's music and dancing. They were double tough and I don't think a night came that some of the bunch wasn't in a fight in one of those saloons. But I never heard of a man getting hijacked in Sour Lake, not in the early days. I saw as much as $10,000 sitting on a crap table, where a man standing outside at the window could've reached right in and taken it. The money was changing hands so fast, the crooks and the gamblers didn't worry about hijacking.

Wages were $3 for a twelve hour work day. Boy could get a nice shave and a bath and haircut for $3. Haircuts just two bits. Room and board a dollar. And yes, there were some women there, women of every type, all types, from the smallest to the largest, and from the tenderest to the toughest; we had lots of fighting among the women. Not killed, just generally beat each other up until somebody'd separate them. Nella Dale and Grace Ashley put on the best bout I ever saw, fought for an hour and fifteen minutes. *And when they quit they didn't have enough clothes left on to wipe out a .22 rifle.*[20]

John Little moved to the Sour Lake area before the boom and watched the dramatic changes take place all around him.

At first when we lived there there were no stores. I was living with my brother and his wife. She had to go over to Beaumont to the stores there. Later they built a pretty nice millinery store in Sour Lake, the Jews come in and run it. But Sour Lake was kind of like a mining town or those gold rush towns. Kind of wild when they start, but finally settle down to moderate times. There were plenty of saloons, and one little [Methodist] church I was affiliated with, had a Sunday School there from the beginning. They had a small building, maybe 18x30. Didn't have a pastor living there; he'd just come in, stay at the Sour Lake Springs Hotel, have a reception there, play the piano and preach on Sunday nights. When he got through, the young people would have a dance there!

Then the honky-tonks came in after the boom. And gambling wide open like in California. At the honky-tonk in the saloon you could see a little show. Cost the oil field workers fifteen cents to get in. They had a little stage and they'd put on these comic plays to entertain the roughnecks. Then after the show they'd stack up the chairs and you could dance. They had square dancing and round dancing. For fifty cents you could get two bottles of beer. Every once in a while there'd be a little fight take place; somebody'd bust a beer bottle over somebody's head, or hit somebody with a six-shooter.[21]

Early Deane, who came to the Sour Lake oil fields in the late fall when it got cold at night, remembered the workers sleeping around the gas flares to keep warm. At first some of them got arrested for being vagrants. But they weren't vagrants, just men looking for work during the day and a warm place to sleep at night. Idle or off time brought on the carousing. "There was a lot of drinking, lots of fighting. But they'd get back on the job the next day or two. They'd 'take Christmas off,' they called it. I saw one fellow around Valentine's Day and he was drunk and I said, 'My God, Bill, you drunk again?' He said, 'No, not again, I'm still taking Christmas.'"[22]

"GOD ALMIGHTY JUST WASHED THE OIL OFF INTO THE WOODS"

Bud Coyle's crew brought in the first well at Sour Lake that signaled the beginning of the boom there. Walter and Jim Sharp had made plans to come up there out of Beaumont and drill in the thicket before anyone else came looking: it was to be a clandestine operation.

It was about two o'clock in the afternoon that we left Beaumont with a good team of horses and a hack. We got on that road and broke two tracers, but we had some hitch ropes and we knew enough to take the hitch ropes and make new tracers out of them. Oh, that road [to Sour Lake] was terrible. We got there at two the next morning. It was about twenty miles, something like that. And we had a well up and going the next morning. We called it Roche #3.

It was a big secret, because Jim Sharp didn't want anybody else to know about it. Some say the Gilbert well was the first to come in there, but we'd been using fuel off our well before they even cleared out that jungle to drill the Gilbert well. Tom Smith and Charlie Dawson drilled it, and we had some two-inch pipe and it hit the cap, hit the pure-D cap rock. We did a fishing job on that well, had some three-inch pipe collars turned down so it'd go inside, but we didn't have any pipes to fit that collar, so Jim sent me after that.

He took me down to Pine Island Bayou and I got in an old boat with a paddle. I had to get to Nome to catch the train there. But the bayou was up and there was no train. So I had to pull off my clothes and wade another bayou, about waist deep. A fellow came along the road with a team, and took me on over to Big Hill. I got out there and Mr. Walter Sharp was there. I told him what we needed and he said he'd go with me. We got out to the pipes but there wasn't any there that we could use. Now there was a junk dealer named Martin that Walter had known up in Corsicana, and Martin had a place at Spindletop. So we went over there and Mr. Sharp made Martin haul that pipe over to the depot, and told him what we'd do to him if he ever got caught with pipe again.

We got over to Sour Lake about four in the morning and it was raining torrents. We opened that well up and estimated it'd make around 5,000 to 7,000 barrels a day. So we shut it off and buried it with sand. Nobody ever knew a thing about it. God Almighty took care of us. He just washed the oil off down in the woods there in the rain. Nothing but a bear could get into that thicket. And that was the first well drilled at Sour Lake, the first finished cap rock well.

Bud Coyle stayed at the Sour Lake Springs Hotel during the boom days when he wasn't on Big Hill or working out at the Sharps' camp. "The front part of [the hotel] had a big old canopy that they drove the hacks under. Long porch and a two-story building and a health resort. It's a wonder to me that everybody who went there and drank that water didn't die. It was nothing on God's green earth but the worst kind of seep water. There was a little old lake, why, it wasn't as big as a fish pond. A little kind of artificial hole. But you could take a beer bottle and knock the bottom out of it and stick it down in that mud and set it afire. And it'd burn until the wind blew it out."[23]

As the boom erupted, so too the rig accidents came right along as they had on Big Hill, and would again at Saratoga and Batson Prairie. And the gas—explosions and poisoned air—were once more the rig worker's worst nightmare. There was the infamous Shoestring District at the Sour Lake fields, dozens of wooden derricks built side by side, built too hastily and too close together. Destroying the pressure below and the air above, the Shoestring took lives as well. "I was drilling a well there," says Bert Stivers, "and my partner was outside the derrick watching me. I told him to motion to me if the derrick started weaving too much. Well, he didn't notice, I guess, and the whole thing fell over with me in it, fell all over me. I just laid down flat and waited and then started crawling out. Didn't get a scratch on me. My wife was in the house not seventy-five feet from that derrick. She heard it fall and she came out screaming. But I told her I was all right."[24]

"I was working one time for Mr. Condon partnered with D. F. Sims and the Sims Oil Company," Frank Hamilton tells the story.

And we were working on a separator, just a big drum that we laid there on the ground. Had a six-inch nipple and six-inch L, then a long nipple about six feet. We dug pits and dropped this L down in there and put another piece of pipe down for the suction. We were using cypress and redwood tanks. And someone left that L loose and when they shot a six-inch stream of oil through there we saw it was loose, and someone hollered to shut off the valve. And this fellow bent over to cut the valve off and when he did the gas caught fire, ignited, tore that L loose, burned him so you couldn't recognize him.

We turned the steam on the fire to blow it out and then we went look-ing for him. We found him under a tree where he'd crawled. He didn't have any feet. Nothing but bones. I got out there to him and he asked for a drink of water. Someone said not to give him any 'cuz it might kill him, but a driller named Johnny spoke up and said to just give him the water, he was gonna die anyhow. He didn't last long, that black flesh just falling off of him. We wrapped him in a sheet and got some quilts and mattresses to put him in a wagon, but he died before we started out. Inhaled that fire right down into his lungs. A terrible thing.

There was no safety, nothing safe. Even when we tuned up a well, run rods in the well, we still didn't have any safety. Elevators on the top hook were liable to fall off any time, and the whole thing go down and you just had to be sure you got clear.[25]

Deadly gas was one of the few things that frightened the tough oil field worker. Charlie Jeffries explains.

That region is sulphurous, and the gas that comes out of the wells is highly impregnated with the mineral. As the pressure was enormous, forc-ing out millions of cubic feet of the poisonous fumes daily, it rendered the place highly dangerous. The fresh gas from the wells, less diffused and highly impregnated with sulphur, that's what the workers dreaded. This kind had hardly any scent, but it was as deadly as a murderer. Its effect when breathed was much like that of chloroform. If a person, or any other living animal, inhaled a few strong breaths of it, he would fall over uncon-scious; and if he lay in it and continued to breathe it, he would die as surely as if chloroformed.

One evening we were working at a bad well. We were pulling pipe and the gas was coming out of the hole, looking like hot air rising from a boiler. We would work awhile until we had as much of the gas as we could stand, then go away a few yards and breathe good air awhile, and then come back and go to work again. I had done this many times during the evening, and after awhile, on getting an extra strong dose, I started for air again. It happened that as I walked away a little breeze blew the gas straight after me, and I drew another breath or two. That proved too much. I got to the edge of the derrick floor, and I remember putting out my hand trying to reach a post for support, but I could not reach it. Over into the mud I went. Next thing I remember, the crew was carrying me out to safety.

I remembered back in mythology that some god or demigod dug out with a stake the eyes of Polyphemus [*sic*], and in my heightened imagination, I reckoned that he suffered no worse than I was suffering right then. When morning came, the men of the place looked at me, and they said I had as bad a case of gassed eyes as they had ever seen. Indeed, they must have been a sight, swollen and red like those of a crawfish, and with tears running out of them like rain.[26]

Hamilton also experienced the poison gas. "It was awful dangerous, you had to watch it especially at night. I was pumping three wells with steam and we'd watch the gas pressure and the gas would get close to the surface and it'd look like smoke. You had to lay down on the ground, generally wet a handkerchief and put it over your nose to keep the gas out of your lungs. I was blind one time for twenty-one days. Had to go to Galveston and open my eyes under water. Stayed in a darkened room the whole time. I know a man named Jack Finnigan and a boy died one night out there in the oil field. We found them the next morning. One fellow had tried to drag the other fellow out of there. Didn't make it out."[27]

Sam Webb and Ed Cotton agree on the horrors of the poison gas that would come up out of those wells. "It'd kill you in a minute if you stayed in it long enough," says Webb. "But the main trouble was going blind. It felt like taking a handful of hot sand or salt and throwing it up in your eyes, felt like that for days at a time. Best thing in the world was a salt solution just as hot as you could bear it, but you thought it'd kill you when you first put it on your eyes. You'd just have to stand it. Scraped Irish potatoes was another thing they used."

"When they brought in the biggest well, they called it The Wild One," recalls Cotton. "When it blew in it was making poison gas, and it came over the town. I was sleeping at the Jordan place and I heard the screaming and I got up and closed the windows down in the house. You could hear people screaming and hollering down there. I had never been on a battlefield, but the town looked like one when I went there after the gas was gone. Dead dogs, dead chickens, cats and horses. Didn't see any people dead but a lot of them with their heads tied up and people leading them around: they were blind. And there was some livestock, horses, just wandering around blind, bumping into things."[28]

"Employers paid good wages for what those boys had to do," Charlie Jeffries concludes, "and slam, bang, clang, they had to have results. *Hence firemen with eyes so badly gassed they could hardly see the steam gauges worked around boilers; hence well crews worked with old rattletrap outfits that were liable any minute to fly to pieces and knock them to kingdom come; hence men worked in the top of derricks, hanging on with one hand, straining with the other to the limit of their muscles to adjust something that had gone wrong."*[29]

MOOCH FRANK

The fascinating characters that appeared on Big Hill were anything but exclusive to that boom. In fact, from California to the Klondike to Batson Prairie, remarkable personalities made their mark on the recollections of those who relive the past, and on the people with whom they came in contact. One of those characters was Mooch Frank, whom Sheriff Billy Bryant remembers as "the best woman fighter I ever saw. We called her Mooch. She was from Cripple Creek, Colorado. And she was every man's hero because she'd come out under her own power, get to drinking, and she was a good fist fighter."

But Frank Hamilton remembers another side of Mooch.

> She was a great character, a pretty woman, a real fighter. She got her name because if any roughneck or pipe liner would get sick and didn't have any money, she'd go out and mooch off the oilmen there. Didn't make any difference who he was, the oil producers were mostly good-hearted men and they'd give her a dollar or more. She'd get enough and go get some doctor and some medicine and food. Out in "the jungle" [the edge of the Big Thicket] she'd cook up some beef and potatoes, and a lot of coffee.
>
> Mooch was a farm girl, did some farming even out there in "the jungle." Later she picked up with another woman, everyone called her Frenchy. She was a redhead, real fighter. Later Mooch died over at Shreveport, and a lot of the oil producers heard about it and they all chipped in and gave her a fine burial. She died from dope, she'd become a dope fiend, and she was in jail. They must've cut her off from the dope and she died in jail. She'd gotten older, and she'd led an awful hard, fast life.[30]

And there was Six Shooter Kate, Jack Ennis's girlfriend according to Early Deane. Kate and Jack spent a lot of time together, but not all of it was happy. In fact, most remember the two spent as much time fighting as they did making up. One night they got in a rip-roaring argument about nothing in particular, and Kate pulled one of her pistols on her erstwhile boyfriend. When he refused to back off from his stance on whatever issue had flared up, she pointed her gun at him right across the table and fired! It missed—most said she knew what she was doing at the moment—and the bullet went right through the wall and into the adjoining bar, missing a complete stranger by inches.

Ed Cotton tells about one of the several times Kate found herself in jail. This time, for whatever reason, Jack Ennis was nowhere to be found: it may have been soon after the shooting! At any rate, she was whining and crying in the jail for somebody to please let her out. Now she was a real beauty according to most of the workers who knew her, and the pitiful sight of her whimpering finally got to an impressionable young man named Adolph Trumley. Young Trumley, about twenty and apparently smitten, strode purposefully from the jail window back to his father's blacksmith shop, got a ball peen hammer and a chisel, went back and broke the lock off Kate's barred door. Kate walked away; Trumley spent a year in jail.[31]

Ed Cotton remembers another character known in Sour Lake as Old Black Cat Jim. "His real name was Jim Morgan, and he owned a bunch of pigs, had a sow that brought some nice pigs, kept them out back of his café, The Black Cat. Well, they died of some disease one night, and the next morning he found them dead and he just threw them over a fence into the thicket. Now Old Joe, another character and a cook at the French Market, was walking by and he stopped and asked Jim what he was doing. And he told him. And Joe asked if he could have those dead pigs, and Morgan said he could. Later that day Black Cat Jim went into town and he saw those pigs in the Market window, with apples in their mouths, all baked up and for sale!"

Speaking of "good eatin'," Cotton says, "everybody ate real good in those days. Lots of beef and steaks, and the prices were good. Big heavy breakfasts of French fried potatoes, steak, eggs. We slaughtered beef and hogs every day, took them razorbacks right off the prairie and out of the thicket, sold them to the French Market. They sold squirrels two for a quarter. You could buy a box of those old time black powder shells for 45 cents, but you hardly ever missed a squirrel with them, that's for sure. Killed every kind of waterfowl, ducks, geese."[32]

And then, of course, there was Dr. Mud. Old Bazile was no longer sturdy when the boom came to Sour Lake. Most described him as tall and thin, gaunt, bent over, hobbled, and so on. He wore a silly white top hat that Houstonian J. Brooks Hamilton presented him one year while rehabilitating at the spa. Hamilton had it left over from the 1892 presidential race when Grover Cleveland won a second term. Somewhere along the way Old Bazile added a long-tailed coat, fancy pants much too short for his gangly legs, a rickety cane and a scraggly beard.

Dr. Mud gained quite a reputation during the forty years he worked at the spa as an entertaining storyteller. He bragged of his activities as a black soldier in the Union army and of his exploits in early Texas, none of which was true, of course. One favorite story went something like this:

> One day Elder Sam Green and I was walking along in the Big Thicket, and I asked him what he would do in a time of danger. "Kneel down and pray," was his answer. About this time I looked up and saw a big ole black she-bear coming out of the woods. "What did you say you would do in a moment of danger?" I asked again. "Kneel down and pray," said the elder. The bear saw us and started charging down the trail. I hollered once more, "What does you do in a moment of danger?" "Why, you just have to kneel down and pray," Elder Sam replied. "No, suh, Elder," I shouted as I started running. "Prayin' might be all right at a prayer meetin', but it ain't nuthin' at a bear meetin'!"[33]

Dr. Mud sold mudpack beauty treatments to improve a woman's complexion, and several concoctions meant to alleviate a variety of "female ills." He sold the women different types of face powder, most of which came from chalky deposits around the Big Thicket. John Little went to him once bothered with a skin cancer. "He'd go out in the woods and find something and mix it up and sell it to me, or anybody who'd come along, I guess. Sometimes it'd cure and sometimes it wouldn't. So he said to me, 'Take this can of mud and rub it all over you, and sit down there in the sun an hour or two.' So I did. And he came around later and said, 'Now go down to that pool yonder and bathe it off.' That pool had sulphur water bubbling up out of the bottom of it, smelled terrible. But I went. Came back and wanted to pay him for the treatment, but he laughed and bowed and said, 'Oh no, Suh. You don' owe me nuthin'. Why, you're an oil magnet.'"

Bud Coyle says the oil companies became curious about Dr. Mud when he would come back to the spa all covered with oil. "So they put scouts on him, followed him out into the woods to see where he was getting that oil. Never did come to anything. And some said he'd sneak out there at night into the thicket, but I don't think he ever did such a thing. I don't think you could've pulled him into those woods at night with an ox team!"

Loither Adams writes that Dr. Mud changed his name to "Old Doctor Mud the Indian" sometime during the boom days because more and more of the patrons at the spa refused to be treated by a black man. But he was always good-natured about it and never had any real trouble. In fact, by all accounts Old Bazile got along well with the ladies. John Little recalls that Dr. Mud would go down where the black girls were "and you could hear them giggling and hollering, 'Now you get out of here. You jest git.'" And there is the popular tale of his encounter with three women from New Orleans—and likely others as well—visiting the spa. When they asked about beauty treatments, he was wont to say, 'Now I'll give you ladies a treatment if you want, but my goodness you sure don't need it!' Quite a charmer, Dr. Mud, right to his dying day in 1903.[34]

Racial incidents occurred in the boom towns, although for the most part they were few and far between, partly because the two cultures kept themselves separate from one another, and partly because for many in southeast Texas their history went back several generations getting along, albeit including the antebellum slavery days. When the Reverend H. S. Gearow organized a boycott of the segregated Beaumont streetcars in 1904, he was met with only lukewarm support, and little change took place. African Americans were not allowed to work in the oil fields, except for the occasional hack driver or teamster making deliveries; for their part, most blacks much preferred working in the sawmills than the uncertain and dangerous oil patch.

Jim Kinnear recalls a serious incident, however, in Sour Lake.

> Some of the oil field workers said they were going to run all the Blacks out of town. They chased them out and I mean the Blacks scattered like birds leaving a cornfield. Then the mob went down to old Ed Ketchum's camp. He was ex-chief of police in Galveston, tough as a boot. They asked him if he had any Blacks working for him, and he said he did. The mob said they were going to run them out of there, and Ketchum said, "Listen, boys, these men are doing work for me that none of you would do and I'd like for you to leave them alone."
>
> Ketchum went into town and bought some birdshot for his shotgun. When the mob returned to run off his workers, old Ed went into his tent, picked up one of those old repeating shotguns, and hollered, "Now you fellows either treat, trade, or travel right now." He fired a shot into them and they broke and run. Never did have any more trouble. But some of the Black women hid out in the woods for awhile 'til they got eat up by the mosquitoes. They came over to the depot and got on the train. When

some men came over to them, they said, "Don't shoot us. We're going to Beaumont."[35]

"A BULLET HOLE RIGHT THROUGH MY STETSON"

A Black man went to court accused of shooting at another man. In the trial a lawyer asked the victim what happened. "Well, that fella pulled a gun on me and I started running. I heard the gun fire and I heard the bullet pass right by me." "Are you absolutely sure you heard that bullet pass you?" asked the lawyer. "Yes, Suh. I heard it twice: once when it passed me and agin when I passed it."[36]

"Got into a little fuss one night, a misunderstanding," relates John Little:

I was standing there in the saloon and the bartender hit this fellow over the head with a beer bottle. The fellow started after the bartender but we held him back. The little city attorney showed up and told us to take the man to the "calaboose." So the night watchman took the fellow out of the saloon and marched him down the street toward the jail. Along the way the fellow claimed he wasn't drunk and he'd pay his fine the next day. So they went into a restaurant so the man could make bond. While they were there the city attorney came in and asked why the man wasn't in jail yet, and the night watchman told him.

The city attorney got mad and grabbed the man to take him on to jail. And when he did the fellow jumped back to get away, and the city attorney pulled his gun to hit the fellow over the head, but the gun went off. And everybody in the place drew their guns! Well, everything calmed down, and the next morning I saw the fellow getting out of jail. I said, "You sure got into it last night." And he said, "Yeah, ruined my hat, too. Look, there's a bullet right through my Stetson."[37]

Ed Cotton witnessed one of the most famous brawls ever to take place in Sour Lake—and no men were involved except as rapt spectators. "They called the one woman Swamp Angel and the other one was Jew Annie. They got into an argument, and they started to fight. Sheriff Billy tried to stop them, and then the county attorney came along. He came up with a proposition: that the two women fight it out and the one that gets whipped pays the fine for both of them. Well, they went to fighting and after awhile Swamp Angel whipped Jew Annie. It was some fight, and after it was over the county attorney just let them both go."[38]

Sheriff Billy Bryant had more than his share of trouble. "A boy and I tied up one night. We were in a dance hall maybe forty feet long and next to the saloon which was that long, too. Well, we got to wrestling down on the floor and neither of us could stay on top of the other. I got one of my fingers in his mouth and we started rolling. Rolled clear across that dance floor and through the saloon and outside into the street. There was a horse and buggy hitched at the rack, and we rolled under the horse, and he jumped and run and rolled that buggy right over us! We caused quite an excitement, that horse running loose through the street and all. Was a good fight, though, except I didn't like much that he nearly bit off my finger."[39]

J. A. Rush came to the Sour Lake oil fields at the age of twenty-four. He remembers the holidays there in those boom days. "I went into town on Christmas Eve. I was batching it during the holidays. Everybody was using their pistols instead of fireworks, shooting off into the air and everywhere. Well, I had to get down on the ground and crawl through the town! There was a fellow across the street from me got shot full of buckshot during the festivities. We got him to the doctor, but he died. Doc testified later that he'd died of a hemorrhage. I think that would've given him a hemorrhage, all right."[40]

> Brains and Eggs
> Boil brains until tender. Remove skins and cut into pieces. Cook in butter until done. Season to taste with salt and pepper.
> Liver and Lights
> Cut liver and lungs into small pieces. Cover with cold water. Add 1 chopped onion and salt to season. Simmer for approximately 2½ hours. Serve with sweet potatoes, greens, and corn bread.
> Pigtails and Turnip Greens
> Clean pigtail thoroughly, cut into sections, salt and pepper to taste, and brown in shortening. Add 1 cup water, cover and simmer slowly for about 1½ to 2 hours or until tender. Serve with turnip greens.
> "Now you got the right scald."[41]

SARATOGA

Hog Killin' Days came with the first blue norther in the late autumn. Aunt Matt—Mattie Naney Evans—was one of the many women of

Saratoga who took part in the annual festival; afterward, far fewer wild rooters were left to roam the Big Thicket countryside. Mattie Jordan had come to the Big Thicket as a child when her family moved there from Alabama, grew up in that wild country, and watched with amazement as it got wilder when oil was struck. Her father, Thomas C. Jordan, gave each of his children 100 acres of land to get in on the oil boom if they wanted; Mattie was a lot more interested in the man who had come to court her. "Nothing to it," she recollects. "I went out of my room into the front room and the justice of the peace married us, and that was all there was to it. We wanted to do it, and not tell nobody nothing about it, but they found out and threw a big *shivaree,* cakes, wine, and stuff. And a whole bunch of people came and we danced all night."

After the wedding, Mattie knew what she wanted, and it wasn't land. She wanted to run a hotel for the booming town, and she got her wish. The Hotel Saratoga, as Doc Stoker remembered it, was operating throughout those wild rush days, although somewhere in the midst of all the confusion it became popularly known as The Vines, likely because of the very same vegetation that covered its walls and fences.[42]

Saratoga had its share of excitement after the first gushers came in east of Pine Island Bayou, as thousands of boomers marched through. Uncle Ben Hooks brought in two wells, the second a gusher on March 13, 1902. The Southern Pacific Railroad bought up 320 acres and started its own Rio Bravo Oil Company. J. M. Guffey and what soon became Gulf Oil brought in a 10,000-barrels-a-day well in 1903. The famous Teel Acre was in Saratoga: a man with a one-acre lease drilled gushers on all four corners of his tiny property causing a general uproar and second boom! The ingenuity on the Saratoga fields included significant advances over Spindletop, including giant levees set up as earthen holding tanks, and the first known use of screens at the bottom of a well.[43]

The boomers came from every direction, and plenty of them had just picked up over at Big Hill or Sour Lake. Many brought their wives and children, who pitched tents next to the oil fields; many more brought the disorder, the violence, the gambling, and the drinking. Saratoga erupted so fast that it had no jail to accommodate the rogue activity. It became one of the first oil towns where the deputies simply handcuffed rowdy citizens to trees, a pattern popularized on Batson Prairie soon thereafter. Although that boom town—it would soon explode nine miles west of the little spa community—overshadowed every chaotic spot in the history of Texas soon enough, for a time all eyes were on Saratoga.

Mattie Evans tells the sad story of her neighbors, Mr. and Mrs. Whitt.

Somebody walked over to their house one day and just shot him. Shot him right where he stood and he fell over on his back. And I heard the shots and went to see what had happened. I saw a friend of mine and I asked her if she had heard the shots and she said, No she hadn't. She invited me in to have oysters and supper. About that time a little boy came running up and shouted, "Mama! Mama! Mr. Whitt got shot!" We all run over there and there he was lying on his back, and Mrs. Whitt was screaming and hollering. She had a big skirt on, and she unbuttoned that skirt—she had it on top of something else—and she pulled it off and put it under his head for a pillow. His pistol was lying there beside him. He never had a chance to use it.

Mrs. Whitt took the pistol off the ground and stood up beside her dead husband, and shouted, "I feel like killing everybody in Saratoga!" Uncle John Hart was there, and he took the pistol away from her and just said, "Now, take him over to Mattie's to lay him out. He loved Miz Mattie." And they brought him up to the hotel and laid him out in a front room. And we kept him all night, and the next day they ordered a coffin and took him over to Beaumont. They buried him in Beaumont.[44]

Ed Cotton was walking down the Saratoga street once "and I heard a shot and I looked up and I saw a fellow running for his wagon and he drove off. And I followed him and he went to Doc Stoker's office and went inside and announced he'd been shot. But Doc Stoker wasn't there, so a man told him to lie down until the doctor arrived. When Doc finally came in he asked the man where he'd been shot. And the man pulled his shirt off and said, 'I've been shot in the back.' The doc saw the hole in his back and so he probed around for awhile and finally said he couldn't find the bullet in there. 'Well,' says the man, 'that's all right, anyway. It don't hurt me now.' And he pulled his shirt back on and tucked it in his trousers and started on his way. Asked the doc if he owed him anything and Doc says, 'No, I haven't done anything for you.' The man drove off in his wagon. Lived sixty more years."[45]

Doc Stoker, "oil field medico," came to Saratoga after the fire on Big Hill, and found himself one of the only real medical practitioners—among a raft of quacks—at the edge of the Big Thicket. He remembers a number of unique characters there, and his own share of oil field experiences.

Irish stew was a favorite of the workers who ate where I did, over in the cook shack behind the hotel. And I have to admit I got so much of it that after awhile I could hardly look an Irishman in the face. But by far the most interesting eating place in the field was a long shed on the other side of the creek where a large Black woman fed the gamblers, whores, and pimps of the town. She was about five feet tall, five and a half feet around, and blacker than night, except for the glistening white of her eyes and teeth. She had a voice like a siren comparable to that of a fog horn. When she hollered "Come and git it," it seemed she was talking to the entire town.

One day she got real sick and they sent for me. When I got to her bedside, she confessed that if she died she didn't think she'd get to Heaven because she'd been "cooking for all these bad women." She got well, but it wasn't long after that she was back cooking for those same "bad women" again. She sent for me a few days later, but when I got there she took me into a small tent where a beautifully set table awaited me: clean, white cloth, and on it was a platter of golden brown fried chicken with all the trimmings, such as I had not seen for many a day. It was her token of appreciation for my keeping her a while longer on this earth.

One afternoon I was called on a labor case to a woman who lived in a tent by the fields. Just a few yards away a fight broke out in another tent filled with gamblers. A knife appeared and one of the men was slashed—deep—across his belly. I heard the sounds of the brawl but had paid little attention, since the baby was coming at that same moment. Just as the infant made its appearance in the world, so too the slashed man stumbled into the tent, holding his intestines in place with two bloody hands! Somehow I managed to deliver that baby while shouting instructions for the wounded man to be carried over to my office. I don't know how it happened to come out the way it did, but they all survived the day!

I remember a man who called himself just "Mac," said he was a sporting man from Beaumont. I had heard of his reputation as a gunslinger in Texas. He came to my office one day to announce his intentions of building "one of the finest gambling houses in this part of the country," commiserating with me at the same time as he noted, "Doc, you are out of your class with this bunch of sons-of-bitches, and so am I. You and I are university graduates, but things are about to get rougher here than anything you have ever seen or heard about before."

Well, he built a large saloon, a gambling house, and a whorehouse within a block of my office. On opening night he invited the public to be his guests and drink all the whiskey they wanted "on the house." By ten o'clock the place was full and by midnight everyone was drunk. Oil men were gambling away fortunes, girls were slipping money out of drunkards' pockets, and arguments turned into fights all over the place. Mac went about trying to stop the fights, and when anyone refused he'd knock them on the head with his old black .45 pistol. And, of course, his bouncers carried the unconscious and the injured to *my* office!

I did not get to bed the night of his opening.[46]

THE MILLION DOLLAR PHOTOGRAPH

One last tale from Sour Lake and Saratoga: a Mr. Craig came to town to establish a photography studio and purchase an oil lease. Papa Stephen Jackson's daughter (also named Stephen!) wanted her picture taken with the famous Dr. Mud, but the exorbitant price was more than her father intended to pay. Instead, Jackson offered Craig one harmless acre of land to take the photo; he agreed and the picture was made. In May, 1903, Walter Sharp and the Savage brothers brought in Wirt No. 1, the biggest gusher ever drilled in Sour Lake. Soon after, an even larger well came in at a stupendous flow of over 18,000 barrels a day. Its name? Craig No. 1. A million-dollar well, a million-dollar photo.[47]

With Sour Lake and Saratoga adding to the peculiar mix that was the Spindletop Era, discovery of the coarse oil beneath the Texas salt dome now began to spread westward to a wide prairie at the edge of the coastal plains. This was Batson Prairie, and it would inherit both the good and the raucously bad from its boom town predecessors. Of the memories that carried down through the century by those who lived out those days, Batson Prairie repeatedly laid claim as the worst of them all, the "coarsest place in Texas."

8

The Coarsest Place in Texas

Bill Douglas stepped gingerly over the fallen tree trunk, his eye cast warily on the clearing ahead of him. The judge let his boot fall silently on the soft needles that covered the ground like a brown carpet. He had discovered this spot some weeks earlier, and had found signs of wild game—droppings, rubs, a scrape—in the vicinity. Tracks marked the wet soil at the edge of the tiny meadow. The shot he could take would be no more than sixty yards.

The judge sat on the trunk and rested his rifle across his lap. He dug his boot toes into the spongy ground for leverage and waited. An hour went by, and a second. Nothing moved. Even the breeze could not wrest its way into the thicket. Douglas's right leg went to sleep, and he carefully, slowly, pulled it up and crossed it over his knee to give it a quick massage. He glanced down casually at his feet. The toe of his boot was covered with an oily sand where he had dug below the pine needles. He bent down for a closer look.

Paraffin soil?

A Beaumont chemist confirmed Douglas's suspicions. Two years later, William L. Douglas and Stephen W. Pipkin organized the Paraffine Oil Company with money from Beaumont businessman William Wiess. They began drilling on October 22, 1903.[1]

BATSON PRAIRIE

From 1891 to 1898 the little town west of Pine Island Bayou called itself Otto, after an early settler in that area. There was a post office bearing that name, a church and two schools by 1897. The schools belonged to a rural district named Batson Prairie after the first settlers, brothers who farmed the land in 1840. There were sixty-eight students.

On October 31, 1903, while the sleepy little community continued apace, the Paraffine Oil crew hit oil at 790 feet. Judge Douglas's belief that paraffin soil, a hydrocarbon alkane compound, was an indicator of petroleum proved correct. The first well produced barely 600 barrels a day; a second, drilled in December, produced 4,000 barrels out of the sandstone at a depth of 1,000 feet. Paraffine's Well No. 3 broke through the cap rock below and gushed at 10,000 barrels.

By this time, in only eight weeks, others had already begun exploration of the area one-half mile north of the Otto post office, including the J. M. Guffey Company making its way up the bayou from Big Hill to Sour Lake to Saratoga. Guffey's Brooks No. 1 came in at a staggering 18,000 barrels a day in January, 1904. By March 4, dozens of rigs were operating in flush production, many crammed up against each other as they vied for the ideal spot where the next gusher would make a man an instant millionaire. On that day alone an estimated 150,000 barrels of Texas crude were pumped to the surface of Batson Prairie—and the little town had moved to the edge of the oil field and changed its name![2]

AT THE END OF THE CORDUROY ROAD

"There was a low flat between the town proper and the field and one man built a walk across so that people could walk without going through all that mud. And right out in the middle of that walk he built a saloon, and anybody who went from the town to the field had to go right through it. Naturally they'd stop and get a cold one when they went through there. I thought that was pretty smart."[3]

Mrs. Ethel Stivers traveled from Ohio to Missouri to Batson Prairie as a newlywed, and her recollections provide a wonderful perspective of those early days from a woman's point of view. She was nineteen.

> We went into Beaumont and bought our furniture and our dishes, and Mr. [Bert] Stivers moved us into a four room house. It was just a shack, but it had four rooms, and I cleaned it top to bottom before we moved anything into it. I was just thrilled to be in Texas because I had never been out of Ohio until then and had always wanted to go someplace. I was very much pleased with everything, except the house at first. We bought one

bed and a rocking chair and two dining chairs and a set of dishes and some stag-handled knives and forks. The dishes cost $15 for 100 pieces. I put up some lace curtains and made the house look livable. Bare pine floors and a wood cook stove.

We started up a Sunday School and we had Sunday School every Sunday and finally got a preacher to come out every once in awhile and we'd have preaching. Big crowds would come, women and children. We built a little building after awhile. Everyone was real liberal with their money those days. And the women got together and went around to the different oil companies and raised money to build the church. And the church was real interdenominational. There were Catholics there and they'd worship with us. We used old Methodist hymnals and we'd sing old songs like "Bringing in the Sheaves." Didn't have any instruments or soloists, but everyone seemed to know the old hymns.

There were oxen everywhere because they could go places the mules couldn't. And there were black bears and deer all over because we lived so near the thicket. At night the people let their oxen loose and they wandered everywhere and would sleep right up against our house. One night I'd been up with a neighbor's sick baby and I was coming home well after midnight. It was real dark and stormy and then there was a huge strike of lightning, and it lit everything up and I was standing in the midst of a bunch of those oxen! It frightened me so that I screamed like a panther. They wouldn't have hurt me, but they sure scared me. I got to my yard in a hurry.

There was a man would come around with all kinds of vegetables in a little wagon and he also carried some canned goods. And another man took a big hay wagon and built a screened room on it and set up a meat market right in that wagon. There was an ice man who came every other day: we had an icebox in the house. And if we needed more groceries than all that, we'd have to go into Batson. But I was always afraid because there were so many saloons there: I would never go alone.

Batson was so overpopulated. And it was always muddy there. It was five miles from Batson over to Saratoga. The roads were built out of pine logs to get up above the mud. They would lay two logs parallel and then would lay split logs with the flat side down. They weren't even bolted together, and we'd bump along on the rounded sides. It was called a corduroy road. The horse would just walk all the way. And the trees were so thick they would strike us in the face, so we had to keep our arms up to keep those limbs away. One time when Mr. Stivers' mother came to visit us a limb struck her and cut her right across the face.

Meat was very cheap there in Batson. Steaks and most cuts of beef and pork were about 8 or 10 cents a pound, and we could buy bear meat and venison. I bought one bear roast but didn't care much for the taste. Very sweet and dark. We ate plenty of venison; there was a boy lived nearby who would go into the thicket and shoot deer and he'd give us the hindquarters, didn't cost us anything then.[4]

Lillian Prince Webb came to Batson as a wide-eyed bride herself.

We named one of the little shacks where we lived Castle Crannie Crow, after the child's game: you'd sit in a swing and sing "Chickama, chickama, crannie crow, went to the well to wash my toe. What time is it, old lady, do you know?" Lived in an old dog[-run] house, they called them. Lived out on the prairie once, 3½ miles from town, no neighbors, nothing. I called it Webb's Corral and made up an address: 711 Coyote Trail, Deep in the Heart of Texas. There were two trails went by and the coyotes would come along yapping at sundown, go into town for awhile, then come back out again around two in the morning. Coyote Trail.

My husband Sam went deer hunting in the thicket and killed his first deer. Brought the meat into town to Old Jim O'Leary. He was a character, an old Irishman, grandest old man that ever was. He always called me Baby Girl. And there was a dance we were all at and O'Leary came over to sit a spell and he asked if we had eaten that meat he processed for us. "Yes," I said real loud, "we got the venison." And he said, "SShhh! Shut your mouth, Baby Girl!" Well, I didn't know Sam had killed that deer out of season. They killed deer around there all the time, it seemed like. Ice the meat down and bring it into town. Deer, squirrels, turkeys, anything you wanted. And go down to the river and catch crabs all day long. And if you could get into that thicket, there was the biggest blackberry bushes you've ever seen; and cane twenty-five feet high, cane brake after cane brake in there.[5]

"They had snakes in there, too," continues Ethel Stivers.

We saw men come out of the thicket with big flannel mouthed moccasins, eight or ten feet long, and they'd tied ropes around their necks to drag them out! We wouldn't go into the thicket, the alligators were so bad. Those big palms were fifteen feet high and the alligators would be in there. Very thick.

The mosquitoes were terrible. We had a mosquito bar over our bed, a regular canopy, and at night when we went to bed we put a smoke pot under the bed and let it smoke real good and then we'd shake the mosquito bar real good. Then we'd rub a little kerosene on our bodies and we'd go to bed. Then about midnight we'd get up and do it all over again! Those small mosquitoes would go right through the screen. And you could hear the sand fleas hopping around on the straw matting on the floor. The children had a terrible time with mosquitoes and chiggers. We'd take coal oil and soak a rag and hang it over the children's bed, because the smell would keep the mosquitoes away, for awhile.

The ladies didn't have much to amuse themselves. No card parties, no picture shows or anything like that. Sometimes we'd get together to work button holes and we'd spend a nice afternoon visiting and having refreshments. One year we had a Christmas tree and everyone exchanged gifts. And on Thanksgiving we decorated our house with palm leaves and holly and some kind of red berries we gathered down at the bayou. We had three big turkeys and a fruit cake and a white cake. And I made a fruit dish out of a meat platter, put a wire handle on it and covered it and had all kinds of fruits and homemade candy. We entertained all of Mr. Stivers' men and their wives and children. We draped moss from out of the woods over the rafters to decorate, made it look beautiful.

There were no doctors in Batson, only over at Liberty or in Beaumont. In many cases when a mother was giving birth we couldn't get the doctor out there in time. It was only a few miles but the roads were so bad. So the other wives would go over and care for her. Lots of children born before the doctor arrived.

The Black folks there were very superstitious, and had lots of homemade remedies for things. My oldest child had an earache and I tried everything but I couldn't ease the pain in his ear. There was a man named Old Smokey, a mule skinner and driver, and he came to my door one day and said, "Mrs. Stivers, if you just take a little wisp of wool and put it in his ear it will stop the earache." And I had tried everything else, so I took a wisp of wool and placed it in my son's ear and the ache went away and he went to sleep. And an old Black woman who worked for me told me whenever I was in trouble of any kind, or if the children were ill, to take an egg and bury it in a wet place. Whatever the trouble was would go away. I never did try that.

Maybe I should have. We went into Beaumont one time, and Mr. Stivers and I took our little white terrier dog with us in the buggy. We let him out so he could run. We came round a bend and there were two hundred wild Texas longhorns, a big old herd of wild steers. And that little terrier tore into them, barking and running at them. Those steers started pawing the earth and started up a stampede and they were coming right at us! That was one of the times I wished I was back in Ohio. Mr. Stivers grabbed up the little dog and we turned and ran for our lives to get away!

Four or five Black women would come by the house every day asking for work. They wanted to do washing; they carried that tub of water on their head and a bucket of water in each hand. They'd get rain water from the pond and walk just as steady as can be and never spill a drop. Carry it a half mile. One of the ladies I kept around, she was a great old mammy to my children. She was so good to the children. We'd pay her fifty cents a day, and we fed her whenever she was at the house. All she ate was fat meat and vegetables, black-eyed peas and fat bacon, and cornbread.

One time I remember we went to Liberty. I had been sitting up all night with a friend's sick baby, and the baby died. There was no cemetery in Batson, and the family was Catholic and there was no priest around. So we took the baby in a hack and I carried the little casket on my lap in the back seat. It was about nine miles but the roads were bad and it took such a long time to get there. We carried our lunch with us, found a priest, and the baby was buried. We ate our lunch and drove back home.

Sometimes they'd bury people just anywhere and there were no markers put up or anything. A lot of those who died were just transients, you know, and they'd get robbed and killed and just left anywhere. Somebody'd find them and carry them off and bury them somewhere. Or they might lay there all day in that hot weather. One I remember in particular lay beside the road all day and clear into the afternoon. Finally somebody came out from town with a big sheet and spread it over him, but they left him laying right there. We had to go around the body until the coroner finally came.

Batson was an awful town. There were so many lewd women, bad women, come in there. I've seen them cross the street to go upstairs at the Crosby House bar, and they wouldn't have an ounce of clothes on—just like they'd come into the world—and they were drunk coming right across the street in the rain and the mud, and up the stairs.[6]

Plummer Barfield recalls the hard lot of the prostitutes in Batson. "They'd get on dope and were always squabbling, lots of fighting, some killed, cut to pieces. One woman died in the depot waiting for the train to get out of there. They just carried her out and buried her in an un-marked grave. And the ladies wouldn't dare go into town. Majority of the roughnecks, they'd see a skirt on the streets, they took it for granted that they were all alike. Somebody's wife might be seen at the post office, but not much. Their kids, well, they didn't fare too rough. People just didn't pay any attention to them at all. Oh, sometimes they'd get hurt by a stray bullet or run over by a horse, maybe."[7]

"The [Texas] Rangers would come in to Batson," says Ethel Stivers, "and they'd clean it up and it would be decent for awhile. Then the gam-blers would come back and start up again. The Rangers would return, the judge would fine everybody $10 and they'd pay it and go back to what they'd been doing. The old judge made his money off the girls, too. Didn't have a jail most of that time. Just chain them up to a tree, men and women, six, seven, eight at a time."[8]

Harry Paramore moved from Spindletop to Batson in 1904, and agrees with Ethel Stivers's assessment of the situation there. "It was a pretty rough place. Had twenty-six saloons in a two-block area. Every one of them had a dance hall and a gambling hall connected with it. There were little concession stands along the sidewalks. The Rangers were there a lot, and they had a little jail for the women built of 2x4s laid flat with a hole in the roof for ventilation. The men, they'd just chain them to a tree. They chained a drunk to a tree one night and when he came to he just climbed the tree, rubbed the chain loose, and walked away."[9]

Preston Mowbray lived in Sour Lake but came over and worked at Batson for a time. "Gus Smith was a lease man, best one around. But he was always getting drunk, and so he'd be chained to a tree most every morning. There were so many wells there by then, and the pumps would break and only old Gus could fix them up right. There was many a time we'd be waiting at the well for Gus to get out of jail or pay his fine so we could get a pump fixed. His boss, Harry Lee, would come out and ask where Gus was. Someone would tell him and we'd go into town and get him off that tree."[10]

Jim Donohoe came to Batson late in its boom days and stayed at the Caledonia Boarding House. "You lay there in bed dodging the raindrops from the leaks. There was so much mud they'd clean the place out with a rake and a hoe. Charged $26 a month for that." He remembers that

> when the prostitutes would get rounded up and thrown in that little
> jail, some of the oil men came around and paid their fines. What they'd do

is go out and live together like they were man and wife. If you asked them if they were married, they'd tell you they had a "sawmill license." Probably no real married couples on the whole main street of Batson.

There were saloons everywhere. The Sarazac and Tom Matson's and the American Bar. Tom Thompson ran a saloon, so did One Quarter Lawson and Monk Fife. The Crosby House was the fanciest place. Doc Harris ran a saloon. He said he was a medical doctor but he never practiced there in Batson. Always wore a flashy vest, and a double watch chain. Kept a shooting iron on his hip. But he was a tender-hearted man all the same. A man named Jack Howard was killed and they brought the body to Doc Harris's place to get it ready for burial. And Howard's ten-year-old son came in and was just standing there by the body. And Harris said, "Gentlemen, you're welcome to leave this body here for now, but seeing as how this little boy is standing here by his father's corpse, what's going to be his impression when he grows up and remembers his father laying dead in a saloon?" They carried him out, and buried him later up in Corsicana.

"EVERY SOB IS HERE THAT COULD GET HERE"

"Mr. Brown ran a saloon on the north end of town," says Donohoe, "and he had a friend who was a gambler and stayed mostly at the south end of town where the gambling went on. The gambler decided to leave Batson and he went to say goodbye to Brown. Mr. Brown asked him how he had liked the place. 'Well,' replied the gambler, 'I wouldn't say that everybody in Batson is a son-of-a-bitch; but I would say that every son-of-a-bitch who could get here is here.'"[11]

Ed Cotton made his way to nearly all of the oil fields and boom towns during those early years, and served as a law enforcement officer for part of the time.

We'd have a round-up now and then in Batson. In those days there were about 33 saloons and gambling joints. There was the Turf Bar and the Crescent, the Standard Theatre and the Klondike. They had roulette, dice games, shaffle-up (that's where they'd put the dice in a leather box and shake it up and toss it from the box), bird cage gambling—all kinds. Each place had eight or ten gambling tables. We'd haul them in on Monday morning and fine them $12.50 each plus $25 for each table. They'd pay the fine and be back in business that night. There were about two hundred prostitutes there. A man would go in a saloon and have beer or whiskey,

then go to the vaudeville show around eight o'clock. After that the girls
would take him into the back and what not.

There was some music in the dance halls, of course. The women didn't
play or sing, they just danced. There was a Black string band, Old Griffin
and his band, and another place there was Kid Fiddler, and Sam Sauer and
Tom Ball also. They'd play everything, waltzes, square dance, two-step,
honky-tonk. Bob Moran was a blind piano player, good a player as there
ever was in Batson. And they had floor managers, what they called them,
big guys would arrange the dancing partners and break up fights. Old
Dutch Wells was one, and Big Mitch. He was about 6-4.

I saw two gamblers playing poker one night and they got to drinking
and arguing. One of them said he could beat the other in poker and quot-
ing the Bible, too! And the other one took that bet, because he said his
father was a Methodist minister and he knew every chapter of the Bible.
First guy bet him $10 he couldn't recite the whole Lord's Prayer, so they
put their money up with the bartender and started off. One guy said "*in*
earth as it is in heaven" and the other said that was wrong, it was "*on* earth
as it is in heaven." Well, they went off down the street still arguing who
was right, looking for someone who had a Bible. Seems to me, betting on
the Bible is a sin.[12]

Billy Bryant, sheriff over at Sour Lake and Saratoga, also spent some
time in the streets of Batson, though not always in law enforcement.

There was a time I got into the saloon business, called it the Turf Bar.
And I had seven men and a woman killed right in the front door of that
saloon. *'Course I hated to see the woman get killed.* She was killed by a boy
who was jealous of her. She was going to a party with someone else, so he
shot her and then shot himself. He was up at the top of the stairs when he
shot himself, and he rolled down the stairs and got wedged in between the
bottom step and the door. We couldn't get the door open from outside, so
we naturally thought he was just holding it, 'cause we'd push on it and it
wouldn't budge. So we finally got a ladder and went in upstairs, found him
like that.

We got a new constable come in there to Batson and he was a fine man,
but I didn't want him around my saloon. So I went to the justice of the
peace, Old Judge Crow, and I made him a proposition. I told him if he'd
keep that new constable away from my door—I didn't want anything bad
to happen to him, after all—why, every Monday morning I'd come to

court and pay a fine for fighting whether there was any fighting in my saloon. He laughed and said okay.[13]

Curt Hamill made his way to Batson Prairie with a wide reputation for the expertise he and his brothers had shown on Lucas No. 1, the gusher that started it all. He wasn't immune to the violence, though. "One night I was going over to town from my house and I passed by a boarding house and there was a man there quarreling with another man who was standing in the door. I passed on by and went into town, and when I came back by that man was laying there dead. The man inside just shot and killed him, left him laying there."[14]

Sam Webb brought Lillian to the wild west town of Batson in 1904. He worked in the oil patch and had some close encounters with the violence there.

One night Charlie Dawson, Pete Hamill, Bob Rose and I were out drinking and we had just come out of a saloon. It was raining and muddy; we were walking along the plank sidewalk about three feet wide, Charlie and me in front of the other two. We passed a Black man going the other way and stepped aside. Hadn't taken but a few more steps we heard a gunshot and Pete hollered, "Bob's been shot!" And Charlie turned and said, "You're joking." But sure enough Bob was on the ground. We took him inside and put him in a bed upstairs over the saloon. In a couple of days he died. Never did do anything about it, never did go looking for the man.

There never was much trouble in Batson between us and the Blacks there. Just skirmishes some, you know. Had a lot of them who were teamsters, and the boys would get out and fight with them some, more for fun than anything. Or there'd be some drinking and somebody'd start up.[15]

"There was an old Black man called Uncle Walsh," says Preston Mowbray. "He wasn't afraid of nobody. Well, the oil field workers went after him one time because he'd been hanging around the derricks, and chased him back to his house at the edge of the thicket. He grabbed his Winchester and crawled under his house, and they couldn't get him out of there. And his neighbor Hack Gainer came along and crawled under the house to get Walsh out. But Walsh handed Hack a shotgun and said, 'You better use this thing when they come again. You gonna die anyway; you might as well die shooting.'"[16]

Frank Hamilton, only eighteen when he came to Batson from Sour Lake, had a close shave. "There were a lot of hold-ups on the road, especially after pay day. We got paid in cash, not checks, you know. We didn't carry any guns on us, though, because the robbers would be liable to beat us to death with them! One time Johnny Palmer and I were walking on the road, right by the old tramp rail track, and I felt something in my back and I heard a voice—a woman's voice!—telling me to throw up my hands. We put our hands up, by golly, but we didn't have but thirty cents between us. She said she had a good mind to shoot us for wasting her time."[17]

"THAT BOLT WENT CLEAR THROUGH HIS HEAD"

"I was walking by the camp with Mrs. Irma Mitchell one day. She'd come along with her husband Mike from Spindletop to Sour Lake to Batson, and Mike was working for Wes Sturm. Well, Mike was arguing with another man, and he was cussing at him, it was really something to hear. And Mrs. Mitchell said, 'I never thought that man would be my husband.'"[18]

For all of the violence and rowdiness, there was actually some oil drilling that went on there at Batson Prairie, too! The crews that came to the west branch of Pine Island Bayou were considerably more experienced: most had been at one or two of the nearby oil fields already. Many of the men had been drilling now for about three years, and some crews had been together much of that time as well. Walter Sharp had one of the best crews around, along with Wes Sturm and Walter Fondren. They worked together smoothly, without the hindrance of "boll weevils" to slow them down.

Plummer Barfield recalls some other "experts" that made their way to Batson Prairie, "from West Virginia and Pennsylvania, exceptionally good looking at those cuttings in the mud bucket and telling you what it was and where it was at. They'd run that sand through their fingers and tell you what to do or not do. Didn't have shakers or chemical methods. They'd just put the sand in a fruit jar, put it in clear water, take a stick and stir it up. Finally a druggist hit upon the bright idea of using chloroform. They'd take those porous rocks that came up and put them in a bowl with chloroform, and that chloroform would force gas bubbles, and sometimes the oil would be showing. Guess a druggist knew a little more about chemicals than a roughneck. They'd be running around the oil field with a bottle of chloroform or high life or turpentine."[19]

And there may have been more families that came along, simply because there were more of the men married by this time. And a few kids could be seen running about on the prairie. Bud Coyle adds another story about Mike Mitchell. "Old Jess Lincoln and some old dead-pecks run one of them outfits. They laid two 1200-barrel tanks down flat and had a dance one night out in the field. Mike and I were over at Wes Sturm's camp, and there was this darned old dog been hanging around. Mike held the dog and I put a tin can on its tail, and we let it go. Durned thing ran right through that dance, scattered girls and boys everywhere."[20]

John Little remembers the time he worked for Mr. Walter Sharp just out of Batson. "He told us to move over to the Trinity River and drill there, and if we got oil he'd pay us each $300 a month. So I got us down to 600 feet and I was coming out of the hole and starting my blocks from above. I looked down from the elevator and I saw my pipes about four or five feet off. I knew something was wrong and I hollered at the man upstairs to hook on the swivel, but before he could it made a burst and threw water all over the derrick, and the pipe started going. Well, we ran in all directions. One fellow ran for his wife, she was nearby in their tent, and I ran for an open space. Sprained my ankle trying to get out of there. That thing blew 300 feet of six-inch pipe and rocks as big as three-gallon buckets. She whistled for about two hours, blowing mud up on top of the pine trees: you could hear it ten miles away. Mr. Sharp came by and told me to kill the well. Some greenhorn loosened a valve and I like to got my brains knocked out when it blew a hose off. Anyhow, we drilled to 900 feet but never got anything out of it but brown sand. Mr. Sharp just shut it down . . . and paid us each $200."[21]

Bert Stivers had a close call on a Batson rig. "I was with Fred Henderson and we were pulling the pipe ourselves and running the engine and he was tailing the rods out, laying them down on the walk. I hollered at him to pull it out so the hook would come down on what we called the headache post, so I could grab it: when I reversed the engines I could come right down that way. But the hook missed the first time. Second time I grabbed it but Fred didn't reverse the engine and the throttle went wide open and I just stepped right out into thin air, sixty-two feet up! He shut that engine off just before my hand would've gone right into that crown block. I'da fallen the whole way and it would have killed me, I guess. I was so scared I just held on to the side of the derrick and couldn't move. They had to get a ladder and come up after me, help me down. When I got to the ground, I said 'That's all the derrick work for me, boys.' Never got up on top of one again."[22]

The poisonous gasses that the Batson wells emitted proved just as deadly as at the other fields. J. A. Rush explains: "Trying to put the connections on a well and get a little too much of the gas. You just had to try and hold your breath until you could step out. Didn't have any controls then, all the gas just flowed on its own. Best you could do was to get it flowing through the separator to the tank, burn your gas there. Used valves and caps and so on."[23]

Billy Bryant concurs. "The Riley No. 1 came in and it gave off the poison gas. We picked up two dead men and dragged them for a long way, but two other guys got knocked out by the gas and we had to leave their bodies where they fell—never could get back to them in time. At the edge of town the gas had killed chickens and hogs, couple horses. Some of the people started moving out."[24]

"Those connections were frail back then," says Plummer Barfield, "and the pressure was 30,000 or 40,000 pounds [psi]. Whatever piece of pipe blew out, why it would go right through a man like a rifle ball. One time a six-inch L blew off a discharge line, went about 300 yards, bounced off a huge tree, glanced off into a tent and killed two women sitting in there drinking coffee. Slug of iron weighed six or seven pounds, went right through both of them."[25]

Adds Bert Stivers: "I had a fireman on a boiler on a lease we called the F&F, and Walter Fondren owned the adjoining lease. The boiler houses were about sixty feet apart. I was standing on the porch of my house about a half-mile away when I saw one of the boilers blow up and heard that explosion after. Boiler went 300 feet in the air. I had my baby rocking in my arms, and I hollered at my wife to take him, that one of my boilers had gone up. I don't even remember if I rode my horse or just ran the whole way. Fondren's fireman had been out of the way, but mine had been right at the boiler house, and it blew him to pieces. There was a bolt went clean through his head and spilled his brains out on the ground. We wrapped the body with soft line to be able to even pick it up: every bone in his body was broken. Buried him the next day."[26]

Lillian Webb offers a poignant postscript to the tribulations of the families of Batson Prairie.

> There was a family living there and one of the girls was a gypsy. They were from a tribe that had settled over in Beaumont, and they were very strict people. Her two brothers ran a saloon. One of the brother's children about seven years old became sick and died in just a few hours' time. I

went up to sit with the family that night, and the mother's grief was something terrible, just calm grief. She didn't cry, she just couldn't understand how and why that child had been taken away from her so soon. We sat up all night and I was wringing rags out of salt and soda and putting them on her little face, to preserve the features, and washing her arms and hands so they wouldn't turn black.

We got thirsty and wanted some soda pop, but everything was closed because it was two o'clock in the morning. So we snuck into one of the saloons and got some soda pop for everyone. We thought we were pretty daring and that we'd committed an awful sin, and we didn't tell anyone for the longest time.

The next morning here came a wagon with a crude little coffin just built out of pine planks, rough pine, and so we lined it inside with white linen. And we put that little body in the coffin and started the long, tortuous drive to the piney woods where there was a little plot of ground that had a rail fence around it; the grave had been dug there. There was no preacher, no singing, nothing. Just the sobs of the mother and father and the little brothers and sisters that were left. I'll never forget going off and leaving that little body there.

Another time there was a baby that lived just in front of us, just about a year old, a cute little fellow. There were seven or eight in that family, and they lived in a tent without a floor. The little fellow became sick and I was taking care of him. And he died in my arms. I was thirteen years old. Well, that taught me never to fear death. There is a beauty in death, just something about it that we should never be afraid. I sat up all night with that baby, and from then on I have never feared anything. It just leads you nearer to God.

Life is not a problem unless you make it a problem. You can just accept anything and make the best of it wherever you are. If you're looking for mud holes you can find them, and if you're looking for a star in the sky you'll find it.[27]

"IF HE DIED, HE WAS JUST DEAD"

"Batson was the worst of all the oil fields in Texas," claims Sam Webb.

No telling on earth how many people were killed there; put them in pits and anywhere else, no telling. One night some of Sharp's bunch went into town, and one of the fellows was carrying a pistol. They were walking through town around midnight and they passed a saloon, and this boy says, "Well, fellas, I think I'll kill that guy there." And he went into the saloon and he shot a guy, just killed him for nothing in the world, not a thing. He lit out and headed for Galveston. They picked him up when he tried to get on a boat there, brought him back to Batson. Jim Sharp paid a lawyer $1500 for him, got Judge Crawford to come down from Dallas. Never had a trial. Turned him loose. He went off to California. Just wanted to have some fun, I guess, but he killed that guy.

There was a woman named Clara White always hung around the saloons there. She killed her husband there, shot him. He was imposing on her, beating her up or something. Nobody cared much that she killed him. They were running a saloon and a dance hall. Nobody much cared.[28]

Says Plummer Barfield: "Why, a guy might get cut in two there, and they'd just put his guts back in there and sew him up. If he lived, he lived; if he died, he was just dead."

Drunk and disorderly seemed to rule the day in Batson. Webb continues:

Sam Davenport had a saloon there, had a little dog used to hang around all the time. The saloon didn't have any plank floor or boards, just sawdust. And that little dog would drink beer. He'd get drunk just like everyone else in there and get under the tables and lay down on his back, feet straight up in the air, and sleep it off.

And a guy named Flanigan, quite a character. Had a good education, good a fellow as you'd ever meet. He was a cousin to the Sharps. But he liked his whiskey too well, couldn't go nowhere because of his drinking. Just got out there and would rough it up with the roughnecks. That was his downfall.

One day Jim Sharp was walking through the town and Flanigan popped his head out of a manhole in the street. Jim just kept on walking.[29]

Bud Coyle couldn't agree more as to the living conditions at Batson Prairie during the boom days of 1904. "They had an eating shack out by the wells, but it got all gassy and we had to move it. There were some pretty good living arrangements there, just a good bed and a good tight house. No bath, the bath was up at the boiler house. But Batson was the toughest place, Oh Lord, that ever was. Ralph Durham, the county attorney, was the only law in that place most of the time. But prostitutes all around, damn old bats there. Old Lady Grace had a place there, and Old

Lady Smith. Grace was from Temple. Had a big two-story place. And then there was 'the jungle' down there, how awful, oh my. About a half-mile back in the woods. Always trouble down in there."[30]

Sometimes the trouble went from tragic to just plain bizarre, as Plummer Barfield can testify.

Mr. Jones was manager for "Crater & Rangam," owned the livery stable. I slept at the stable and it was my duty to unharness and take care of the horses, and go out in the event of an accident and haul the wounded, the crippled or the dead to the livery stable—it became an undertaker's parlor in those days. We even had a hearse, a hexagon-shaped vehicle that was built by the Columbia Carriage Company. The only embalmer was over at Beaumont. We'd send for him but I'd start the embalming process before he arrived, and on a number of occasions I'd finished the job by the time he got there. I couldn't do much for the wounded or the mutilated, though. Never got an embalming license or nothing, never took an exam because I never knew any of those big words.

We used to make our own coffins right there. They came from the factory all knocked down, four sides and two ends, and the hardware in a little box. We just nailed them together. Buried most of the dead in un-marked graves. Some of them got a Christian burial and some were just buried by the roughnecks. Sometimes me and a Black man would bury them out at the cemetery.

One time another boy and I set out to bury a man at the Pine Lake Cemetery. We were hauling him out there at night and the dark caught up with us and it was raining and the creeks were high. We decided that we'd gone far enough, so we pulled over to the side of the road and we found a stump hole that was partially dug, so we just buried him deep enough that the hogs wouldn't root him up. Don't know who he was, but like they'd say, "he was off the payroll anyway." I pronounced a little benediction, you know, quoted a little scripture: wouldn't want to just drive off like you was leaving a dog.

One night in the winter it was dark and it had been raining. There was a roughneck killed in the field. Guess he fell off a derrick. And I went to the field and loaded up the body in my wagon. Started back to the livery stable and about half way I met a bunch of men on the road with lanterns just milling around. They stopped me and asked me what I had and I told them I had a body. And they said to throw him out because they had other work for me to do! They drug the body off and left it by the road. And they pointed to a tent that had a light on inside and a bunch of lanterns around it, and said for me to go over there. Inside the tent was a dead woman and her dead baby!

I loaded them up and took them to the livery stable and unloaded them and put them on what we called cooling boards. And some roughnecks showed up and told me that when I went back to the field I'd find two more bodies there about 100 yards from that tent. So I went back down the road and picked up the man I'd left there before and brought him to the livery stable. Didn't have any more cooling boards, so I told the old man Cyrus Jones what had happened. He managed the stables.

Well, I went out on the road again and found out what had happened. The woman and the baby had been sick and were in the tent, and some rattlebrained drunks had seen the lamp in the tent and had shot at it. They killed the woman and her baby, shot right through the baby's head and the woman's breast. Then the roughnecks and the rigrunners nearby caught the two drunks and hung 'em from a sweet gum tree! So I cut them down from the tree where they were still hanging and took them back to the livery stable.

Five bodies. One night.[31]

"ONE MOB, ONE RANGER"

"The Rangers were Captain McDonald[32] and Captain Brooks, Lott Tumlinson, Winfred Bates, and Clyde McDowell—finest bunch of men I ever met."[33]

January 20, 1904
Mr. J. S. Cullinan, Beaumont, Texas
Dear Sir:
Recalling our conversation on the necessity of the State taking timely action to prevent the threatened outbreaks of lawlessness around Batson, I beg to say that the Governor has ordered Capt. Brooks of the Ranger force to go there to cooperate with the local officers, if necessary to this end. He is a careful, capable officer from whom much good can be expected, in the performance of his duties.
Yours truly, J. S. Hogg[34]

John Abijah Brooks was born in Kentucky in 1855. He served with the Texas Rangers after the Civil War and rose to captain by 1891. During the years 1901–1906 he was one of the fabled "four captains" and worked out of an Alice office. His district covered all of South Texas and most of East Texas, including Batson Prairie. In his autobiography, Ranger William Warren Sterling recalls the conversation that set off the arrival of Brooks's Company A in the boom town.

> In December of 1903 my father and I were passengers on a Southern Pacific train en route from Beaumont to Houston. Occupying the two seats facing us were former governor James Stephen Hogg and his business associate Jim Swayne of Fort Worth. . . . As the train passed Sour Lake Station, the gentlemen's conversation centered on the lawless conditions that had arisen in Hardin County since the discovery of oil. Sour Lake had simmered down somewhat but Saratoga and Batson Prairie were running hog wild. And Batson held a thin edge over the others for sheer deviltry in the rough. Human life there was cheap. Shootings and cutting scrapes were common occurrences while thieves stole any property that was not guarded day and night. It was claimed that a boiler with steam up had recently been hauled off from a drilling rig without the owner's knowledge or consent.
>
> My father, who had been in all three fields, stated that the local officers were both unwilling and unable to cope with the situation. I have never forgotten Governor Hogg's next statement. Pointing his finger toward the new oil fields, he said in emphatic tones, "There is only one way to stop that lawlessness. If I were still governor, I would have Rangers in Batson before sundown tomorrow. When I get to Houston, I am going to wire [Governor S. W. T.] Sam Lanham and urge him to send them there."

It worked. After a quick trip to Batson on his own, the diminutive, mustachioed Brooks reported the need for Rangers, and Adj. Gen. John Augustus Hulen responded in kind. Brooks went to Batson accompanied by Sergeant Winfred Bates and Privates Lott Tumlinson and Clyde McDowell. They took a train from Alice to Liberty, and a hack to Batson Prairie. They stayed in a local hotel the first night, but the place was such a crude excuse for accommodations that they bought a tent and pitched camp in a grove of trees at the edge of town thereafter.

Their first encounter with the local law enforcement was a big, hulking deputy sheriff whose reputation for brutality preceded him in the streets. He had purportedly killed a drunk one day and laughed that he enjoyed "seeing 'em kick." When he first laid eyes on Captain Brooks, who stood about five feet, four inches and weighed some 125 pounds, the deputy figured he would be any match for this tiny Ranger. He was wrong. When Brooks found the deputy beating up a dance hall girl a few days later, a faster draw got the drop on the hulk and a swing of the pistol dropped him unconscious like a sack of mud. "120 Pound Ranger Whips 220 Pound Deputy" was the newspaper headline that followed. Chained to a tree, the deputy started to threaten Brooks the next day but finally thought better of it.

The local constable and a justice of the peace were similarly ousted by the Rangers, and the local businessmen were impressed enough by the advent of law and order that they hastily erected a town jail for the occasion. The first occupant was a Scot named Simpson, a saloon keeper and brawling drunk who was likeable most of the time. When the Rangers arrested a particularly detestable pimp that same evening, they made sure he landed in the jail with the Scot, who obliged them by "taking care" of his cell mate during that night. As Sterling concluded, "The Scots are a very thoroughgoing people."[35]

A number of instances arose in 1904 that brought the Texas Rangers to Batson Prairie more than once. Bud Coyle, Ed Cotton, and Hardeman Roberts each contribute a story.

"I went from Sour Lake to Batson Prairie," says Roberts,

> and that was some place then. Got there all tired out one night, ate supper and found a little tent with no floor and few cots right next door to a clapboard saloon with a gambling house in the back. Went to bed, but was awakened by an argument that started in the gambling house. They commenced to throwing beer bottles and then they started shooting. One of the shots hit right under my cot and knocked a hatful of dirt up on top of me. I left.
>
> I saw three men killed and another shot there in two fights on a Fourth of July. I had gotten up and started over to get some breakfast when two men—named Bets and Mexican Joe—shot it out in front of me. Just shot each other to pieces. I went on to work. When I came to the old Carver House to get lunch, there was a fight started up there. Pearl Bredon killed Slim Johnson and wounded Bob Campbell, a friend of mine, in the shoulder. Later, Porter Lawson killed Pearl Bredon.
>
> Well, there wasn't much law there.
>
> I was there when Captain Bill McDonald of the Texas Rangers came in to clean up Batson. He was a little, dried-up fellow, stepped out of a hack in front of the hotel. The sheriff and the county attorney met him,

and a big crowd gathered. The captain announced, "My name's McDonald, the State sent me here. I want a change made in twenty-four hours." The sheriff offered to assist but McDonald kind of hung his head sheepishly and replied, "That's all right. I'll take care of it." Sure enough things changed fast.[36]

"There were a lot of gunfights back then," says Ed Cotton.

One time I saw two pistols emptied at each other right there in the street, and neither one of them was hit. I arrested one of the fellows on the spot and went to get the other one who'd run off. I went to his house to get him and his wife told me I had to wait until he changed his clothes.

One time a big fight started because someone hit a porter is all. There was a pool table and the dance hall and the saloon all together, and the fight started in the back when someone knocked the porter down while he was carrying a tray of about eight bottles of beer. The men and the women were fighting, and the floor manager couldn't handle it. They were throwing billiard balls and breaking pool cues over each other's head, and they were scattering all over the place. Two women were fighting under the pool table and they pulled it down on top of them. They were pulling wood off the walls—the place hadn't even been finished yet—and hitting each other with the boards. The bartender pulled out a shotgun and shot at a fellow and blew an eighteen-inch hole in the wall.

The Rangers got there, and it stopped.

Bud Coyle's story involves boom town gang activity.

You couldn't hardly go up there to Batson without a gang robbing you. And so the Rangers came in and, "We're going in and running them s.o.b.s out of town." All the gamblers took off with their women and the pimps and others and took off into the woods. But a fellow named Lang stayed, him and his bartender, and they would walk up and down in front of their saloon. And a boy walked up and shot one of them right in the stomach. And before the Rangers could get there a mob was gonna hang the boy for the killing. Someone told Jim Sharp that they were going to hang the boy, who worked for him. Sharp had two 30-30 rifles and a six shooter, and I had a shotgun. We went to a fence where the mob was coming to hang the boy. They never got over that fence. Jim would have killed them as fast as they crossed that fence.

And there was another fellow in a saloon with two girls and he wouldn't leave. He had a shotgun and every time somebody'd stick their nose inside he'd take a pot shot at them. Captain Brooks just walked right in that door and closed the place down. Someone asked the fellow why he didn't shoot Brooks, and he says, "Why, I knew he was a Ranger just the way he walked in that door, and I wasn't about to shoot him."

This fellow came down from Liberty and he told me he wanted to see "the jungle." That's what they called the mean hang-out over in the thicket. It was the worst place in the whole world. I said we'd wait until Sergeant Bates got there and maybe we'd go down if he was going. And the man didn't know who Bates was, and I told him he was a Texas Ranger. And he asked me if I was yeller to go down to the jungle without the law. I said, "Dadgum right I am! Why, a man's a fool to go down to the jungle without the law, without a Ranger. Why, I wouldn't go down there with a deputy or a constable, just a Ranger. You're liable to never come back."[37]

"The Rangers didn't stay there all the time; they would come in and out. But now I'll tell you, when they would come in, they would clean up the place, and it would look pretty decent for a while."[38]

OCTOBER 2, 1904

"The real fire was in Batson Prairie when those big tanks caught fire from lightning."

They built those big underground tanks. That was before the days they got to building so many iron tanks because they were too costly, and they couldn't get the steel. They were probably fifteen feet deep and maybe a hundred yards square. Then they pumped about a foot or so of water in the bottom, and the oil would ride on the water. They covered these tanks over with planks and left a funnel in the top for the gas to go out. They didn't realize it was a perfect trap—pointed straight up at the clouds.

When the storm got there and got close enough for them to form a sort of circuit, why, Bam!, the lightning come down and the thing exploded and set the fire. *Burned up two million and seven hundred and fifty thousand barrels of oil.* Ten of those tanks burned, and the whole Batson field.

The first day it caught fire, that old heavy oil was hard to burn, and there were plenty of men around tried to put the fires out. One boy was throwing dirt on the fire when a spark set another tank on fire, and it burned right down to the water and the water started to boil and the whole thing blew. And that boy started running and he ran clear across that prairie, said he thought the fire was right behind him the whole way. Never looked back. Just ran.

There was an excursion train out of Galveston and Houston, and a bunch of ladies came out to see the oil fields and they got in a hack and came out to see the fire. The hack broke down, and it started raining soot and ink. The ladies had to wade back in the mud with that stuff raining down on them the whole time. I was up at the depot when they came in. Some of them had their shoes in their hands, and if they weren't the awfulest-looking, drab bunch you ever saw. They were just as black as if they had been dipped in ink. All horrible. Funniest thing I ever saw.[39]

Curt Hamill shares a poignant moment from the holocaust that destroyed the Batson oil field. "During that last fire we lost a man. He was married, separated from his wife at the time, and caring for his children. He was up in the derrick and whether he fell or jumped, he was burned to death. I took care of his children for some time, and a bartender friend of mine found the man's parents back in some other state. I gave him $500 and he took the children to their grandparents. They were glad to take them in. . . . That was the saddest scene, seeing that man burning up, laying out there, burned, boiled in the oil, and we couldn't get to him at all."[40]

HUMBLE, TEXAS

In any big new petroleum field two things invariably happen. The output of the greatest of gushers is a fleeting thing. The doom note is sounded from the moment the oil begins to appear. No other mineral presents such a spectacle of transitory life. It is fugitive, migratory, and cannot be renewed.[41]

That Texas oil is such a headache.[42]

In the fall of 1902 George Hart spudded in a well in far northeastern Harris County, Texas. It blew out soon after, as did several other wells on "the hill" over the next year. But in the summer of 1904, C. E. Barrett of Houston brought in a promising well, a "flank production" well on the outer edge of the southeast Texas caprock. When the Higgins Oil and Fuel Company brought in a high-volume gas well in October, the interest in that new field began in earnest. D. R. Beatty's producing well gushed on January 7, 1905, at 8,500 barrels a day and a depth of 1,012 feet. In February alone the Humble field brought up a half million barrels of green crude oil, and by the spring an explosion prevention device—the first of its kind—had been invented by ingenious oil field workers. A boom was on.[43]

Most of the roughnecks who worked there that first winter came from the salt dome fields of Big Hill and Sour Lake and from the burned prairie near Batson. Other fields were opening across Texas at the same time, and by the summer of 1905 the state had seen a significant shift in the oil-producing centers; no longer was the world's focus on Spindletop.

But though the stories from Humble go beyond the scope of the epoch of Spindletop, there are connections. Bill Farish and Lee Blaffer, the men who would put Humble and Humble Oil Company on the petroleum map, had first made their plans in a hotel room in Beaumont in 1901. The Sturms, Sharps, and Hamills made their way to Humble in 1905. So did J. M. Guffey's Gulf Oil and the Texas Company, establishing lucrative wells there. Frank Leovy, future CEO of Gulf Oil, happened on William Mellon and his wife at the Beaumont depot in 1904: Mellon had come to investigate the new Texas fields that were opening. Leovy helped them with their baggage and accommodations, and went to work for the grateful multimillionaire. Many of the same names and similar stories can be found traced in the oily sands of 1904 and 1905, and many of the stories told out of Humble sound strikingly familiar to those from Big Hill to Batson.[44]

So one story seems appropriate to complete these anecdotes of the first oil fields of Texas. From the dribbling novitiate that was Corsicana to the explosions that rocked a world, and on to a century of prolific, and productive, petroleum discoveries across Texas, the stories reach as deep as the wells around which they were told. Walter Cline tells his Humble story of Bill Farish:

> Well, a swabbing in the early days of Humble consisted of tying a gunny sack around the top of your bailer and letting it down slowly through the fluid and then pulling it up more quickly, or as quickly as you could, with the old horse [engine] we had, and pulling a jag of oil out ahead of it. And the sulphur gas was terrifically poisonous.
>
> I was swabbing this well which Lee Blaffer and Bill Farish owned, and I'd let the bailer down and the wind was blowing back toward where the driller had to stand, and I'd kick the clutch in, then I had me a little piece

of rubber hose that I'd throw over the brake and the clutch and I'd walk back behind the engine where I could get to the throttle to shut it off in case anything went wrong, and let this sulphur gas blow where the driller was supposed to be and I was not. Mr. Farish didn't think much of the idea; he was a big, husky fellow, and he got a little impatient at my apparent delaying tactics. "I know how to run that thing. I'll bail it," he said. I said, "Mr. Farish, that sulphur'll knock you out. It'll knock anybody out."

"Well, it won't knock me out," he replied. So he goes in and starts swabbing. And you could see this gas roll out and this little soft breeze just a-blowing it right down his throat. And he stood it for quite a little while, and he started up with another jag and his knees began to buckle like a fellow who's taken a haymaker in a fight. I ran over to the engine and shut it off right where it was and started in on the derrick floor. We'd swabbed out some bad, muddy water and it was an inch or two thick on the derrick floor and when Farish fell, he fell smack on his face with his nose right down in that stuff.

If you ever saw an ordinary well digger wrestling with a big load of human being, you should have seen me trying to get Mr. Farish off of that thing and out into a pine thicket where I could ride him a little bit and pump some of that stuff out of him. I got a little assist from two or three of the boys that worked on the rig. They'd been well out of range of the gas and had run over and helped me drag him away. We turned him over and gave him a little first aid and jumped up and down on that big set of lungs he had and finally knocked some good air in him.

Later there was a big party and Bill Farish was the honored guest and the main speaker at a fancy hotel conference. He spotted me in the hotel lobby—hadn't seen me for a long time—and came over and greeted me. He asked me to sit with him at the head table, and one of the people in charge told him that wouldn't be possible because of all the really important men who were going to be there. Bill Farish said, "I don't give a damn what or who you got coming. I'm gonna sit with Walter Cline. Now if you want me to sit up there you make room for him. If not, I'll sit down at the table where he's sitting."

We had a nice visit that evening.[45]

9

Tall Tales and Oil Talk

Since that oil well came in on his place, why, he's got so much money he can't hardly spend it. He bought three new axes, and had a bunch of money left over!

— From Mody C. Boatright, Texas Folk and Folklore

From the sawmill workers in the Deep South to the lumberjacks of the Far Northwest, and in working camps all over the country, tall tales have been a favorite pastime around a camp fire or a boiler. Cowboys have told stories since their beginnings; the wonderful mix of Irish, Mexican, and African American anecdotes filled the long, wearying hours of a cattle drive to Abilene or Laramie. The Klondike Gold Rush, like its ancestor at Sutter's Mill, contributed its share of exaggerated stories.

The oil field camp was no different: the roughnecks took their own sense of braggadocio and created larger than life characters with incredible feats of strength and ingenuity to their credit. The two most popular characters of the oil patch at the turn of the century were Paul Bunyan and Gib Morgan. Bunyan and his famous big blue ox named Babe came out of the logger camps of Minnesota, Wisconsin, and California. Gib Morgan was a real person—though a character, to say the least—whose achievements became legendary in his own time, due in large part to his own telling of them!

Gilbert Morgan was one of three boys born and raised in Western Pennsylvania in the 1840s. Gib joined the Tenth Pennsylvania Infantry at the outset of the Civil War, where he became known as "the Minstrel of Company A." Signed up and discharged as a private, his own stories spoke of selfless bravery in the heat of many battles. Records indicate his service during most of the war as a teamster. After wandering about in search of a career and a fortune, during which time he enhanced his storytelling prowess, Gib spent the years 1872 to 1894 in the oil fields as a driller. He worked across the Midwest, from Ohio to Indiana and finally in West Virginia, where most of his tales are based. Over the last fifteen years of his life, Gib Morgan lived in a variety of veteran's retirement homes, where he was a popular spinner of tales until his death in Tennessee. By the turn of the century, and in places like Corsicana and Spindletop, the Gib Morgan stories grew to huge proportions at the hands of the Texas roughnecks.[1]

The Paul Bunyan stories transformed the oversized lumberjack into a Texas-size driller and derrick builder, to no one's surprise. Although the Big Hill camps preferred the Gib Morgan versions, Bunyan found his way to the tentside swaps at Sour Lake, Saratoga, and Batson. A third legendary oil patch worker named Kemp Morgan appeared in the stories of J. Frank Dobie, the most famous Texas storyteller of them all. This character may have been an adaptation of one or both of the others, or a Gib Morgan story passed down with a slurred first name.[2]

Mody Boatright, a gifted storyteller, and Frank Shay have bequeathed the following stories, which have been only slightly modified; Paul Bunyan's mosquitobees tale is an adaptation from a yarn by Dell J. McCormick. In all great tall tales, there is an insurmountable problem that only a legendary hero can solve. It takes material greater than any normal human can muster, and an ingenuity far beyond average. And our hero always figures it out. Here is a sampling of the terrific, entertaining tall tales from the Texas oil fields.

"GIB'S BIGGEST RIG"

It was fitting that the biggest oil rig ever built should be built in the biggest state in the union.

There was a certain region down in Texas where the oil rockhounds figured there was oil under the ground, but they hadn't been able to get to it. They had sent their crack drilling crews and production men, but the formation above the oil sand was so cavy that they hadn't been able to make a hole. They would start with a twenty-four-inch bit and a case with a twenty-two-inch casing. Then they would make a few more feet of hole and would have to set a twenty-inch casing. They would cut a little more ditch and then they would have to case again. And it would go on like that until the casing became too small for the tools to go through, and after all that expense they would have to abandon the hole.

They showed Gib the logs of all the wells they had tried to make, and said, "Gib, do you think you can make a hole down to the oil sand?"

Gib looked at the logs a while, and then he said, "If you'll put up the money, I'll put down the hole." And they made the deal.

First Gib went over to Pittsburgh to see the Oil Well Supply Company and told them how to make the special tools he wanted, some big tools and some little tools. Then he went to Texas and started putting up the rig.

The derrick covered an acre of ground, and because Gib expected to be there for some time he fixed it up nice. He weatherboarded it on the outside and plastered it on the inside. It was so high that he had it hinged in two places so that he could fold it back to let the moon get by. It took a tool dresser fourteen days to climb to the top to grease the crown pulleys. That is the reason Gib had to hire thirty tool dressers: at any time there would be fourteen going up, fourteen coming down, one on the top and one on the ground. A day's climbing apart he built bunk houses for the men to sleep in. These bunk houses had hot and cold showers and all the modern conveniences.

By the time the derrick was up, the tools began to arrive from Pittsburgh. The biggest string of tools reached to within ten feet of the crown block. The drill stem was twelve feet in diameter. At the first indication of caving Gib cased the well with thousand-barrel oil tanks riveted together. This reduced the hole to twenty feet. He put on an eighteen-foot bit and made about fifty feet of hole before he had to case again. Down about five hundred feet he had to go to a smaller bit, one about six feet in diameter. At a thousand feet he was using standard tools. At two thousand feet he was using his specially made small tools and casing with one-inch tubing. But he hadn't figured it quite fine enough, for he hadn't got the oil sand when the smallest drill he had wouldn't go through the tubing.

But that didn't stump Gib. He brought in the well with a needle and thread.

"GIB'S BOARDING HOUSE"

Gib Morgan, more as an accommodation to his friends than anything else, put up a boarding house for oil field workers. The thing that made the place famous was his buckwheat pancakes. The men would crowd his place every morning and demand more and more hot cakes. Gib had to enlarge his dining room and get more and larger griddles. But he still couldn't keep ahead of his trade.

So he finally had to build a new plant altogether. He bought a dozen of the largest concrete mixers he could find and steam engines to turn them and set them on a hill a mile away. Into these mixers the workmen dumped flour and milk and eggs and other ingredients—the exact recipe is still a trade secret—and when the batter had reached a certain creamy consistency it was turned into a pipeline leading to the kitchen. The griddles were bottoms of 43,000-barrel oil tanks, each heated by a gas well underneath it.

At first Gib had trouble keeping the irons greased, but he solved that problem by strapping sides of fat bacon to the feet of his workmen. Seven big strapping men skimmed over the hot surface of each griddle continuously. They were followed by another crew who handled the batter hoses leading from the pipeline. Another crew with shovels turned the cakes over, and a fourth took them up and tossed them to the waiters.

Melted butter and maple syrup flowed through the pipes along the half-mile counters, and at each seat were spigots from which the customer drew as much as he wanted.

Gib fed twenty-five thousand oil field workers at a time. So many people came out of mere curiosity to see Gib's place that they were about to crowd out the regular customers, so Gib had to put up a sign: "Only Drillers and Tool Dressers Fed Here."

"GIB'S HOTEL"

After Spindletop came in Gib Morgan saw the thousands of people that were crowding Beaumont without any place to stay, so he decided he would put up a hotel for the general public. The building was forty stories high with ten high-speed elevators to bring the people up and down. When they stepped out of the elevator, no matter which floor, there was a narrow gauge railroad with a train waiting to take them to their rooms. In each room was a number of taps—one for ice water, one for bourbon, one for rye, and one for scotch, one for Tom Collins, one for old fashioned, and so on.

But the most remarkable thing about the hotel was its adaptation to the climate. Gib had noticed that throughout Texas and Oklahoma when a guest came in, he always asked for a south or east room. He never wanted a north or west room. So Gib built his hotel without any north or west rooms. Every guest who registered would be assigned to a south or east room. This would go on until all the rooms were filled. Every guest would go to bed in a room with a south or east exposure. But when those who had gone to bed first would wake up in the morning, they would look out through north or west windows and see the railroad tracks.

Gib's hotel was mounted on a turntable, but by the time his guests found out, they were so pleased with the service, especially the spigot service, that they didn't mind.

"GIB IS A FARMER"

Gib's ventures into agriculture were less successful, but because his planting was done in spare time for recreation, his failures were of little consequence.

Once he decided to make a home garden. He thought it would be an economy of land and labor to plant his corn and beans together so that the bean vines could run on the corn stalks. Somehow the timing went wrong. The corn grew faster than the beans and pulled the vines up by the roots.

When he was living in Texas, Gib put in a big field of popcorn. It was a good crop that year, and he harvested all the popcorn he could pack into his barn. Then along in late summer came the hottest day in forty years. Gib was lying in the shade of a hackberry tree trying to keep cool when he heard a series of explosions that sounded like musketry in battle. He looked up in time to see the roof blown off the barn and the popcorn spouting like a twenty-thousand-barrel gusher, only white.

As the popped corn grains fell to the earth, Gib's old gray mule thought they were snowflakes, and he froze to death.

"GIB'S GUNS"

Gib Morgan was one of the busiest men in the world. If he hadn't been, he couldn't have done all the things he did—not in one man's lifetime.

Yet he did manage to find time for a little recreation now and then, generally fishing or hunting.

His fame as a hunter depended in some part upon two very remarkable and famous guns he owned, both of which he had designed himself and had had manufactured at no inconsiderable cost. One was a fine rifle with a telescope sight, the first ever placed on a gun. He used to hunt wild pigs with it—javelinas they called them in Texas. He could climb a mesa or even a slight hill, and survey the country for thirty miles around. If there was a drove of javelinas anywhere within that radius, he could focus his telescope sight on them and draw them up to where he could hear them grunt. The rest was easy. All he had to do was pull the trigger. He couldn't miss them. But shooting at such long range, he found that the meat would often spoil before he could get to it. He thought and studied a while and then it occurred to him to salt his bullets. After that he had no trouble.

Equally famous was Gib's fowling piece, a twenty-four-barrel shotgun. He designed it for shooting passenger pigeons that used to fly over the Neches Valley in such numbers that they blotted out the sun. When a flock passed over, even if it was twelve o'clock sun time, the cows came home to be milked and the chickens went to roost.

Gib never would forget the first time he shot his gun. It had just come away from the gunsmith's a few days before, and Gib had been waiting for the pigeons. One day they came. He got out his new fowling piece, loaded all twenty-four barrels to the muzzle, and rushed to the woods. By that time it was too dark for him to see more than ten feet in front of him. He raised the gun to his shoulder, pointed it toward the sky and fired all twenty-four barrels.

That was the last he knew for some time. When he came to, he thought his folks must have picked him up for dead and buried him alive. He began struggling, however, more from instinct than conviction, and after an hour or so he saw sunlight. He had been knocked through the top soil and three feet into the hardpan and buried in pigeons seventy-two feet deep.

That surely was a lesson for him. After that he loaded his gun only half way to the muzzle.[3]

"KEMP MORGAN, THE TEXAS OIL DRILLER"

A solitary man of gigantic proportions plodded wearily across the sandy plains of East Texas. He led a long string of pack mules loaded with curious tools and equipment. From time to time the man would pause in his tracks and smell the air, sniffing like a hound dog trying to pick up a scent. From his sniffing he learned two things: first, that there was no oil in the vicinity and, secondly, that a sandstorm was brewing from the west.

Coming upon a small clump of saplings he unloaded his mules and tied them to the trees. Then he prepared his supper of razorback hog bacon and beans. The supper over he prepared for the night and the coming storm. He knew enough about the country to know that the storm would probably come up after he was asleep and be over before the coming of the morning. Covering his nose with his blanket he dozed off into a sound sleep.

The next morning when he awoke his mules were nowhere in sight. Peering up and down the plains he could see no trace of them or their hoof prints. Then he heard a loud braying in the air and looking up he saw what had happened. So intense was that sandstorm that it blew the soil away from under the mules and they were left hanging by their tie ropes forty feet in the air. Bending the saplings over by sheer strength he let the mules down, reloaded them and resumed his search for the liquid gold.

In a manner of speaking the man was a man nobody knew. He was Kemp Morgan, the greatest of all oil well drillers. No one really knew the man because he worked alone. There was no gang, no matter how expert, that could equal him in effort and endurance. The strongest driller could not stand Kemp's tour of duty. He was a complete gang all by himself. First he prospected for oil and found it, then he spudded-in, drilled and, when a gusher came up, he capped and cased it and built his own derrick. Whether he worked for himself or for a great corporation was never known for Kemp Morgan was a silent man and not given to boasting.

Men stood apart and watched him in action, wonderment writ in large letters on their stupid countenances. He used tools and gadgets entirely unknown to them and it was only when he had thrown equipment away as outmoded that they learned of his labor-saving devices. Some they were able to adapt to their own puny efforts but a great many more had to be abandoned because no one was big enough or strong enough to work with them.

He was, as has been pointed out, a complete oil gang all in one. After he had located oil with his sensitive nose he would take a sharpshooter, a long handled shovel, and begin spudding in. Men who had seen him at work insisted he could work a sharpshooter faster and make better time than a No. 1 gang could with a standard drilling rig. It was only when he got to tough digging, that is, hard rock, that he would put up his drill, mount his bull wheels, hang his walking beam and start his engine. Once he started his engine he would go on a double tour of duty, that is, for twenty-four hours a day, until he struck oil. When he had brought in a gusher he would build his own derrick, cap and case the hole, build the tanks and turn the whole affair over to a regular gang. Then he would move out and look for another oil field. Every oil field in operation today in Texas and Oklahoma was started by Kemp Morgan. He is, or was when he was alive, the only man in the oil fields who could not be called a boomer. Kemp Morgan was responsible for boomers and all the more intelligent boomers followed him about to see where he was to dig next so they could be in on the boom.

Many are the stories that oil drillers tell of Kemp Morgan. He could sight so accurately no plumb line was necessary; he took but a few hours to build a full size derrick and when he drove nails he had to restrain his great strength for fear of demolishing the whole derrick. He could drive any nail with a single tap of his hammer and when he was angry he very often drove the hammer itself deep into the hard wood.

There was one time that he lost his patent drill. He was drilling into soft digging when he noticed that the drill worked slower and slower as it went down. After a while it stopped completely and investigation showed that he had gone into an alum mine and the hole had shrunk right up around the drill and held it fast. Another time his drill was deflected by some unusually hard substance and came out in a rubber mine in Brazil. The hole gushed pure rubber and Kemp cut it off in ten-foot lengths and sold it to a rubber manufacturer who promised him he would found an industry at Akron, Ohio. One winter when it was pretty cold Morgan kept right on drilling and brought in a twenty-inch gusher. The oil froze as it left the ground. The oil underneath pushed the frozen column up straight into the air. Another man would have torn his hair out. Not Kemp Morgan. He sawed it off in three-foot lengths and shipped it to the refinery on flat cars, effecting an enormous saving on tank cars.

Most drillers when they bring in a duster, a dry hole, just abandon it and try somewhere else. Old Kemp Morgan knew about other things than oil drilling. He knew that no Kansas farmer could ever dig a post hole in his hard-bottomed soil. He would get his hands around the duster hole and pull it up, four feet at a time, saw it off and ship it to Kansas.

Ask any Kansas farmer what he thinks of the Kemp Morgan Portable Post Holes.

Kemp Morgan invented most of the tools and gear now used by the high-speed drillers. His finest invention was the rubber drill. After the hole was spudded-in and the steel drills started he would watch it until he got sleepy. Then he would remove the steel drill, substitute the rubber drill and get it bouncing properly and go off to bed. Another of his inventions was a drum around which steel drills could be wound. This saved a great amount of time for others when a drill had to be changed. Before that the drill pipe had to be brought up in sections and unjointed and stacked on the derrick. For his own part he never used either method. If a drill needed changing he simply lifted the two thousand feet of pipe and held it in the air until the drill was changed. Sometime in his life he must have been a cowboy, for once when his boiler blew up he sprang on it, thumbed its safety valve and rode it back to earth. But he was always a quick thinker. Once when he was shooting a well, that is, exploding a charge of nitroglycerine at the bottom to speed up the flow of oil, he brought out a gusher. He was totally unprepared for it and all he could do was to sit upon the pipe until it was capped.

"KEMP MORGAN AND BULL MORRISON"

There was one man who worked for Kemp Morgan, and his name was Bull "Cook" Morrison. He was working in a restaurant in Beaumont when he met Morgan. He was cooking almost nothing for the oil boomers but T-bone steaks. One day Bull saw two boomers come in followed by the tallest man he'd ever seen. The waitress, a gal named Mayme, went over to the table where the two boomers sat and asked for their order.

"I want, Dearie," said the first, "a piece of roast about four pounds, and I want it rare. You get me, Kid? Rare."

"Listen, you boll weevil," Mayme replied, "when you come in here you leave your chewin' gum at home, and talk polite. It's a long time since I was a kid and I expect some respect outa you."

The second boomer said, "You go look in that icebox of yours and pick out the biggest chunk of meat you have. Tell your bull cook to scorch it, got it?"

Mayme gritted her teeth and smiled a crooked smile. "Yes, sir," was all she said. She walked over to the table where the tall stranger sat, and he was glaring at the two smart mouth boomers. They put on their best bluff faces and stared back. "What'll you have, mister?" asked Mayme, seething.

"Ma'am," said the man, "please bring me a couple of steaks well done, and I'd be obliged." Then, loud enough for everyone to hear and while looking right at the other two customers he added, "Bring me the sharpest steel knife you have. Then bring me two wild longhorn steers in here and I'll just cut off what I need."

Mayme smiled. The two boomers stared down at the floor. Bull Morrison quit his job as a cook and went to work for the tall stranger. His name was Kemp Morgan.

As Kemp and Bull headed out of town for Big Hill, Morrison asked if Morgan was a driller. "I'm the full crew," he responded. "I'm the driller, the toolies, and the roughneck. I cap and I case, I rig, I pull, sight, and rig the derrick. Then when I have time I build the tanks."

Bull thought Kemp might be a bit loco.

"I don't have much time for cooking, though," Kemp Morgan continued. "I like the way you shoot a steak and I want you to cook for me. Whaddaya say?"

Bull thought a minute. "Well, I've had four wives and they all left me because I was always making the wrong decision. So I'll come with you."

Kemp and Bull spent a week buying supplies and getting ready to go drilling. Most of the equipment was so big only Morgan could lift it on to the truck. Bull Morrison bought the food for their camp. Kemp had decided to bring in the biggest gusher in history, and make enough money to buy the Mail Pouch Tobacco Company. He knew how much the roughnecks liked their chewin' tobacco, and he aimed to take the stuff and soak it in corn shine liquor. He thought the oil field workers would like that.

So Kemp Morgan went out on the hill and stuck his nose up in the air and commenced to sniffing for oil. Morrison didn't smell anything, and Kemp told him he was a pretty fair cook but a rotten oil prospector. "Why, Bull," he said one day, "under your big flat feet is the biggest oil field that ever was." Bull looked around and all he saw were some dry holes, dusters, in that field. But Kemp Morgan went to work.

After spudding in, Kemp started off with a sixty-inch hole and drilled one mile down. Then he stopped and told Bull to cook him up a T-bone steak for breakfast. While he was eating breakfast, a sandstorm blew in and the two men shut themselves in the cook house until it was over. When they went outside the wind had blown the dirt off the whole well, and it was sitting there sticking a mile in the air. Kemp cut the well into four-foot lengths and shipped them off to the Midwest to sell as post holes.

Then he went to work with a seventy-five-inch drill, the biggest hole ever drilled in the country. Some say there were bigger ones, but don't believe everything you hear. Morgan drilled to fifty thousand feet and come up dry. But at fifty thousand feet and three inches he brought in the biggest gusher that ever was. And not only that, but all the dusters in that field started gushing at the same time, too! Well, Kemp knew he had to cap them all so he went to work, capped and cased, and raced from one to the next. He lost about a half-barrel of oil altogether.

Kemp Morgan then set about to build a derrick over his gusher, the biggest derrick that ever was. But as big as it was, every time he'd let the oil gush it'd spout right out the top anyway. It took ten days for the oil to reach the top and then three weeks for it to rain back down to the ground. It spouted so high that St. Peter and all his angels would raise Hell about the oil shooting through the floor of Heaven.

Kemp Morgan made a fortune and bought the Mail Pouch Tobacco Company, all right, just like he said he would. Then he took all that tobacco and soaked it in corn shine liquor. But he chewed it all before he could get around to selling it, and lost his fortune that way.[4]

"PAUL BUNYAN, OIL FIELD WORKER"

"In loosening a connection the man using the wrench will sometimes take it off the fitting and remark that it should be 'handy,' meaning that it should be loose enough to be taken off by hand. His companion will then try it and, if it is too tight, will remark, 'You pulled it green, Bud. It may be handy for Paul Bunyan, but not for me.' This is a favorite expression among the early pipeliners, and any job too difficult for a man to do is considered a good one for Paul Bunyan, strong man of the oil fields and pipeliner deluxe."[5]

John Lee Brooks tells about the legendary American hero who walked the oil fields at the turn of the century:

> Paul Bunyan is known in practically all phases of the oil game, as well as in other trades where he can find the tough characters as his comrades and fellow workers. He is never seen in a white-collar job, but is always out where there is "something doing," and with no time for effeminacies of dress or manners. Pipeliners tell of Paul's big camp for which he laid a pipeline to furnish buttermilk for his men. According to some stories he was a giant with only one arm, and that was in the middle of his chest! His

tongs were so heavy that four men were required to carry them. The tank builders say that Paul's first tank was so high that a hammer which he dropped from the top one day wore out two handles before it hit the ground.

As a driller Paul Bunyan is quite as striking a figure. He was equally at home on a rotary or on a standard rig; in fact, he devised most of the implements and practices of the trade. His naïve humor is seen in the names used since by every driller, toolie, and roughneck: the headache post; Maude, the heavy breakout tongs; bull wheel and calf wheel; the lazy bench, and many others. . . . For his own convenience, to allow him to leave the rig occasionally, he invented a way of winding the drill pipe around a big steel drum. His boilers were so big that anyone who carelessly went near the injectors was sucked up inside.

As a rig builder, as the oil field carpenter is called, he demonstrated clearly that he was supreme. He could sight so accurately that no plumb line was necessary. The arduous job of "pulling," "running," and "sighting" a derrick took Paul only one day, thereby saving two days of the usual time, as well as the labor of at least two men. The customary hatchet was too light for him; his weighed eight pounds and drove any nail to the head at a single blow. He could build a pair of the great wooden bull wheels in half a day, hang the massive walking beam by himself, and "skid a rig" several yards over by hand. If any timber, or even the crown block, fell off the structure, Paul naturally caught it by hand and saved the wood as well as the heads of the crew below.

Bunyan was such a powerful and tireless worker, and so considerate of his men, that he used to let them sleep half the tour while he alone did the work of five men. He could dig faster with a sharp shooter (a long narrow spade) than any crew could drill, but since he could never find anyone to call his bet, he did not try this feat. In fits of anger he would drive his sixteen-pound hammer so deep into the ground that oil often came to the surface: this practice was deplored by the operators because it called for the very inconvenient and wasteful task of dipping the oil out of the hole!

Paul did not waste his time with derricks of the usual size. His structures towered far above their conventional neighbors and had telephone connections for each member of the crew. (After drilling started, you see, the derrick men were able to come down only twice a month, for payday.) On one occasion Paul decided to break the record for the tallest derrick in the world. He built the structure up so high that he and his crew moved to Heaven and lived there while they finished their work. That well was dug to China before he stopped.

Perhaps the strangest of all Paul's experiences came as the result of an accident. One day he carelessly allowed himself to be caught in the steel drilling cable while the bit was being lowered into the hole. Before he could be stopped he found himself at the bottom of the well in a large cavity in a very warm atmosphere. "It was hot as Hell down there," Paul described it later. He soon found that he actually *was* in Hell. Walking on deeper into the mountain cave, he met the Devil, who greeted him warmly—for even Hell had heard of Paul Bunyan!

While Paul was there, he settled a certain question that had been bothering him. Some time before, a roustabout who held a grudge against Paul had sneaked up on him from behind and cut off his leg and thrown it down a well. Paul had never grown accustomed to his wooden leg, so he asked the Devil if he'd seen the leg and could he have it back. The Devil told him he couldn't have it back, because it was still roasting on the coals.

The Devil took Paul all around his place, and at last showed him the harem. The beauties were so ravishing that Paul tried to carry one along, and the Devil in a rage chased him back up the well to the surface.

One of the few wells Paul Bunyan never brought in.[6]

"PAUL BUNYAN AND THE BIG THICKET MOSQUITOBEES"

One of the worst times Paul Bunyan ever had was the time he was drilling around Sour Lake and the Big Thicket. It was nearly all bayou land, and though Paul didn't know it at the time it was a famous breeding ground for mosquitoes. Not the tame, puny little kind you find back in New Jersey, but huge evil-looking insects that measured fifteen or sixteen inches from tip to tip.

The present day mosquitoes are mere pygmies compared to the ones that attacked Paul and his crew during the spring of 1903 at Sour Lake oil field. They appeared in swarms and began to make life miserable for everyone in the camp. It was no use covering the bunks with mosquito netting. The huge insects would dive through it like it was tissue paper.

Paul told his friend Ole to fit all the doors and windows with heavy chicken wire but even that didn't work. Great holes appeared in it overnight, and soon there were more mosquitoes inside the bunkhouses than outside. The smaller mosquitoes would crawl through the chicken wire holes and help the larger ones saw an opening with their sharp beaks, like two men working at the ends of a crosscut saw. The beaks were as sharp as razor blades in spite of the daily wire cutting, and Paul soon found out the reason. Down behind the blacksmith shop the mosquitoes had set up six grindstones, and while one turned the grindstone the others held their beaks over the wheel until all the rough edges were worn off. They had worn out three of Ole's best grindstones before Paul put an end to that.

Paul finally decided to fight them with bumblebees. He sent Brimstone Bill out to the other side of El Paso to find the largest and fiercest bees he could find. Bill did a good job, all right, and brought back six hundred of the largest bumblebees the men had ever seen. He tied their wings to their backs and brought them back overland on foot. It was quite a feat, crossing eight hundred miles of Texas desert. And he never lost a bee.

Paul turned the bees loose the day they arrived in camp. Everybody expected a battle royal, but nothing happened! In fact, the bumblebees took a liking to the mosquitoes from the start and became as friendly as ants at a picnic. The bachelor mosquitoes took a fancy to the young lady bumblebees and soon they were intermarried left and right. The worst of it was that the offspring were twice as bad as either parent! They had stingers fore *and* aft and got the men both coming and going. It soon became dangerous to go out into the Big Thicket alone, and the men armed themselves with axes and shotguns to fight off the attacks of the savage "mosquitobees" as the men called them.

These young mosquitobees grew to such a huge size that they began to attack the camp itself and make off with large sacks of flour and barrels of sugar. Hot Biscuit Slim put all the sugar barrels that were left in a small storehouse back of the cook house and tightly bolted the door, but a great swarm of the worst mosquitobees came down on it one day and carried away the sugar—storehouse and all!

Paul was away in Beaumont for a time and his men didn't know what to do. It became a matter of life and death when the giant insects attacked the big dining room and started eating all the food before the men could sit down for dinner. Ole, the Big Swede, got the men together and led an attack against the mosquitobees, while seven roughnecks stood at the doors to block any escape. They killed more than half the swarm in the ensuing battle.

The rest escaped through the windows and went for help. Doc Johnnie Inkslinger bound up the wounded men and handed out double-bitted axes to beat off an attack should the swarm return. They did not have to wait long. In less than an hour all the giant mosquitobees swarmed the camp. They attacked the men in battle formation and drove them from the dining room and the bunkhouse. Step by step the men were driven back. The weary oil field workers finally hid beneath the giant pancake griddle that Paul had brought with him to camp, hoping the eighteen inches of thick boiler plate would protect them.

About that time Paul showed up in camp and saw the men's dire predicament. As he watched, the swarm attacked the griddle from above, diving down and driving their sharp beaks through the boiler plate with enough force to reach the men huddled beneath. Several of Paul's men were badly punctured. But Paul got an idea. He ordered the men to take their axes and bend the beaks that came through the griddle until they were flat against the under side. In that way the mosquitobees were held fast to the griddle itself. More and more of the mosquitobees plunged their stingers through the griddle, and Paul and his men bent each one as it came through. Paul himself bent 285 of the beaks while his men bent the other 15. In a short time every last mosquitobee that hadn't been killed in the Great Dining Room Fight was stuck in the griddle.

The angry buzzing above began to grow to a deafening roar as the mosquitobees saw they were trapped at last and unable to escape. Suddenly the huge griddle itself began to tremble and seemed about to topple from its foundations. The men ran out from under it, but Paul stayed there and pushed with all his considerable strength against the bottom of the iron plate. Without warning it broke loose and the vast swarm of mosquitobees rose in the air, carrying the heavy pancake griddle with them!

With thankful shouts the oil field workers cheered as the griddle soared away over the treetops of the Big Thicket, the swarm angrily buzzing as they dragged their flying prison with them. Nothing more was heard of the giant insects until an oil tanker two hundred miles to the south reported seeing the swarm struggling through the air with the giant griddle weighing them down. They finally sank to the bottom of the Gulf of Mexico. Not a single mosquitobee escaped. Paul had saved the Sour Lake camp.[7]

MYSTERY OF THE OIL SLICK

One of the strangest phenomenons that was ever brought to the attention of man was the Great Oil Slick. For as long as man can remember the men that sailed the Gulf of Mexico knew that this great oil slick was ever present just off the coast several miles just out of the mouth of Sabine Lake.

The oil was often washed to shore in small bubbly balls. Mixed with salt water, they were often found and had gained a gray powdery color, due to the salt water and the sun. The sun had bleached them while lying on the beach.

These small bubbles of oil were almost worth their weight in gold to those that were fortunate enough to find them. For you see, they were crudely refined into oil and could serve as a lubricant for the wheels of carts and wagons, mixed with other available fats. They were also highly prized for their uses for medical purposes.

Also, the greatest of this discovery served a far better purpose, if that is possible. For it has been recorded that when the great hurricanes and the normal storms in this area of the Gulf prevailed, all ships would hurriedly gather into the slick to weather the storms. No ships were ever reported lost that once reached its haven. The oil was so thick and the area so large that the great waves calmed and the ships could not be tossed about. The only threat was to the masts and decks. If all was secured, little or no damage was realized.

Ships at times would leave the supposedly safe harbor of Galveston to seek the security of the slick.

The impressing, almost impossible, reality came when on January 10, 1901, the incredible gusher of Spindletop came in! Almost immediately a new world was founded. A new industry was born, but the Great Oil Slick died.[8]

OIL PATCH TALK

Spudding In—To begin the process of digging an oil well. In Scandinavia, a *spud* is a tool used for digging ditches or rows in gardens. From it comes the Anglicized word, *spade.*

There are pipeliners of varying importance, the least of them being the *boll weevil,* or the new man. The roughest and the dirtiest work is thrown his way, but he endures it until another boll weevil enters the gang. Some men, however, because of their inability or their reluctance to learn the trade, always remain boll weevils. Any mistake by a pipeliner is a *boll weevil stunt,* and the penalty for pulling such a stunt is drinks for the gang. A shorter name for a mistake, derived from the penalty, is *coffee.*

Another type of pipeliner is the *snapper,* the man who always looks for the easiest job, or the *snap.* A snapper could always be found walking the streets, but a man who could "hit the ball" always had a job. Equally detested is the man who seeks after "pull," in order to win promotion. A man who works steadily and efficiently is a *real pipe hand*.

And a job, no matter how small, is called a *contract*. The contract most detested by the pipeliner is ditch digging, and he would much rather lay pipeline all day than to dig. The first thing the ditch digger does is to *spud in*, the term used universally in the oil fields, especially in the drilling. To begin digging any hole or ditch is to spud in. The tools used by the ditch digger are the long-handled shovel and the *sharp shooter*, a slender-bladed digging spade with a short handle. The first layer of the ditch is dug with the sharp shooter, and the dirt that is left is *crumbed* or *doodled* out with the shovel, and the ditch is left clear of dirt. In especially hard ground a pick is used.

Another contract less distasteful to the pipeliner is the repairing of pipeline leaks. When the line walker spots fresh oil near a pipeline, the gang is sent to find the leak. The man who finds it says that he has *got production*. A clamp is usually placed on the leak, but sometimes it is patched by a welder.

The *laying of the screw-joint* is an interesting procedure. The joints of pipe have threads on each end, and both ends are screwed into a *collar*, the name used to designate the simplest form of union. The collar is usually already screwed firmly on one joint of the pipe, the end of which is raised from the ground and placed on the *lazy board*, a square piece of lumber with a broken spade handle attached for convenience in carrying. The *stabber* fits a small pipe wrench in one end of the joint of pipe that is to be *rolled in*, and the other end of the joint is placed in the collar. The joint is lined up so that it will "roll" easily, and then the *jack*, a crude two-legged wooden tool, is placed under the joint next to the stabber, who screws in the pipe as far as it will roll.

The tools usually used in *making the pipe up* are pipe wrenches called *chisel tongs* because a square metal key, or chisel, placed in the jaws of the tongs, grips the pipe. A common type of chisel tongs is the *scissor tongs*, so called because the hands open like scissors. One pair of these tongs, the *back ups*, is placed behind the collar and the lazy board, with the handles on the ground to keep the pipe from recoiling. Two other pairs of tongs are placed on top of the joint of pipe to make it up and each is operated by one to three men, depending on the size of the line.

The *pusher* usually "pounds" or "packs" the collar with a hammer and the *hook men* "hit" the hooks in time with the beats of the hammer. When the pipe rolls easily, the hook men "break out," or hit at alternating beats of the hammer, but when the pipe rolls harder, they "break in," or strike in unison. When the pipe is made up, the *collar packer* "rings 'em off," and the whole gang moves on to the next joint.

A pipeline gang usually consists of the *back-up man, the collar pounder,* who is also the *lazy board man, the hook hitters, the jack man, the stabber,* and two or three men who manhandle the joints of pipe and "spell off," or relieve, the other men. Every man in a gang is usually capable of handling any job. If there is more than one man on each pair of hooks, the one on the end of the handles is called the *hook pointer.*[9]

You are in a *boom* if a lot of work is going on, whether drilling or production. If you cannot handle your job, it "eats you up." If you get in trouble, you are in a *bind.* When you try to do a job and it goes wrong, you may be told you "twisted off," which comes from the name for a drill pipe failure. This expression is also common in poker games.

If any kind of equipment fails, the operator will say it "swarmed" (as a bee colony separates) or more commonly, it "cratered." This last word comes from the description of the worst kind of *blowout* or wild well, where a huge crater is formed.

When a man says he is ready to "flange up" he is about through. This common saying comes from the necessity of using a flange union to complete nearly all pipe connection jobs.

During a boom, when the edge of the field is discovered by a rig encountering the producing sand below the salt water horizon, they have "hit the Gulf of Mexico" or "the suitcase sand." The roughnecks know that before long there will be a "suitcase parade" of layoffs or transfers.

One of the more unusual sayings could be heard when explaining that a rig worker had given up and headed home. Perhaps rather than embarrassing the poor fellow for quitting, it was simply noted that "he went to Fort Worth with a load of goats."

A well that fails to produce oil or gas is a *duster* or *dry hole.* A gas well is a *blue whistler.* A well or field that has to be pumped is "on the beam," the "walking beam," that is.

A roughneck who loses his girl to another has been "drilled around." If someone passes him up for a better job, he has been "sidetracked" or "bypassed."

An oil company that has a hard time financially and has to use patched-up equipment is a *po' boy outfit.* The community of houses built up around a major oil company headquarters is called the *camp.* The company-owned houses built to accommodate the key men are usually in a group. The privately owned houses where the hands live are officially the "employees' camp," but the people who live there sometimes call it the "po' boy camp," although many of the po' boys have a nicer spread than the company houses.

Any kind of faked or altered reports are "boiler housed," referring to the alleged practice of pumpers "gauging their tanks in the boiler house."

A *tool pusher* is in charge of one or more drilling rigs. The name originated in the days when his main job was to keep the rig supplied with drill bits or tools and the day driller was the king of the rig.

A *farm boss* is in charge of producing and treating oil after the wells are completed. All gangs and pumpers work under him. The name probably started in the early days when a producing unit, now referred to as a lease, was called a farm, which it usually was.

A *rotary driller* is foreman of a drilling crew. He is more often called a *rig runner, well digger,* or *digger.* A roughneck will say he is "running days." The 4:00 P.M. to midnight shift is called "evening tour" (pronounced *tower*), and midnight to 8:00 A.M. is the "morning tour" or the "graveyard shift." The driller operates the drawworks and rotary to drill the hole or run pipe in or out. Next to the driller is the *derrick man,* who works in the derrick when the pipe is being run in or out of the hole. He is also the pump repair man. They say he "works derricks."

The two rotary helpers are the legendary *roughnecks.* When making a "trip" (out and in the hole with the drill pipe) one is a "pipe racker," who guides the stand of drill pipe coming out of the hole to its proper place on a platform and "stabs" it in the joint hanging in the rotary going in the hole. He also latches the breakout tongs and helps handle the slips. The other roughneck works the "boll weevil corner," which is always the first job for an inexperienced man. He latches on the backup tongs coming out of the hole and the makeup tongs going in the hole if a star post is used. A roughneck is emphatically a skilled laborer.

The fifth man in a drilling crew is the *fireman* or "pot fireman." He fires the boilers with gas or oil, repairs the boiler feed pumps, and helps the roughnecks during trips. Two of his most important jobs are to make coffee and to wash the crew's overalls in a "blow barrel," usually a fifty-five-gallon oil drum connected to water and steam. It is rough on the overalls but gets them clean.

The foreman of a gang is a *roustabout pusher.* His crew consists of three more roustabouts. Their duties are to connect oil wells to the gas-oil separators and lease-stock tanks, maintain all producing equipment, and keep the producing properties cleaned up. A gangpusher is said to be "pushing a gang" while a roustabout is "in the gang."

A *lease pumper* is called a pumper even if every well in the field is flowing. It is his duty to regulate the flow of the wells, gauge the tanks into which the wells produce, treat oil water emulsion, and report on "gauge tickets." A *rig builder* erects and dismantles derricks and has nothing to do with the drilling rig. The name originates from these days of wooden derricks when the rig builders built the derrick and then hewed out a walking beam, made a bull wheel and sampson post for standard pumping rigs.

A *dry watchman* watches a rig that had been shut down or "stacked." The *crum boss* is custodian of the bunkhouse. A *swamper* is the name for a driver's helper. The *dauber* is a welder and a *pump doctor* is the repair man.

A wide, smooth-faced, flanged pulley on the end of the drawworks lineshaft is the *cathead,* and the rope that runs on it by friction is the *catline.* A very heavy set of chain tongs used only on hard-to-break drill collars is called *Old Maude* or the "bull tongs." A rotary made so that the center can remain still while the outside turns is called "double deck." When it is used to make up pipe going in the hole, the chain tongs are engaged by an erect tool called the *star post,* which fits into the moving outside ring of the rotary while the weight of the drill pipe in the hole is carried by "slips" resting on the rotary. Some rigs make up their drill pipe with a "spinning line," which turns it by friction and is pulled by the cathead.

The steam engine–driven hoist that raises and lowers pipe in the hole by means of a wire rope run through the crown block on top of the derrick is called the *drawworks.* While running or pulling pipe the hook below the traveling block supports the "elevators," a device that latches around the pipe by means of steel loops called "elevator bails." While drilling or "making hole," the drill pipe is supported by a *swivel* and *kelly joint* or *grief stem* suspended from the hook and screwed into the drill pipe. The kelly joint is a square, hexagonal, or grooved hollow forging that slides through and fits snugly in the rotary drive bushing. The *rotary* is a turntable controlled by the driller and usually turned by a chain from the drawworks.

The rotary hose connects the swivel to the top of the *standpipe,* a pipe run up a corner of the derrick. The bottom of the standpipe connects to reciprocating *slush pumps* or "mud hogs" and drilling fluid or *mud* is pumped through the drill pipe and bit all the time it is rotating on bottom.

If a well is being drilled and the drilling mud pumped down the drill pipe enters the formation instead of flowing back up the hole, the crew is "losing returns." When the end of an old catline or bull rope unravels, it becomes "soft line."

Finally, heavy pieces of pipe that run adjacent to the bit on the bottom of the drill pipe are *drill collars*. And when anything is lost in the hole, it is a *fish* and all devices used to recover material dropped in the hole are *fishing tools*. Some of the most creative work done by the drilling crews, and most of the innumerable patents from the oil patch at the turn of the century, had to do with fishing tools!

Thus, it is possible to make some sense of a description of drilling for oil such as this one supplied by Winfrey:

"The wire line drum, drum pulley, and brake wheel make up the bull wheel. When sucker rods are pulled, the bull wheel is connected to the band wheel in the belt house by the bull rope, a heavy manila rope or small wire line. The band wheel is belt driven by some kind of prime mover. While the rig is bobbin' the pump down in the well is suspended from the end of the walking beam by the sucker rods and beam hanger. The walking beam rocks on the sampson post riding the saddle bearing. A post set under the walking beam to catch the weight of the sucker rods in case the pitman breaks on a rig is the headache post."[10]

Absolutely.

Epilogue

"Oh, that I were as in the months of old, as in the days when God watched over me; when his lamp shone upon my head, and by his light I walked through darkness; as I was in my autumn days, when the friendship of God was upon my tent; when the Almighty was yet with me, when my children were about me, when my steps were washed with milk, and the rock poured out for me streams of oil!"

—Job 29:2–6 RSV

1951. Another time. Another generation. Another world:

There was the sputter and cough of an engine in the drive. A grease-spattered Ford with flapping fenders came to a stop with a shrill squeal of old brakes and seared tires.

Jett Rink sprang out. His face was grotesque with smears of dark grease and his damp bacchanalian locks hung in tendrils over his forehead. He leaped from the car and began to run as he landed, without a pause, and he limped a little as he ran.

He came on, he opened the door of the screened veranda, he stood before the company in his dirt and grease, his eyes shining wildly. They stared at him in shocked suspense, relaxed as they were against the cushions, glasses in hand. Leslie thought, Now he is really crazy. Something terrible is going to happen. The man stood, his legs wide apart as though braced against the world, the black calloused hands with the fingers curiously widespread as they hung, his teeth white in the grotesquely smeared face. He stared at Bick with those pale blue-white eyes and there was in them the glitter of terrible triumph.

Bick did not even rise from his chair. Very quietly, sitting there, he said, "Get out."

Jett Rink spoke four words only. His voice was low and husky with emotion. "My well came in."

The words shot geyser-swift out of Jett Rink's mouth like the earth-pent oil his labors had just released. "Everybody said I had a duster. You thought old Spindletop and Burkburnett and Mexia and those, they was all the oil there was. They ain't, I'm here to tell you. It's here. It's right here. I got the laugh on you. . . . My well come in big and there's more and bigger. They's oil under here. They's oil here on Reata and someday I'm going to pay you a million dollars or ten and you'll take it because you'll need the money. I'm going to have more money than you ever saw—you and the rest of the stinkin' sons of bitches of Benedicts!"[1]

AFTERMATH

The figures of oil production tell the last chapter of the story, when the salt-dome boom in Southeast Texas began to wane:

1902	18,083,658 bbls	Valued at $3,998,097 ($ .22 per bbl)
1903	17,995,572 bbls	Valued at $7,517,479 ($ .41 per bbl)
1904	22,241,413 bbls	Valued at $8,156,220 ($ .39 per bbl)
1905	25,236,189 bbls	Valued at $7,552,262 ($ .30 per bbl)[2]

Although the quantity of oil continued to increase in 1905, due in large part to the new field on Batson Prairie, the valuation dropped. All of the numbers dropped again in 1906 and 1907; by the end of the decade these areas had generally closed down or were already being re-opened as shallow fields.

The shift had begun west and northwest: the Humble field alone produced 2.9 million barrels *per month* in 1905 while Spindletop barely eked out 145,000 at the same rate. Even Humble had had its first gush of oil that would now diminish. With the flush production behind it, Humble oil fields produced in all of 1907 what it had produced monthly two years before. In 1913 another small boom took place when oil was reached at 2,700 feet, but by 1919 that phase was over. A decade later hundreds of wells were producing from below 5,000 feet, an unheard-of depth just twenty-five years earlier.[3]

On Batson Prairie the decline continued to 1924, when several flank producers added to the annual totals. To the northwest of the old field, and at more than 3,600 feet, new oil gave the area a lift for the remainder of that decade, only to see another decline. The thirties and forties saw little change, but new additions and more than one thousand wells brought some life in 1935, 1949, and again in 1951. Still, the annual yield in 1953, one hundred years since its inception, was a meager 111,000 barrels. The town of Batson fluctuated with the prairie oil field. At its height after 1903 Batson claimed more than 1,000 residents; most of the time it hovered closer to 200.[4]

Saratoga remained somewhat more consistent after the boom moved on. The railroad continued to come through but shifted its commerce to lumber, and finally abandoned the Bragg-Saratoga link in 1934. Oil and gas wells opened briefly in the early fifties but had little long-term impact on the community. The population, like Batson, never again rose above 1,000 and generally numbered less than 500.[5]

Sour Lake did somewhat better than its declining neighbors to the north. The oil field produced at a constant rate over the next several decades, though never again at the impossible levels of the boom years. Texaco maintained an active presence there for the rest of the century, and a new field actually showed some promise in 1948. The hotel and spa eventually burned down—again—and this time they were not rebuilt. The sour springs lake dried up, and there was not even a glimpse left of the spot where Dr. Mud had delivered his beauty treatments so long ago. The community kept its population up over 3,000 for many years, then declined to half that during and after World War II.[6]

Although Big Hill did not fare well after 1902 except for attempts in the 1920s (a successful year in 1925), 1930s, and 1950s to drill much deeper, the city of Beaumont diversified and returned to its glory days before the oil boom "interruption." The Neches River was cut in 1908 to provide a channel to the coast; pipelines studded the landscape on their way to Port Arthur. Texaco, Gulf, and Exxon (Humble) kept up significant activity there, and the Gulf States Utilities Company established headquarters in Beaumont in 1925. The population of "the Queen of the Neches" in 1950 stood at 94,014, and it claimed a place among the ten largest communities in the state. The Tyrells' estate and the McFaddin House were being restored as historic sites, and the names of the boomers could be seen in new street names and city parks. On a downtown corner stood the Texas Energy Museum, a cooperative result of Great Western Oil and the citizens of Beaumont.

Just to the south of the growing city, the fourteen buildings that comprised Gladys City deteriorated or burned into oblivion, except for the old Log Cabin Saloon, which managed to stand on its own for decades after the boom.[7]

In the decades that changed Spindletop and southeast Texas, the names changed as well. The next "generation" of oil men included Harry Wiess, brothers Tom and Bill Lee, Marrs McLean, Howard Hughes, Sr., and Ross S. Sterling, a future Texas governor. Everette Lee DeGolyer, Walter Fondren, Harry Phelan, and Miles Frank Yount joined forces in the rediscoveries that followed the World War I years. Next came Glenn McCarthy and Michel T. Halbouty, the Campbell brothers and a whole new generation of roughnecks, land men, and "doodlebuggers."

New corporations struck it rich: Southern Pacific's Rio Bravo, Yount-Lee, Stanolind Oil and Gas, and Hughes Tool Company, just to mention a few who joined the ranks of Texaco, Humble, and Gulf. And Texas opened its subsurface in remote places never heard of before the twentieth century except to locals: Glenn Pool, Ranger, Kilgore, Burkburnett, and the fabulous oil fields of the Permian Basin.

"The most important product of Spindletop was men. Men to man the industry which gave birth to an age more glorious than man's mind had ever heretofore imagined."[8]

CENTENNIAL

"Exploration is somewhere between poetry and shooting craps."
—Joe Foster, Houston Geological Society meeting,
January 10, 2000

Big Hill is barely recognizable now, overgrown with shoulder-high weeds and brush, a smattering of gas and oil wells peeking around the flora. A highway bypass cuts right at its edge; across that avenue is a replica of Gladys City, the Boom Town Museum. Some sixty yards from its entrance gate stands the Spindletop Monument, a tall, pink granite obelisk first unveiled in 1941 on the site of Lucas No. 1 but since moved when the shifting sands threatened to topple it. The marker states that "On this Spot on the Tenth Day of the Twentieth Century a New Era in Civilization Began. Petroleum has revolutionized industry and transportation; it has created untold wealth, built cities, furnished employment for hundreds of thousands, and contributed billions of dollars in taxes to support institutions of government. In a brief span of years, it has altered man's way of life throughout the world."

The city of Beaumont has grown out to Big Hill, and Park Avenue and Highland Avenue are still thoroughfares moving traffic both ways. The "Reservation" is long since gone, and "Deep Crockett" is only a narrow, crooked street lined with dilapidated warehouses. Red Town, out to the northwest, is but a street's name anymore: the mile-long road runs along a city aqueduct but shows no sign of its rowdy past.

A few short miles west of Red Town is Sour Lake. Fannin Street has changed little in a century, still barely two-way, graveled, bumpy, and four blocks long. Three dozen buildings stand sullenly together within shouting distance of the encroaching Big Thicket. Just west of the town a historical marker points to the original location of the Sour Lake Hotel, but a visitor sees nothing save mossy trees, thick underbrush, and a lonesome gas well on a dirt carpet.

Two state highways take the traveler north and just east across Pine Island Bayou to Saratoga, passing at least two signs that point off the beaten path to what was once the crusty corduroy road that sliced through the thicket. What's left of the town is quaint at best, but even the historical marker has been ripped off its post, and nothing remains from 1904.

Batson is a four-way stop under construction to be widened, presumably, for the increasing tractor-trailer traffic that hauls timber and petroleum products between Houston and Jennings. The prairie is difficult to spot, but has little to offer when discovered just north of *the* intersection.

Humble, twenty miles west and to the San Jacinto River, has become an industrialized city in its own right, situated on a national highway, crowded with malls and automobile dealerships, golf courses galore, and wooded bedroom communities that serve Houston to the south.

The character of the boom town days may be gone, but the ghosts of those frontier characters still remain for the visitor who looks hard into the shadows. Walter Sharp is there, barking instructions to a crew while idly tossing a coin in the air, a stub of a cigar chomped between his teeth; his brother Jim stands along a fence line, Winchester in hand to discourage would-be encroachers on his property. Curt Hamill and his two brothers dangle from phantom derricks, pulling pipe and drilling deep into the salt dome and its sands.

George W. Carroll meanders down the main streets of old Beaumont, nodding at the merchants who stand in their doorways. He still waves to Will Armstrong and G. W. O'Brien, still takes his carriage to Perlstein's smithy. Jim Hogg and Jim Roche swap political jokes in the Oaks Hotel lobby, and the depot is crowded with a ghostly mob of motion and sound and chaos.

Mooch Frank walks the streets, too, and Billy Bryant wanders from drunk to drunk in Sour Lake, chaining them to trees when the jail is full. Ras Landry keeps order the old-fashioned way, Six Shooter Kate still stays in trouble all the time, and Old Black Cat Jim Morgan raises pigs by the Big Thicket. The two Doctors Davis keep their osteopathic clinic open, and Doc Stoker runs from office to oil field in the middle of the night, delivering babies in downtrodden tents or sewing up bloody gashes on a roughneck's forehead.

The dashingly handsome Californian, Scott Heywood, peers out over the fields in search of the next gusher's location. Frank Trost sets up his old wooden camera on its tripod for yet another photograph that will sell well in Houston and Galveston.

Bazile Brown, "Dr. Mud," sends a young man to the pool to wash off the mudpack from his damaged shoulder: "You're an oil magnet!" he calls after him.

And Captain Lucas stares a hard stare in the direction of Big Hill while holding his wife's hand on their front porch, convinced more than ever that the Sunday School teacher is right: there is oil down there.

And the one-armed Sunday School teacher walks ramrod straight out from the wagon to the edge of the field, a dozen eager, smiling children close behind. Pattillo Higgins gathers them in a tight circle around a small indentation in the ground, and lights a match just above it. There is a soft explosion, a momentary puff of smoke, and a little girl named Gladys squeals with delight. It's another beautiful Sunday afternoon on Big Hill.

Notes

CHAPTER 1. GETTING THERE

1. Christine Moor Sanders, *Captain George Washington O'Brien and the History of the Gladys City Company at Spindletop*, pp. 11–12.
2. Ibid., p. 41*n* 33.
3. J. E. Brantly, *History of Oil Well Drilling*, p. 21.
4. Ibid., p. 88; also, Carl Coke Rister, *Oil! Titan of the Southwest*, p. 38.
5. Brantly, *History of Oil Well Drilling*, p. 212; C. A. Warner, *History of Texas Oil and Gas Since 1543*, pp. 45–49.
6. Brantly, *History of Oil Well Drilling*, p. 216.
7. Ibid., p. 217; also, Warner, *History of Texas Oil and Gas*, pp. 188–92.
8. John O. King, *Joseph Stephen Cullinan: A Study of Leadership in the Texas Petroleum Industry, 1897–1937*, pp. 71–72.
9. Rister, *Oil!* pp. 43–44.
10. Lawrence Goodwyn, *Texas Oil, American Dreams: A Study of TIPRO*, p. 14; Daniel Yergin, *The Prize*, p. 116.
11. Ruth Knowles, *The Greatest Gamblers*, p. 29.
12. Brantly, *History of Oil Well Drilling*, pp. 218–19.
13. King, *Joseph Stephen Cullinan*, p. 73.
14. Ibid., pp. 75–77.
15. Brantly, *History of Oil Well Drilling*, pp. 216–19.
16. King, *Joseph Stephen Cullinan*, p. 79; also, Rister, *Oil!* p. 45.
17. King, *Joseph Stephen Cullinan*, pp. 92–94.
18. Ibid., pp. 69–72.
19. Robert C. Cotner, *James Stephen Hogg*, p. 539.
20. Ibid., pp. 442–43.
21. Ibid., pp. 436–38.
22. King, *Joseph Stephen Cullinan*, pp. 77–78.
23. Cotner, *James Stephen Hogg*, pp. 506–508.
24. Pattillo Higgins, transcript of audiotaped interview, included in The Texas Pioneers of Oil Collection, Center for American History, University of Texas at Austin. Hereafter cited as TPO, with interviewee's name.
25. Robert McDaniel and Henry Dethloff, *Pattillo Higgins and the Search for Texas Oil*, p. 42.
26. Sanders, *Captain George Washington O'Brien*, p. 13.
27. TPO—Pattillo Higgins.

28. McDaniel and Dethloff, *Pattillo Higgins,* p. 43.

29. Ibid., pp. 41-44.

30. Ibid., p. 45.

31. TPO—Clint Wood.

32. McDaniel and Dethloff, *Pattillo Higgins,* p. 46.

33. William Kennedy article in *Beaumont Journal,* Mar. 23, 1895.

34. McDaniel and Dethloff, *Pattillo Higgins,* pp. 47-48.

35. TPO—Plummer Barfield.

36. McDaniel and Dethloff, *Pattillo Higgins,* pp. 51-53.

37. Flagler Rockefeller to Pattillo Higgins, July 9, 1896, Pattillo Higgins Papers, Tyrrell Historical Library Archives, Beaumont, Texas.

38. Reid Sayers McBeth, *Pioneering the Gulf Coast; A Story of the Life and Accomplishments of Capt. Anthony F. Lucas,* p. 37; also, James Presley, *A Saga of Wealth: The Rise of the Texas Oil Men,* p. 41.

39. James Clark and Michel T. Halbouty, *Spindletop,* p. 281.

40. Everette L. DeGolyer, "Anthony F. Lucas and Spindletop," *Southwest Review* 30 (fall, 1945); also, Presley, *A Saga of Wealth,* pp. 41-42.

41. McDaniel and Dethloff, *Pattillo Higgins,* p. 58.

42. Presley, *A Saga of Wealth,* pp. 42-44.

43. McDaniel and Dethloff, *Pattillo Higgins,* p. 59; Presley, *A Saga of Wealth,* pp. 42-43.

44. Clark and Halbouty, *Spindletop,* p. 56.

45. Lloyd Wendt and Herman Kogan, *Bet A Million! The Story of John W. Gates,* pp. 207-209.

46. TPO—Pattillo Higgins.

47. King, *Joseph Stephen Cullinan,* p. 89.

48. TPO—Pattillo Higgins.

CHAPTER 2. SPINDLETOP!

1. Cf. John Edward Weems, *A Weekend in September* (New York: Holt, 1957); and, Andrew Forest Muir, *William Marsh Rice and His Institute: A Biographical Study,* ed. by Sylvia S. Morris (Houston: Rice University Studies, spring, 1972).

2. TPO—Curt Hamill.

3. Curtis G. Hamill, *We Drilled Spindletop!,* p. 10.

4. TPO—Allen Hamill.

5. TPO—Curt Hamill.

6. Clark and Halbouty, *Spindletop,* p. 43.

7. Brantly, *History of Oil Well Drilling,* p. 244.

8. Hamill, *We Drilled Spindletop!,* p. 16.

9. Oct. 26, 1900, *Beaumont Journal.*

10. TPO—Curt Hamill.

11. Hamill, *We Drilled Spindletop!,* pp. 18-20.

12. Ibid., pp. 22-24.

13. Clark and Halbouty, *Spindletop,* pp. 46-47.

14. Ibid.

15. Hamill, *We Drilled Spindletop!*, p. 25.

16. Dec. 21, 1900, *Beaumont Journal.*

17. Brantly, *History of Oil Well Drilling,* p. 240.

18. Jan. 2, 1901, *Beaumont Journal.*

19. Hamill, *We Drilled Spindletop!*, p. 27.

20. Clark and Halbouty, *Spindletop,* p. 51.

21. Ibid., pp. 52–53.

22. Curt Hamill, *We Drilled Spindletop!*, pp. 27–29.

23. Knowles, *The Greatest Gamblers,* pp. 32–35; Apr. 10, 1901, *Beaumont Daily Enterprise;* also, Yergin, *The Prize,* pp. 85–88.

24. TPO—Plummer Barfield.

25. TPO—Wilbur Gilbert.

26. Presley, *A Saga of Wealth,* pp. 47–48.

27. TPO—Pattillo Higgins.

28. McBeth, *Pioneering the Gulf Coast,* pp. 37–38.

29. Clark and Halbouty, *Spindletop,* pp. 157–58.

30. Rister, *Oil!,* p. 59.

31. Clark and Halbouty, *Spindletop,* pp. 70–71.

32. Jan. 11, 1901, *Beaumont Journal.*

33. Clark and Halbouty, *Spindletop,* pp. 60–62.

34. Ibid., p. 64.

35. TPO—Curt Hamill.

36. TPO—Allen Hamill.

37. Jan. 14, 1901, *Beaumont Daily Enterprise.*

38. Hamill, *We Drilled Spindletop!*, p. 30.

39. Ibid.

40. TPO—Allen Hamill.

41. Mody C. Boatright and William A. Owens, *Tales from the Derrick Floor,* p. 45.

42. Hamill, *We Drilled Spindletop!* pp. 31–32.

CHAPTER 3. THE WORLD GONE MAD

1. E. W. Mayo, "The Oil Boom in Texas," *Harper's Weekly,* June 22, 1901, p. 624.

2. TPO—Frank Redman.

3. Hamill, *We Drilled Spindletop!*, pp. 70–76.

4. W. Scott Heywood, "My Recollections of Spindletop," *Oil Magazine,* Jan., 1951, pp. 17–18.

5. Clark and Halbouty, *Spindletop,* p. 108.

6. Cotner, *James Stephen Hogg,* p. 526.

7. McBeth, *Pioneering the Gulf Coast,* pp. 18–19.

8. TPO—Curt Hamill.

9. Clark and Halbouty, *Spindletop,* pp. 94–96.

10. Jan. 15, 1901, *Beaumont Journal.*

11. Clark and Halbouty, *Spindletop,* p. 186.

12. Yergin, *The Prize*, pp. 230–31.

13. Clark and Halbouty, *Spindletop*, pp. 161–63.

14. TPO—Clint Wood.

15. Clark and Halbouty, *Spindletop*, pp. 184–86.

16. Yergin, *The Prize*, pp. 92–94.

17. McBeth, *Pioneering the Gulf Coast*, pp. 37–38.

18. Upton Sinclair, *Oil!*, p. 393.

19. Clark and Halbouty, *Spindletop*, pp. 75–76; also, Stephen B. Oates, *Visions of Glory: Texans on the Southwest Frontier*, p. 153.

20. Mayo, "The Oil Boom in Texas," p. 625.

21. TPO—H. P. Nichols.

22. TPO—Clint Wood.

23. Apr. 10, 1901, *Beaumont Daily Enterprise*.

24. TPO—Clint Wood.

25. Clark and Halbouty, *Spindletop*, pp. 75–76.

26. Boatright and Owens, *Tales from the Derrick Floor*, p. 59.

27. Rister, *Oil!*, pp. 59–63.

28. Clark and Halbouty, *Spindletop*, p. 76.

29. TPO—Hiram Sloop.

30. Apr. 3, 1901, *Beaumont Daily Enterprise*.

31. TPO—Benjamin "Bud" Coyle.

32. Walter B. Sharp to Mrs. Sharp, Jan. 18, 1901, Walter Benona Sharp Papers, Rice University.

33. "Howard Hughes, Sr.," *New Handbook of Texas*.

34. TPO—Edgar Eggleston Townes.

35. Walter Cline in Boatright and Owens, *Tales from the Derrick Floor*, pp. 189–90.

36. TPO—Sam Webb.

37. TPO—Clint Wood.

38. TPO—Sam Webb.

39. TPO—James William Kinnear.

40. Paul Isaac, "Municipal Reform in Beaumont, 1902–1909," *Southwestern Historical Quarterly* 78, no. 4 (1975): 412n 6.

41. TPO—Bud Coyle.

42. TPO—Wilson Hudson.

43. Boatright and Owens, *Tales from the Derrick Floor*, p. 117.

44. Thelma Johnson et al., *The Spindle Top Oil Field: A History of Its Discovery and Development*, p. 62.

45. R. T. Hill, *Journal of the Franklin Institute*.

CHAPTER 4. QUEEN OF THE NECHES

1. William Owens, *Fever in the Earth*, pp. 35–39.

2. "Beaumont, Texas," *New Handbook of Texas*.

3. Apr. 4, 1901, *Beaumont Daily Enterprise*.

4. Clark and Halbouty, *Spindletop*, p. 86.

5. Apr. 5, 1901, *Beaumont Daily Enterprise.*
6. TPO—Frank Redman.
7. TPO—Bud Coyle.
8. TPO—Will Armstrong.
9. Clark and Halbouty, *Spindletop*, pp. 82–83.
10. TPO—Frank Redman.
11. TPO—Daniel Walter Davis.
12. Marilyn D. Trevey, "Social and Economic Impact of Spindletop on East Texas" (MA, Lamar University, 1971), pp. 101–103; also, Janice J. Reitz, "Social and Economic Impact of the Spindletop Oil Boom on Women's Fashion in Beaumont, Texas" (MA, Lamar University, 1982), p. 123.
13. TPO—Harry Paramore.
14. W. T. Block, "Daily Spindletop Diary," Jan. 21, 1901, from *Galveston Daily News.*
15. TPO—Curt Hamill.
16. TPO—E. E. Townes.
17. TPO—H. P. Nichols.
18. Clark and Halbouty, *Spindletop*, p. 188.
19. Trevey, "Impact on East Texas," p. 128; also, Reitz, "Impact on Women's Fashion in Beaumont, Texas," p. 165; and, Clark and Halbouty, *Spindletop*, p. 91.
20. Clark and Halbouty, *Spindletop*, p. 92.
21. TPO—Daniel Walter Davis.
22. Advertisement in *Beaumont Daily Journal*, 1901–1903.
23. TPO—Hiram Sloop.
24. Trevey, "Impact on East Texas," pp. 63–65; also, *Blue Book of Texas (Beaumont Edition, 1908–1909).*
25. Trevey, "Impact on East Texas," pp. 35–37.
26. Betty Cutler Barrington, "A Sketch of the Life of James Edmund and Laura Emma Thweatt McGlaun," *Southwest Texas Genealogical and Historical Journal* 7, no. 4 (1977).
27. Reitz, "Impact on Women's Fashion in Beaumont, Texas," p. 80; also, TPO—Curt Hamill.
28. Reitz, "Impact on Women's Fashion in Beaumont, Texas," pp. 95–96.
29. May, 1901, *Pittsburgh (Penn.) Leader,* in Everett A. Martin, "A History of the Spindletop Oil Field" (MA, University of Texas, 1934), pp. 44–45.
30. TPO—Hiram Sloop.
31. George Parker Stoker, *Oil Field Medico*, pp. 2–9.
32. TPO—H. P Nichols; Daniel Walter Davis; James William Kinnear.
33. TPO—Will Armstrong; Frank Redman.
34. TPO—Daniel Walter Davis.
35. TPO—Sam Webb; Bud Coyle.
36. Clark and Halbouty, *Spindletop*, pp. 193–94.
37. TPO—Bud Coyle.
38. John O. King, *The Early History of the Houston Oil Company of Texas, 1902–1908*, pp. 6–7.

CHAPTER 5. DARK SIDE OF THE MOON

1. Mayo, "The Oil Boom in Texas," pp. 624–25.
2. Sinclair, *Oil!*, pp. 47–48.
3. TPO—E. E. Townes.
4. TPO—Frank Redman.
5. TPO—Ray Sittig.
6. TPO—H. P. Nichols.
7. Trevey, "Impact on East Texas," p. 104.
8. TPO—Will Armstrong.
9. TPO—Bud Coyle.
10. TPO—Will Armstrong.
11. TPO—Daniel Walter Davis.
12. TPO—George Walker Weller.
13. TPO—Hiram Sloop.
14. TPO—Harry Paramore.
15. TPO—Bud Coyle.
16. TPO—Wilson Hudson.
17. Clark and Halbouty, *Spindletop*, pp. 102–103.
18. TPO—Frank Redman.
19. Mar. 23, 1904, *Beaumont Journal*.
20. Clark and Halbouty, *Spindletop*, p. 83.
21. TPO—Daniel Walter Davis; Will Armstrong.
22. TPO—Daniel Walter Davis.
23. TPO—Will Armstrong.
24. Nena McDonald, in Reitz, "Impact on Women's Fashion in Beaumont, Texas," p. 123.
25. Stoker, *Oil Field Medico*, p. 20.
26. Clark and Halbouty, *Spindletop*, pp. 189–91.
27. Frank Andrews, "Law and Order," Oct., 1901, *National Oil Reporter*.
28. Thompson, *Spindletop Oil Field*, pp. 38–39.
29. TPO—Bert Stivers.
30. Trevey, "Impact on East Texas," pp. 131, 179.
31. TPO—Bill Philps.
32. TPO—Hiram Sloop.
33. A derogatory term for the town's African American citizens.
34. Trevey, "Impact on East Texas," p. 109; May 20, 1901, *Beaumont Journal*.
35. TPO—Daniel Walter Davis.
36. Reitz, "Impact on Women's Fashion in Beaumont, Texas," p. 82.
37. TPO—Daniel Walter Davis.
38. TPO—R. R. Hobson.
39. TPO—Daniel Walter Davis.
40. Stoker, *Oil Field Medico*, pp. 27–31.

CHAPTER 6. THE BLACK GOLCONDA

1. TPO—Guy Finley; also, Boatright and Owens, *Tales from the Derrick Floor*, pp. 16–17.
2. TPO—Harry Paramore; Bud Coyle; Wilson Hudson.
3. TPO—Bud Coyle.
4. TPO—Curt Hamill.
5. TPO—James William Kinnear.
6. TPO—Will Armstrong; Ashley Weaver.
7. TPO—George Walker Weller.
8. TPO—Frank Dunn.
9. Clark and Halbouty, *Spindletop*, p. 92.
10. Clark and Halbouty, *Spindletop*, p. 124.
11. Ibid., pp. 125–26.
12. The following descriptions are based on information from *The Spindletop/Gladys City Boomtown Museum* brochure and guide (1992).
13. Robert Haynes, *Catching Shadows: A Directory of Nineteenth-Century Texas Photographers*, p. 83. Luther C. Lane may have also ventured down from Corsicana: the name "Hughes & Lane" appears on oil field pictures taken around Sour Lake and Batson.
14. TPO—E. E. Townes.
15. The Log Cabin Saloon as last standing building of Gladys City, in *Spindletop/Gladys City Boomtown Museum* brochure and guide.
16. May 2, 1901, *The Nation Magazine*.
17. Trevey, "Impact on East Texas," pp. 125–27.
18. TPO—Harry Paramore; also, Jan. 21, 1901, *Galveston Daily News*.
19. TPO—George Walker Weller.
20. TPO—Daniel Walter Davis.
21. TPO—William Ed Cotton.
22. TPO—Wilbur C. Gilbert.
23. Ibid.
24. Richard O'Connor, *The Oil Barons*, p. 107.
25. Ibid., pp. 108–12; also, Robert D. Henriques, *Bearsted: A Biography of Marcus Samuel, First Viscount Bearsted, and Founder of Shell Transport and Trading Company*, pp. 300–23.
26. Ibid., p. 109; also, Presley, *A Saga of Wealth*, pp. 63–65.
27. Harvey O'Connor, *Mellon's Millions*, p. 7f.
28. Yergin, *The Prize*, pp. 118–28; also, Kendall Beaton, *Enterprise in Oil: A History of Shell Oil Company in the United States*, pp. 43–55.
29. Yergin, *The Prize*, p. 128.
30. The "rule of capture" law continues at the end of the twentieth century in Texas, not with oil deposits but rather groundwater, which accounts for 57 percent of the water used in Texas. Whereas regulations came about in the 1920s governing oil production, the Texas Supreme Court ruled unanimously in *Sipriano et al. v.*

Great Spring Waters of America, Inc. (May 6, 1999) that a landowner could pump as much water as desired, regardless of the harm done to his neighbors.

31. William Owens in Boatright and Owens, *Tales from the Derrick Floor,* pp. 60–62.
32. Sinclair, *Oil!,* pp. 156–57.
33. Clark and Halbouty, *Spindletop,* pp. 118–19.
34. TPO—Ethel Stivers.
35. Clark and Halbouty, *Spindletop,* p. 119.
36. Jewel Gibson, *Black Gold,* p. 287.
37. Stoker, *Oil Field Medico,* pp. 32–33, 41.

CHAPTER 7. BIG THICKET OIL

1. Loither I. Adams, *Time and Shadows,* pp. 60–62; also, W. T. Block, *From Mud Baths to Millionaires, 1835–1909,* pp. 49, 94, 133.
2. Adams, *Time and Shadows,* pp. 51–53.
3. Ibid., pp. 56–58.
4. Ibid., pp. 120–21.
5. Stoker, *Oil Field Medico,* pp. 42–45.
6. TPO—William Ed Cotton.
7. W. T. Kavanaugh, in Block, *Mud Baths,* p. 41; also, Boyle House, "Spindletop," *Southwestern Historical Quarterly* 50, no. 1 (1946): 37.
8. Adams, *Time and Shadows,* p. 74; also, Block, *Mud Baths,* p. 71.
9. TPO—Mrs. V. B. Daniels; also, *Mud Baths,* p. 116; and, Alice Cashen in Frances Abernethy, *Tales From the Big Thicket,* p. 141.
10. Adams, *Time and Shadows,* p. 135.
11. Wanda A. Landrey, *Boardin' in the Thicket: Recipes and Reminiscences of Early Big Thicket Boarding Houses,* pp. 139–40.
12. Block, *Mud Baths,* p. 167f.
13. Jan. 25, 1904, *Houston Post.*
14. Adams, *Time and Shadows,* pp. 79–81.
15. Charles Jeffries, "Reminiscences of Sour Lake," *Southwestern Historical Quarterly* 50, no. 1 (1946): 25–27.
16. TPO—Frank Hamilton.
17. TPO—Sam Webb.
18. TPO—William Ed Cotton.
19. TPO—Frank Hamilton.
20. TPO—William H. "Billy" Bryant.
21. TPO—John Little.
22. TPO—Early Deane.
23. TPO—Bud Coyle.
24. TPO—Bert Stivers.
25. TPO—Frank Hamilton.
26. Jeffries, "Reminiscences," pp. 30–31.
27. TPO—Frank Hamilton.
28. TPO—Sam Webb; William Ed Cotton.

29. Jeffries, "Reminiscences," pp. 32–33.
30. TPO—Billy Bryant; Frank Hamilton.
31. TPO—Early Deane; William Ed Cotton.
32. TPO—William Ed Cotton.
33. Mody C. Boatright, *Texas Folk and Folklore,* p. 167.
34. TPO—Bud Coyle; also, Adams, *Time and Shadows,* p. 62; and Block, *Mud Baths,* p. 94.
35. Isaac, "Municipal Reform in Beaumont," p. 412n 7; also, TPO—James William Kinnear; and Wanda A. Landrey, "Lawlessness in the Big Thicket" (MA, Lamar University, 1971), pp. 35–36.
36. Boatright, *Texas Folk and Folklore,* p. 172.
37. TPO—John Little.
38. TPO—William Ed Cotton.
39. TPO—Billy Bryant.
40. TPO—J. A. Rush.
41. Landrey, *Boardin',* pp. 150–55.
42. Stoker, *Oil Field Medico,* pp. 46–49.
43. Ibid., p. 45; also, *New Handbook of Texas;* and, Adams, *Time and Shadows,* p. 225.
44. Boatright and Owens, *Tales from the Derrick Floor,* pp. 114–15.
45. TPO—William Ed Cotton.
46. Stoker, *Oil Field Medico,* pp. 42–44, 60–61.
47. Adams, *Time and Shadows,* pp. 79–81.

CHAPTER 8. THE COARSEST PLACE IN TEXAS

1. Landrey, "Lawlessness in the Big Thicket," p. 39.
2. "Batson Oil Field," and "Batson Prairie, Texas," *New Handbook of Texas.*
3. TPO—Harry Paramore.
4. TPO—Ethel and Bert Stivers.
5. TPO—Lillian Prince Webb.
6. TPO—Ethel Stivers.
7. TPO—Plummer Barfield.
8. TPO—Ethel Stivers.
9. TPO—Harry Paramore.
10. TPO—Preston Mowbray.
11. TPO—James Donohoe.
12. TPO—William Ed Cotton.
13. TPO—Billy Bryant.
14. TPO—Curt Hamill.
15. TPO—Sam Webb.
16. TPO—Preston Mowbray.
17. TPO—Frank Hamilton.
18. TPO—Bud Coyle.
19. TPO—Plummer Barfield.
20. TPO—Bud Coyle.

21. TPO—John Little.
22. TPO—Bert Stivers.
23. TPO—J. A. Rush.
24. TPO—Billy Bryant.
25. TPO—Plummer Barfield.
26. TPO—Bert Stivers.
27. TPO—Lillian Prince Webb.
28. TPO—Sam Webb.
29. TPO—Plummer Barfield.
30. TPO—Bud Coyle.
31. TPO—Plummer Barfield.
32. Although several of the Batson folks talk about William Jesse McDonald being there, neither of his biographers make any reference to his presence in the oil fields during the boom days.
33. TPO—Billy Bryant.
34. TPO—John Stephen Hogg to Joseph S. Cullinan, Jan. 22, 1904.
35. W. W. Sterling, *Trails and Trials of a Texas Ranger,* pp. 78–83.
36. TPO—Bud Coyle; William Ed Cotton; Hardeman Roberts.
37. TPO—William Ed Cotton.
38. TPO—Bert Stivers.
39. TPO—Hardeman Roberts.
40. TPO—Curt Hamill.
41. Isaac Marcosson, *Black Golconda; The Romance of Petroleum,* p. 306.
42. William A. Mellon, in Craig Thompson, *Since Spindletop: A Human History of Gulf's First Half-Century,* p. 22.
43. "Humble, Texas," *New Handbook of Texas.*
44. Clark and Halbouty, *Spindletop,* pp. 183–202; also, Thompson, *Since Spindletop,* p. 20.
45. Walter Cline, in Boatright and Owens, *Tales from the Derrick Floor,* pp. 191–92.

CHAPTER 9. TALL TALES AND OIL TALK

1. Mody C. Boatright, "Gib Morgan, Minstrel of the Oil Fields," *Texas Folklore Society* 20 (1945): 65f.
2. George Sessions Perry, *The Hackberry Cavalier,* p. 62.
3. Boatright, "Gib Morgan," pp. 65–66, 89, 94.
4. Perry, *Hackberry Cavalier,* pp. 63–75.
5. Orlan L. Sawey, in Boatright, *Texas Folk and Folklore,* p. 321.
6. John Lee Brooks, in Boatright, *Texas Folk and Folklore,* p. 315–19.
7. Dell McCormick, *Tall Timber Tales,* pp. 99–105.
8. Adams, *Time and Shadows,* pp. 279–81.
9. Sawey, in Boatright, *Texas Folk and Folklore,* pp. 322–29.
10. James W. Winfrey, in Boatright, *Texas Folk and Folklore,* pp. 331–35.

EPILOGUE

1. Edna Ferber, *Giant,* pp. 363–65.
2. Rister, *Oil!,* p. 77; also, Charles A. Warner, "Texas and the Oil Industry," *Southwestern Historical Quarterly* 50, no. 1 (1946): 24.
3. "Humble Oil Fields," *New Handbook of Texas.*
4. "Batson Oil Fields" and "Batson, Texas," *New Handbook of Texas.*
5. "Saratoga, Texas," *New Handbook of Texas.*
6. "Sour Lake Oil Fields" and "Sour Lake, Texas," *New Handbook of Texas.*
7. "Log Cabin Saloon," *Spindletop/Gladys City Boomtown Museum* brochure and guide, p. 14.
8. Everette L. DeGolyer, 1951 speech, Fiftieth Anniversary Commemoration records, Beaumont, Texas.

Bibliography

PRIMARY SOURCES
THE PIONEERS

The Texas Pioneers of Oil Collection, Center for American History, University of Texas at Austin. These audiotapes were transcribed in the mid-1950s from interviews with men and women who had lived in the boom days of 1901–1904 in Southeast Texas. The following thirty-six interviews were used extensively in this research:

William L. Armstrong
Plummer Barfield
W. H. "Billy" Bryant
William Ed Cotton
Benjamin "Bud" Coyle
V. B. Daniels
Mrs. V. B. Daniels
Daniel Walter Davis
Early Deane
James Donohoe
Frank Dunn
Guy Finley
Wilbur C. Gilbert
Allen Hamill
Curtis Hamill
Frank Hamilton
R. R. Hobson
Wilson M. Hudson
James W. Kinnear
John Little
Preston Mowbray
H. P. Nichols
Harry Paramore
Frank Redman
Hardeman Roberts
J. A. Rush
Ray Sittig
Hiram C. Sloop

Bert Stivers
Ethel Stivers
Edgar E. Townes
Ashley Weaver
Lillian Prince Webb
Sam Webb
George W. Weller
Clint Wood

REMINISCENCES

Cashen, Alice. "Boom-Town Tales," *Tales from the Big Thicket.* Francis E. Abernethy, ed. Austin: University of Texas Press, 1966.

A Daily Spindletop Diary. W. T. Block, ed. Galveston: *Daily News,* 1994.

Doran, Michael, ed. "Early Beaumont: The Reminiscences of Frank C. Weber." *Texas Gulf Historical and Biographical Record.* November, 1981.

Hamill, Curtis G. "Spindletop: A Narrative by Curt Hamill" (audio recording). Produced by Casey Martin, 1964.

————. *We Drilled Spindletop!* Houston: n.p., 1957.

Heywood, W. Scott. "Autobiography of an Oil Man." *Oil Magazine,* June, 1941.

————. "My Recollections of Spindletop." *Oil Magazine,* January, 1951.

Jeffries, Charles. "Reminiscences of Sour Lake." *Southwestern Historical Quarterly* 50, no. 25 (1946): 25–35.

Landrey, Wanda A., ed. *Boardin' in the Big Thicket: Recipes and Reminiscences of Early Big Thicket Boarding Houses.* Denton: University of North Texas Press, 1998.

McBeth, Reid Sayers. *Pioneering the Gulf Coast; A Story of the Life and Accomplishments of Capt. Anthony F. Lucas.* New York: n.p., 1918.

Sharp, Walter Benona, and Estelle Baughton. Letters and Papers. Woodson Research Center, Rice University, Houston.

Sterling, William W. *Trails and Trials of a Texas Ranger.* Norman: University of Oklahoma Press, 1968.

[Stoker], George Parker. *Oil Field Medico.* Dallas: Banks Upshaw Company, 1948.

ARTICLES AND NEWSPAPERS

Andrews, Frank. "Law and Order." *National Oil Reporter.* October, 1901.

Beaumont Daily Enterprise. Articles from 1901–1904.

Beaumont Journal. Articles from 1901–1904.

Galveston Daily News. Articles from 1901–1904.

Houston Post. Articles from 1901–1904.

Mayo, E. W. "The Oil Boom in Texas." *Harper's Weekly* 45 (June 22, 1901): 624f.

"Oil Wells in Texas." *Scientific American* 84 (February, 1901): 116.

"Texas Oil Craze." *The Nation* 72 (May 2, 1901): 350–51.

Treherne, Edward W. "The Great Texas Oil Fields." *Cosmopolitan* 31 (July, 1901): 251–60.

SECONDARY SOURCES
SIGNIFICANT RESOURCES

Boatright, Mody C., and William A. Owens. *Tales from the Derrick Floor.* New York:
Doubleday and Company, 1970.
Clark, James, and Michel T. Halbouty. *Spindletop.* New York: Random House, 1952.
O'Connor, Richard. *The Oil Barons.* Boston: Little Brown Company, 1971.
Presley, James. *A Saga of Wealth: The Rise of the Texas Oil Men.* New York: G. P.
Putnam, 1978.
Rister, Carl Coke. *Oil! Titan of the Southwest.* Norman: University of Oklahoma Press,
1949.
Yergin, Daniel. *The Prize.* New York: Simon & Schuster, 1991.

FOLKLORE

Adams, Loither Iler, Jr. *Time and Shadows* [Jefferson and Hardin Counties].
Lumberton?, Miss., 1971.
Block, W. T., Jr. *From Mud Baths to Millionaires, 1835–1909.* Atascosita: Atascosita
Historical Society, 1995.
———. *Mud, Gushers, and Sour Lake "Molasses": A Tale of Texas' Second Oil Boom Town.*
Nederland, Tex.: W. T. Block, 1990.
———. *Sour Lake, Texas.* Atascosita: Atascosita Historical Society, 1995.
Boatright, Mody C. *Folklore of the Oil Industry.* Dallas: Southern Methodist University
Press, 1963.
———. "Gib Morgan, Minstrel of the Oil Fields." *Texas Folklore Society* 20 (1945).
———. *The Golden Log.* Dallas: Southern Methodist University Press, 1962.
———. *Texas Folk and Folklore.* Dallas: Southern Methodist University Press, 1954.
Cox, S. E. J., Sr. *Girls, Gushers, and Roughnecks.* San Antonio: Naylor Company, 1972.
McCormick, Dell J. *Tall Timber Tales.* Caldwell, Idaho: Caxton Printers, 1977.
Perry, George Sessions. *The Hackberry Cavalier.* New York: Editions for the Armed
Services, 1944.

HISTORIES

Goodwyn, Lawrence. *Texas Oil, American Dreams: A Study of TIPRO.* Austin: Texas
State Historical Association, 1996.
History of Petroleum Engineering. Dallas: American Petroleum Institute (API), 1961.
House, Boyce. *Oil Boom: The Story of Spindletop, Burkburnett, Mexia, Smackover,
Desdemona, and Ranger.* Caldwell, Idaho: Caxton Printers, 1941.
Johnson, Thelma, et al. *The Spindle Top Oil Field: A History of Its Discovery and
Development.* Beaumont: n.p., 1927.
Knowles, Ruth. *The Greatest Gamblers.* 2d ed. Norman: University of Oklahoma Press,
1978.
Marcosson, Isaac. *Black Golconda; The Romance of Petroleum.* New York: Harper &
Brothers, 1924.

Oates, Stephen B. *Visions of Glory: Texans on the Southwest Frontier.* Norman: University of Oklahoma Press, 1970.

Olien, Roger M., and Diana Davids. *Life in the Oil Fields.* Dallas: Texas Monthly, 1986.

———. *Wildcatters.* Dallas: Texas Monthly, 1984.

Rundell, Walter, Jr. *Early Texas Oil.* College Station: Texas A&M University Press, 1977.

Spindletop/Gladys City Boomtown Museum. Lamar University, 1992.

Spindletop, Where Oil Became an Industry. Beaumont: Spindletop Fiftieth Anniversary Commission, 1951.

Warner, Charles A. *History of Texas Oil and Gas Since 1543.* Houston: Gulf Publishing, 1939.

TECHNICAL

Ball, Max W. *This Fascinating Oil Business.* New York: Bobbs-Merrill, 1940.

Barton, Donald C. and Roland B. Paxson. "Spindletop Salt Dome and Oil Field, Jefferson County, Texas." American Association of Petroleum Geologists (AAPG) *Bulletin* 9, no. 3 (1925): 594–612.

Brantly, J. E. *History of Oil Well Drilling.* Houston: Gulf Publishing, 1971.

Dumble, Edwin T. "Age of Petroleum Deposits: Saratoga, Texas." *Science* 23 (1906): 510–11.

Forbes, Gerald. *Flush Production: The Epic of Oil in the Gulf Southwest.* Norman: University of Oklahoma Press, 1942.

Gardner, Frank J. *Texas Gulf Coast Oil.* Dallas: Rinehart Oil Company, 1948.

Halbouty, Michel T. *Petrographic and Physical Characteristics of Sands from 7 Gulf Coast Producing Horizons.* Houston: Gulf Publishing, 1937.

———. *Salt Domes: Gulf Region, United States and Mexico.* Houston: Gulf Publishing, 1957.

Henley, A. S. "Big Hill Salt Dome, Jefferson County, Texas." AAPG *Bulletin* 9, no. 3 (1925): 590f.

"Introduction to Gulf Coast Oil Fields." Houston Geological Society, 1947.

Kennedy, William. "Coastal Salt Domes." AAPG *Bulletin* 1, no. 1 (1917): 34–59.

Owen, Edgar Wesley. *Trek of the Oil Finders: A History of Exploration for Petroleum.* Tulsa: AAPG, 1975.

Palacas, James G. "Hydrocarbons in Estuarine Sediments." AAPG *Bulletin* 56, no. 1 (1972): 1410f.

Roberts, W. H., and Robert J. Cordell, eds. *Problems of Petroleum Migration.* Tulsa: AAPG, 1980.

Sawtelle, George. "Batson Oil Field, Hardin County, Texas." AAPG *Bulletin* 9, no. 9 (1925): 1277–82.

"Texas Gulf Coast Composite Study." Houston Geological Society, 1946.

Vittrup, Lawrence. "Drilling in Steeply Dipping Oil-Producing Sands." AAPG *Bulletin* 31 (1947): 2040–44.

BIOGRAPHIES

Cotner, Robert C. *James Stephen Hogg.* Austin: University of Texas Press, 1959.

DeGolyer, Everette L. "Anthony F. Lucas and Spindletop." *Southwest Review* 30 (June, 1945).

Henriques, Robert David. *Bearsted: A Biography of Marcus Samuel, First Viscount Bearsted, and Founder of Shell Transport and Trading Company.* New York: Viking, 1960.

House, Boyce. "He Started It All." *Texas Industry Magazine,* September, 1946.

King, John O., *Joseph Stephen Cullinan: A Study of Leadership in the Texas Petroleum Industry, 1897–1937.* Nashville: Vanderbilt University Press, 1970.

McDaniel, Robert and Henry Dethloff. *Pattillo Higgins and the Search for Texas Oil.* College Station: Texas A&M University Press, 1989.

O'Connor, Harvey. *Mellon's Millions.* New York: John Day, 1933.

Sanders, Christine Moor. *Captain George Washington O'Brien and the History of the Gladys City Company at Spindletop.* Beaumont: C. M. Sanders, 1992.

Wendt, Lloyd and Herman Kogan. *Bet a Million! The Story of John W. Gates.* Indianapolis: Bobbs Merrill, 1948.

CORPORATE HISTORIES

Beaton, Kendall. *Enterprise in Oil: A History of Shell Oil Company in the United States.* New York: Appleton, 1951.

James, Marquis. *The Texaco Story: The First Fifty Years, 1902–1952.* New York: n.p., 1953.

King, John O. *The Early History of the Houston Oil Company of Texas, 1901–1908.* Houston: n.p., 1959.

Larson, Henrietta M., and Kenneth W. Porter. *History of the Humble Oil and Refining Company.* New York: Harper, 1959.

Thompson, Craig. *Since Spindletop: A Human History of Gulf's First Half-Century.* Pittsburgh: n.p., 1951.

UNPUBLISHED

Landrey, Wanda A. "Lawlessness in the Big Thicket." MA, Lamar University, 1971.

Martin, Everette A. "A History of the Spindletop Oil Field." MA, University of Texas, 1934.

Proctor, Mary Lou. "History of Hardin County." MA, University of Texas, 1950.

Reitz, Janice J. "Social and Economic Impact of the Spindletop Oil Boom on Women's Fashion in Beaumont, Texas." MS, Lamar University, 1982.

Rowe, Ina May. "Development of Oil at Sour Lake." MA, Southwest Texas State Teachers College, 1939.

Trevey, Marilyn D. "Social and Economic Impact of Spindletop on East Texas." MA, Lamar University, 1971.

FICTION

Bader, Bonnie. *Big Strike at Spindletop*. New York: Silver Moon, 1994.
Bredeson, Carmen. *Spindletop Gusher*. Brookfield, Conn.: Millbrook Press, 1996.
Donahue, Jack, and Michel T. Halbouty. *Grady Barr*. New York: Arbor House, 1981.
Ferber, Edna. *Giant*. New York: Doubleday, 1952.
Gibson, Jewel. *Black Gold*. New York: Random House, 1950.
Hancock, Sibyl. *Spindletop*. Burnet, Tex.: Eakin Press, 1980.
Leigh, Eliza. *Prairie Ecstasy*. New York: Zebra Books, 1993.
Light, Linda. *Passions and Prejudice. The Secrets of Spindletop* Richmond, Ky.: Spindletop Productions, 1997.
Owens, William A. *Fever in the Earth*. New York: Putnam, 1958.
Sinclair, Upton. *Oil!* New York: A & C Boni, 1927.
White, Pablo. *Blossoms of Steel*. Artesia, N.M.: n.p., 1995.

OTHER

Advantages and Conditions of Beaumont and Port Arthur of Today. New Orleans: n.p., 1902.
Beaumont Souvenir Magazine. 1903.
Bigbee, North. "Spindletop." *Texas Star Magazine*, October, 1941.
"The Big Thicket of southeast Texas, a History, 1800–1940" (video). Austin: Forest Glen TV Productions, 1988.
Clark, J. Stanley. *The Oil Century: From the Drake Well to the Conservation Era*. Norman: University of Oklahoma Press, 1958.
Gard, Wayne. *The First One Hundred Years of Texas Oil and Gas*. Dallas: Texas Mid-Continent Oil and Gas Association, 1966.
Haley, James L. *Texas From Spindletop through World War II*. New York: St. Martin's Press, 1993.
Haynes, David. *Catching Shadows: A Directory of Nineteenth-Century Texas Photographers*. Austin: Texas State Historical Association, 1993.
Hidy, Ralph and Muriel. *Pioneering in Big Business, 1882–1911*. New York: Harper and Brothers, 1955.
House, Boyce. "Spindletop." *Southwestern Historical Quarterly* 50, no. 1 (1946): 36–43.
Isaac, Paul. "Municipal Reform in Beaumont, 1902–1909." *Southwestern Historical Quarterly* 78, no. 4 (1975): 409–30.
Knowles, Ruth. *The First Pictorial History of the American Oil and Gas Industry, 1859–1983*. Athens: Ohio University Press, 1983.
Landrey, Wanda A. *Outlaws in the Big Thicket*. Quanah, Tex.: Nortex, 1976.
Linsley, Judith W. and Ellen W. Rienstra. *Beaumont, a Chronicle of Promise: An Illustrated History*. Woodlands Hills, Calif.: Windsor Publications, 1982.
McKay, Seth and Odie B. Faulk. *Texas After Spindletop*. Austin: Steck-Vaughn, 1965.
Marcosson, Isaac. "The Black Golconda." *Saturday Evening Post*, April 19, 1924.
New Handbook of Texas. Austin: Texas State Historical Association, 1996.
O'Connor, Harvey. *The Empire of Oil*. New York: Monthly Review Press, 1955.

Owens, William A. "Boom in Batson: Birth of an Oil Field." *Drilling Magazine.* December, 1957.

———. "Gusher at Spindletop." *American Heritage.* June, 1958.

Perry, George Sessions. *Texas: A World in Itself.* New York: McGraw Hill, 1942.

Prindle, David F. *Petroleum Politics and the Texas Railroad Commission.* Austin: University of Texas Press, 1981.

Rundell, Walter, Jr. "Texas Petroleum History: A Selective Annotated Bibliography." *Southwestern Historical Quarterly* 67, no. 2 (1963): 267–78.

Schaadt, Robert L., ed. *History of Hardin County, Texas.* Silsbee, Tex.: Curtis Co., 1991.

Shaffer, Roger. *Spindletop Unwound: The William Pelham Humphries Lawsuit.* Plano, Tex.: Wordware, 1997.

Solberg, Carl. *Oil Power.* New York: Mason/Charter, 1976.

"Spindletop" (audio recording). Sung by Mitch Torok and Ramona Redd. In *Ballads of Texas,* vol. 1. Houston: Texas Specialty Records, 1972.

Spratt, John S. *The Road to Spindletop: Economic Changes in Texas, 1875–1901.* Austin: Steck-Vaughn, 1955.

Standard Blue Book of Texas, 1908–1909 (Beaumont Edition).

Stratton, Florence. *The Story of Beaumont.* Houston: Hercules Printing and Book Company, 1925.

Tait, Samuel W., Jr. *The Wildcatters.* Princeton University Press, 1946.

Tarbell, Ida. *The History of Standard Oil Company.* New York: McClure, 1904.

Taulbee, Dena. *James Meaders and the Spindletop Lawsuits.* Lexington, Ky.: D. Taulbee, 1986.

Walker, John H. and Gwendolyn Wingate. *Beaumont: A Pictorial History.* Virginia Beach, Va.: Donning, 1983.

Warner, Charles A. "Texas and the Oil Industry." *Southwestern Historical Quarterly* 50, no. 1 (1946): 1–24.

Index